D1027950

a
reader's
guide
to the
poetry
of
richard
wilbur

a
reader's
g u i d e
to the
poetry
of
richard
wilbur

by
rodney stenning edgecombe

the university of alabama press
tuscaloosa and london

designed by erin t. bradley

The drawing used as a design motif is an ex-
cerpt from an illustration by Richard Wilbur in
More Opposites, copyright © 1991 by Richard
Wilbur, reproduced by permission of Harcourt
Brace & Company.

∞

The paper on which this book is printed
meets the minimum requirements of American National Standard for Information Sci-
ence-Permanence of Paper for Printed Library
Materials, ANSI Z39.48-1984.

Library of Congress Cataloging-in-Publica-
tion Data

Edgecombe, Rodney Stenning.
A reader's guide to the poetry of Richard
Wilbur / Rodney Stenning Edgecombe.
p.   cm.
Includes bibliographical references and index.
ISBN 0-8173-0715-X
1. Wilbur, Richard. 1921- —Criticism and
interpretation—Handbooks, manuals, etc.   I.
Title.
PS3545.I32165Z65   1995
811'.52—dc20   94-37229

British Library Cataloguing-in-Publication
Data available

For Diana Fallon

contents

note to the reader

The high permissions fees requested by Richard Wilbur's American and British publishers have prevented me from using quoted material in this study. I accordingly ask the reader to keep Wilbur's *New and Collected Poems* (San Diego: Harcourt Brace Jovanovich, 1988; or London: Faber and Faber, 1989) at hand and to cross-refer my commentary with the text of each poem. All page references to *New and Collected Poems* are abbreviated as "NCP."

acknowledgments

I should like to thank the following librarians at Jagger Library, University of Cape Town, for their invaluable help in securing texts and tracking references. In uninvidious alphabetical order, they are Pene Beamish, Pat Golding, Colleen Harford, Rosalind Maree, Shanaz Morris, Evelyn Rossmeisl, Celia Walters, and Tiziana Zambonini. Paul Meyer, no longer a librarian at Jagger, also helped a great deal, and so did Richard Wilbur himself, who wrote to explain the identity of Tywater. My thanks go also to B. E. Cohen, who copyedited this manuscript, and Suzette Griffith, project editor, at The University of Alabama Press.

a
reader's
guide
to the
poetry
of
richard
wilbur

introduction

In various interviews and manifestos, Richard Wilbur has stressed that he composes (and perceives) all his poems as units, not as the components of a suite or other collective structure: "I never make a book, in the sense that a poet such as William Butler Yeats made a book. . . . With me, a book is simply the clutter of poems which have accumulated over a certain number of years."[1] And again: "The unit of my poetry, as I experience it, is not the *Collected Poems* which I may some day publish; nor is it the individual volume, nor the sequence or group within the volume; it is the single poem. Every poem of mine is autonomous, or feels so to me in my writing, and consists of an effort to exhaust my present sense of the subject."[2] Taking its cue from his declarations about the integrity and autonomy of each item of his output, my study offers itself as a critical accompaniment to those poems as they unspool chronologically before the reader from the earliest collection, *The Beautiful Changes*, to the "new" segment of *New and Collected Poems*.[3] While I try to say something about each lyric in turn, my claim to comprehensiveness must stop there. Any one of Wilbur's collections has such resonance and allusiveness and formal complexity that, were it to be fully explored, it would require a book to itself. All I can do in a guide of this limited scope is to gesture here and pause there and expect the reader to fill in the many lacunae I leave in my wake. Furthermore, in order to make more space for the original poems, I have been forced to disregard the many fine translations interleaved among them.

Wilbur has at last published something close to the *Collected Poems* he mentions above, and I have taken him at his word, treating the 1988 volume as an assembly of individual utterances. I have also followed the sequence of lyrics in each of the independent collections gathered in that volume, altering only its reverse chronology, which starts with the most recent poems and works back to *The Beautiful Changes*. To have followed this temporal regression would have been to forfeit the chance to monitor changes in the poetry, changes that (on Wilbur's own admission) have tended in the direction of greater simplicity and immediacy. But while I have been so bold as to invert the order of collections, I have at the same time taken care to retain the sequence of poems as it occurs in each, since I do not subscribe to the poet's self-deprecating remarks about his method of compilation: "When I organize a book, since the poems are all—as I say—one-shots, and don't amount to variations on a theme, I use the crudest possible methods of organization. I'll say, well, that was a long poem; let's rest them with a short one. Or, that was a heavy poem; let's have something trivial" (Irv Broughton, "An Interview with Richard Wilbur," in *Conversations*, pp. 142–43). Wilbur's cognizance of his readers in this regard is better viewed as tact than as crudity: a rhythm of alternating weight and length seems to me to be a perfectly respectable rhythm to strive for. And even then the sequences he has devised prove on examination to be much less mechanical and arbitrary than he makes them sound. It is sometimes the case that one group of poems will explore a particular mode of imagery, say, while another might balance or qualify the statement made by its predecessor. A good many felicities of placement and transition would have been fudged if I had reshuffled the lyrics.

Having said that, however, I must hasten to add that, even though I have opted for a reader's guide format, my study is nonetheless colored and shaped by what I perceive to be two central themes that recur throughout the poetry. No matter how unitary Wilbur's sense of the individual poem, each is the product of a unifying sensibility and is shaped by governing attitudes and assumptions. He himself observes that there "are certain things I find that I will not say, and there are certain matters to which I keep coming back" (Peter Stitt, Elessa Clay High, and Helen McCloy Ellison, "The Art of Poetry: Richard Wilbur," in *Conversations*, p. 183).

The first theme to which I shall recur throughout my commentary is one that almost all Wilbur criticism hitherto has addressed and that the poet himself has termed the "quarrel with Poe"—the resolved balance of the concrete and the spiritual that rejects any Manichean fissions of the two. It is a topic that all Wilbur's commentators have had to confront, but its most definitive treatment has come from Peter Stitt: "Wilbur's ideal is a union of the two realms, a mingling of them, so that we deal with a spiritualized reality. The tension that exists in a Wilbur poem is between these two poles; what the poet seeks is a point of balance between them, where neither is slighted or lost."[4] There is of course nothing especially new about such a program, which, following Carlyle, we could call a quest for "natural supernaturalism." But although precedents exist in the work of several Romantic poets, Wilbur is unique among the writers of his generation in his readiness to posit a world of the spirit, to marry it with matter, and so to confer a luminousness on things that materialists would otherwise seek to deny.

The second theme I have chosen to emphasize has not been treated quite so exhaustively, but it can be construed as a sort of corollary (or even an allotrope) of the same concern. Not only does Wilbur synthesize the tangible with the immaterial, but he also reconciles the region with the metropole, rendering native materials through an international legacy of form. This can best be illustrated by a dream of his adolescence:

You ask for "a dream," and I am not sure whether to give you one which I understand or one which I do not. When I was sixteen I dreamt of the appearance of an equestrian figure—a cowboy, I think—on the road which led past the gate of the walled vegetable-garden and rounded the manure-house behind the barn. The figure gestured to a range of hazy blue mountains, Rockies-like, which had never appeared behind the pine-grove before. In a deep, oracular voice, which seemed to be speaking close to my ear, the rider said, "Those are the Old Catica Mountains." I woke up with a feeling of awe, but with no comprehension, and forty years later I feel the same about that comparatively uneventful dream, wherein large and craggy Western forms are glimpsed above a New Jersey farm's horizon.[5]

About the meaning of that dream I am as uncertain as Wilbur himself, but because it illustrates an important idea behind this study, I shall conscript it as a parable. It reveals two noticeable features—the way in which the farm setting is scrupulously documented (the cowboy located by careful directives among the buildings), and the way in which the alien presence of the mountains intrudes upon that setting, enriching it and amplifying its horizons. Thus do regionalism and internationalism combine to form a distinctive compound. Wilbur's regionalism is open and unprovincial, the analogue of his earthbound spirituality. Some remarks on the two antithetic poles he straddles will help us to get his medial position in focus.

The eighteenth century was the heyday of cosmopolitan attitudes. Halfway through it, Dr. Johnson began *The Vanity of Human Wishes* with a "pan," sweeping in a vast cinematic arc from China to Peru and relying on this comprehensiveness to validate his characterizations of general nature. This "extensive view" is antiregionalist. No nook of the globe can offer itself as a possible resource of the spirit, for the world is itself unstable, and mutability and transience are its *necessary* features. The ideal of the *cives mundanus*, priding him- or herself on an inner strength that exalts the values of the spirit above the contingencies of time and place goes back to Seneca, and it lies at the heart of most Stoic thought, not least Dr. Johnson's.

Seneca's universalism finds an extreme antitype in the thought of William Carlos Williams, a poet readier than most regionalists to project the region as a cultural entity sealed off from, and unreceptive of, the pressures of internationalism and the cosmopolitan modes it engenders. David Ferry has pointed out that Williams was worried by the international character of *The Waste Land*, "its abandonment of 'the locality which should give it fruit'; and related to this is the disillusionment he found in that poem, which, in Williams's view would inevitably follow from its internationalism, its indifference to locality."[6] Indeed, Williams conceives America as a monolithic region whose borders are defined by a consciousness that rejects or strongly modifies the options of a European (and, by implication, a metropolitan) culture. This is how he puts his case: "From the shapes of men's lives imparted by the places where they have experience, good writing springs. One does not have to be uninformed, to consort with cows. One has to learn what the meaning of the local is, for universal purposes. The local is the only thing that is universal."[7] This is fine as a shibboleth, but it is obviously too intemperate to be useful.

As we might expect, Wilbur's stance is altogether more balanced:

> I react wistfully, as Miss Calisher does, to the French farmer's salute to letters; though such a man may not be a great reader himself, he testifies to an ancient feeling, long predating popular literacy, that the writer does a fundamental job in society. That feeling is not unheard-of here, but it is rarer, and I think that some of the reasons are obvious: our huge, diverse, ethnically jumbled and forever altering country does not have a deep-founded collective reality in relation to which a writer can seem widely functional. . . . I think that Robert Frost was the last American writer to be taken as representative of us all: because of his excellence, his patriotism, his venerability, his mentor style, his stemming from our British and New England origins.[8]

Like all Wilbur's critical pronouncements, this is wise and just, but it is not unproblematic. By privileging the Northeast as the *fons et origo* of American culture, he opens himself to attack by multicultural critics, even though his reference to the European connection is balanced by a crucial sense of patriotism, of the rootedness that enabled Frost to *adapt* such classical forms as the eclogue to mediate his localist, New England vision—a vision, after all, that has played a major (if not an exclusive) role in American literary history. Community, the foundation stone of regionalism, is for Wilbur the matrix of his poetry, and while he admits that Frost speaks for all and to all Americans, he also acknowledges that the culture he addresses is in fact an aggregate of regionalisms: "I think this is true of America, where beneath so much surface homogeneity there lies a radical commitment to diversity and to the toleration of dissent. We are not a settled and monolithic nation" (*On My Own Work*).

An American regionalism that defines itself through combat with the European metropole and its antitype, an openness to the heritage of Europe, are not, however, irreconcilable. Both Frost and Wilbur show that these apparent contrarieties can be resolved in synthesis. Both are blessed with a bifocality that keeps a steady eye on the regional object and yet feels no sense of cultural betrayal or compromise in mediating these perceptions through "international" form. The synthesis these poets achieve was also to some extent affected by the Nashville Fugitives. As Louis Rubin has noted, the movement did not at first seek to put down regionalist roots, but these soon grew out of the Agrarian manifesto:

> Rebelling from the United Daughters of the Confederacy tradition in Southern letters, they had found self-conscious sectionalism a hindrance to their own

literary development. In the later years of the decade [the twenties], however, as they thought more and more about the role of poetry and the arts in American life, their attitude changed. . . .

At this point the four leading Fugitive poets turned to the South. . . . In the history of the South they perceived the image of a region that had for many years resisted the domination of the machine, persisting in its agricultural ways even after military conquest, and well into the present century, and only then, in the 1920's, beginning to capitulate fully to the standards of American industrial society.[9]

Here we detect that recurring impatience with the materialism of the metropole and the redemptive vision of a regionalist culture wedded to the soil.

Wilbur is a poet acutely conscious of both poles in the argument. In an essay entitled "Regarding Places," he gives an account of a walk in the New England countryside with a friend, a friend so caught up with his internationalist art that he cannot respond to the local detail before him. Wilbur's vision is by contrast a covalent one—he is able to respond to his immediate setting *as well as* to the abstractions that obsess the cyclopean artist walking with him: "But my friend from New York, an excellent abstract artist, walks through our Berkshire woods smoking Gauloises and talking of Berlin. It is too bad that he cannot be where he is, enjoying the glades and closures, the climbs, the descents, the flat stretches strewn with Canada Mayflower. . . . The elaborate arrangement of the hop hornbeam's leaves would engage my friend's exquisite sense of line and pattern, if only he would see it, but he will not."[10] Later in the same essay, he mentions a motel in South Carolina, equally displaced, unnative, unendued. Here the usurping metropole is not Berlin but Paris, reduced to a suite of predictable photographs. The effect is the same, however—that impoverished sense of belonging, that blunting of response to locality:

> Within were an office, a restaurant that did not offer grits on the breakfast menu, and, for the rest, long corridors lined with identical rooms in which hung pictures of the Pont Neuf and the Arc de Triomphe. . . . In bed that night, I imagined that I heard crying out from beneath the asphalt, asking to be a place again, a place in Carolina. And I had the bad fancy that we Americans might be becoming a race which, for all its restless motion, moves by preference through . . . an anaesthetic modular world in which we are at home only because things are everywhere the same (*Responses*, p. 155).

If there is something of Hopkins in this impassioned sense that an inscape has been "unselved" by the uniformity of Hiltonism, that is because Wilbur has regionalist sympathies as vivid as the English poet's, however different his conception and practice of poetic form.

Wilbur's mediate position between the extreme and finally impractical regionalism of poets like Williams (not to mention the multicultural critics who succeed him) and the geographically unrooted position of exiles like

T. S. Eliot can perhaps be ascribed to his New England heritage, the mediateness of which is apparent in the very name "New England." Frank Wells has characterized its nineteenth-century culture as something based on the "curious marriage of provinciality and cosmopolitanism whereby they remained provincials in heart and cosmopolitans in mind."[11]

Wilbur documents such mental cosmopolitanism in "The Genie in the Bottle," an essay whose title has by now acquired the dignity of proverb. Here he stresses objective form as a source of self-extension and discipline:

> The use of strict poetic forms, traditional or invented, is like the use of framing and composition in painting: both serve to limit the work of art, and to declare its artificiality: they say, "This is not the world, but a pattern imposed upon the world or found in it; this is a partial and provisional attempt to establish relations between things."
>
> There are other less metaphysical reasons for preferring strictness of form: the fact, for example, that subtle variation is unrecognizable without the preexistence of a norm; or the fact that form, in slowing and complicating the writing-process, calls out the poet's full talents, and thereby insures a greater care and cleverness in the disposition of words. In general, I would say that limitation makes for power: the strength of the genie comes of his being confined in a bottle.[12]

"Strict poetic forms" are unlikely to be yielded by regionalist culture, if only because the folk art that produces, say, an artless ballad is not an art concealing art by any Horatian sleight of hand. Nor are more self-conscious artists forging new forms as an act of anticolonial faith likely to manage much by way of strictness. Self-evolved laws will fit the contours of the self instead of challenging its habits and velleities.

Yet at the same time, Wilbur's creed has little bearing on that of Wallace Stevens, even in spite of the points of contact between them. Form imposes pattern on the world, and yet the world is there tractably or reluctantly to receive it, not to be displaced by the artifact that denatures its materials as it admits them to the alternative permanence of art. In "The Genie in the Bottle" Wilbur also objects to the artistic confusion of windows and doors:

> If art is a window, then the poem is something intermediate in character, limited, synecdochic, a partial vision of a part of the world. It is the means of a dynamic relation between the eye within and the world without. If art is conceived to be a door, then the dynamic relation is destroyed. The artist no longer perceives a wall between him and the world; the world becomes an extension of himself, and is deprived of its reality. The poet's words cease to be a means of liaison with the world; they take the place of the world. This is bad aesthetics—and incidentally, bad morals (p. 7).

If the word becomes the world (though this is not Wilbur's meaning), it will follow that the floodgates of cosmopolitanism will open; everything will acquire the potential to pass for something else because it lacks a local habitation and a name. Better the regionalist's sense of an experienced *part*, the sense of offering what is known in the confidence that knowledge confers authenticity. This is one implication of Wilbur's "partial view of part of the world."

However, the limitation that discipline imposes must not be confused with circumscription. I cannot agree with Stephen Stepanchev that Wilbur's strenuous and committed submission to form makes for airlessness: "It can, no doubt, be said that his commitment to traditional techniques is confining; the postulates of the verbal and metrical system that he has adopted rule out a great deal of everyday experience and also the sort of technical experimentation that sees every poem as a challenging new genre."[13] This, it goes without saying, is based on false assumptions. Everyday experience, the staple experience of regionalism, is not "ruled out" by formal discipline; if anything, it is heightened by the challenge of established form. Genres, furthermore, are institutional and evolutionary, seldom the creation of a single poet, and Stepanchev's notion that an innovative poet regards every utterance as a "new genre" cannot bear inspection.

We have seen Wilbur claim that poetry can at best offer "a partial and provisional attempt to establish relations between things." Partiality, while on the one hand it conjures up notions of sectionalism, also suggests affectionate, paternal bias. A love of matter instinct with values of the spirit is very different from the materialism that some imagistic poets espouse. Up till now my emphasis has fallen squarely on Wilbur's regionalism as revealed in the transcriptive fidelity of his poems, a fidelity enlarged and strengthened by his readiness at the same time to embrace a "cosmopolitan" variety of forms and techniques, many of which are not the outgrowths of an indigenous American tradition. Indeed, his regionalism itself is flexible and adaptive. We see him in his first collection, newly arrived in Europe from America, somehow managing to create a stabilizing spirit of place amid the bewilderment and disruption of a war-ravaged continent. In middle age, granted an opportunity to spend some time in Rome, he seizes it not as a chance to accumulate the fragmentary perceptions of place a tourist might gather, but to learn Italian, to read Dante, and so to effect the cultural saturation that is a strength of regionalism (cf. *Responses*, pp. 73–74). In such resolves we have cosmopolitan regionalism revealed to perfection: openness and inwardness balanced and synthesized.

Nor do the balance and synthesis stop there. One could go so far as to expand the idea of regionalism not only to fit continents (as Williams expands it), but also to embrace the world in all its tangible reality—what one might term *terrestrial regionalism*. For materialist poets, the term would be meaningless, since they have no ontological alternative to the materials they explore. But Wilbur, for whom the realm of the spirit is real, does in fact have a choice—that of disregarding "the dome of many colored glass" as some idealist poets before him have done or, alternatively, of effecting a synthesis of matter and soul. There is nothing extreme about him, however, and in this, as in all things, he manages a *via media*. While he clearly respects the thinking of Edgar Allan Poe in these matters, there can be no doubting its remoteness from his own: "Vagueness and indefinitiveness were, in Poe's aesthetic theory, indispensable to the highest art, because they estrange the reader from mundane fact and meaning, and presumably set him adrift toward the spiritual and dim" (*Responses*, p. 51). In Wilbur, on the other hand, there is no estrangement, no drift, and no dimness. Facts are lovingly and attentively documented; metaphor in his hands becomes a precise and clarifying instrument. He is a regionalist of the earth, with all the regionalist's locality and calm attachment. And yet, as in the case of Wordsworth, the reality of the region glows with an additional, immanent radiance, the radiance of the "God, who is our home." Both poets imbricate the material upon the spiritual. One can even detect an affinity between Wilbur's position and the organicist theory of A. N. Whitehead:

> The materialistic starting point is from independently existing substances, matter and mind. The matter suffers modifications of its external relations of locomotion, and the mind suffers modifications of its contemplated objects. There are, in this materialistic theory, two sorts of independent substances, each qualified by their appropriate passions. The organic starting point is from the analysis of process in the realisation of events disposed in an interlocked community. The event is the unit of things real. The emergent enduring pattern is the stabilisation of the emergent achievement so as to become a fact which retains its identity through the process.[14]

A sense of "interlocked community" is the hallmark of Wilbur's terrestrial regionalism. There is that stalwart commitment to the created world, tangibly there, assailed by poems that define both it and themselves in real and tactile encounters, but synthesized with spirit as region is synthesized with metropole.

I have spoken again and again of Wilbur's mediate position between alternative extremes, a position that connects him to other poets of transition, especially those who wrote during the Age of Sensibility. Thomas Gray is chief among these writers encusped on opposing modes of thought and technique, and I believe that it is Gray above all whom Wilbur most resembles. Both rank among the great craftspersons of English poetry, and both, distilling crystalline poems with the utmost care, have been stigmatized for sacrificing energy to the pursuit of perfect form. Attentive reading of both writers will nonetheless show that their consciousness of poetic heritage, far from weakening the impact of their verse, actually canalizes its intensity. I shall thus draw parallels between Gray and Wilbur throughout this study, not so much because I wish to establish a conscious debt of influence—"In a Churchyard" contains the only *explicit* allusion to the earlier poet—but because I am struck by their similarities of habit, thought, and procedure.

Also, because eighteenth-century verse, beautifully turned and artistically conscious as it is, responds gratefully to rhetorical analysis, so too, in my opinion, does Wilbur's. I have therefore taken pains in this survey to highlight the elegance of the poetry by invoking the tropes and figures by which that elegance is often secured. Wilbur is an expert in the field of Renaissance poetry and the greatest translator of Molière that the world has known. We should therefore feel no surprise when these interests feed and nourish the formality of his verse.

one

the
b e a u t i f u l
c h a n g e s
and
o t h e r
p o e m s
(1 9 4 7)

by claiming that the "accent of our native country dwells in the heart and mind as well as in the tongue,"[1] the Duc de la Rochefoucauld has suggested that we are all to some extent regionalists, conditioned in crucial ways by circumstances of birth and culture. However, because many poems in Wilbur's first collection record his experiences as a soldier in Europe, his native accents of heart and mind sound for the first time in an alien milieu. One might have expected laments of dislocation and puzzlement, and yet even the earliest poems testify to his knack of adapting and adopting, of naturalizing his responses by acts of sheer attention. John Reibetanz has claimed that in his early poems Wilbur "assumed the ideals of a culture, but one that was urban and international rather than rural and local."[2] That is a part of the truth, but it needs to be qualified. Possessed of a wide-ranging, "internationalist" sensibility, he was able to enter into the milieux that the war brought with it and thus to strike notes of authentic locality in his European poems, even as he carried his American circumstances into them (in "Tywater" and "Mined Country," for example). From the start, that crucial balance of habitation and distance gave the poems their regional-cosmopolitan flavor and set him on a course of integrating opposites from which he has never wavered.

"Cicadas" (formerly "Cigales"), the opening lyric (NCP, p. 337), is in many ways a typical effort—detailed, attentive, and concerned to fix an exact sensuous nuance. We are invoked almost collusively at the start, the demonstrative in the reference to evenings spanning the poet's and the reader's experience in an intimate way. Whereas Reibetanz claims that the poem is "very stiffly trying to involve us in [its] world by direct reference to us" ("What Love Sees," p. 68), I find that the pronouns relax rather than stiffen the diction and moreover build an experiential bridge. The night is presumably a Mediterranean one, but we can recognize its similarity to hot nights of our own experience, no matter what our location might be. Wilbur evokes satiety of a rich, sensuous order, with an amplitude almost Keatsian. Its source is not immediately disclosed; we are simply given the data of repleteness: sounds that, like the amplified frequencies of a gramophone re-cord, owe their existence to friction and attrition; sounds that, like the clogged utterances of a record losing speed, cannot be construed and that have ended with harmonic finality—the fullness of the quiet obviously sug-gests a full close (a perfect cadence). In these are embodied the languor and ripening promise of summer that even the leaves—the media of sibylline prophecy—are too parched to whisper.

It is not Wilbur's habit to stop there, however. Evocation leads almost at once to meditation, or at least to meditation on meditators, people who have sought emblematic values for the cicada. Their method is not Wilbur's, though. Simple signs are signs of simplification—they reduce a complex, baffling reality. Emblem verse, with its tendency toward patness, is not easily practiced in a post-Darwinian world. The elegant stealth with which Wilbur begins forging emblematic links in this lyric therefore seems all the more remarkable. At the very moment he calls traditional iconographies into ques-tion, he sets about constructing his own. One is reminded of Auden's praise for Marianne Moore—"The approach of her poetry is that of a naturalist, but, really, their theme is almost always the Good Life. . . . Occasionally . . . the moral is direct, but, as a rule, the reader has to perceive it for himself."[3]

The brisk, discursive mode of the third stanza, not unlike that at the end of D. H. Lawrence's "Bat," is designed to jolt us into a sense of how prob-lematic any simple emblem-mongering is likely to be. Having languidly suc-cumbed to the spell of Wilbur's evocation, we are galvanized by this change of tone. The swiftly disposed preterite verbs displace the present tense of lassitude supplying, as in an encyclopedia entry, a resumé of the meanings imposed upon the cicada. We are no doubt meant to recall that in China it symbolizes "continuity between man, his ancestors, and his descendants,"[4] while in the more sinister context of the Tithonus myth,[5] it conveys an ever-withering longevity. Wilbur's reference to ants also momentarily conflates the cicada with the grasshopper of Fontaine (the French *cigale* covers both insects), presenting it as a type of the self-absorbed hedonist. That these disparate myths should cancel each other out serves Wilbur's purpose to perfection—the song cannot be construed in any simple way. The rapidly adduced moralizations slide off the subject as soon as they are applied, just as its noise eludes any attempt at onomatopoeia. But while the cicada defeats the redactions and reductions of apologue and verse fable, its very mysteriousness makes it a recurring source of interest to different people with different cultures, and hence the binding quality of the air/aria, which creates a cohesion comparable to the languid stickiness of the summer night.

As a French entomologist discovered, the insect cannot hear, and this deafness in itself becomes emblematic. Deaf to our questions like Keats's urn, it teases us out of thought. Deaf, and yet not dumb. The cicada becomes an oracular voice, the center of a quest for meaning. At the very moment that the insect's deafness is asserted, the aural cohesion of rhyming "air" with "hear" begins paradoxically to seal up the stanza. The tree becomes by extension the *fagus* of *sub tegmine fagi* motif of pastoral, the cannon an instance of the technology of war. So, at the very moment of revoking all past inadequate efforts to give significance to the song, the poet's parable reveals how science, as much as the spirit, is baffled in its search for meaning.

A similarly deft and unobtrusive kind of emblem can be found in "Water Walker" (NCP, p. 338). The title of the poem (a meditation on transfiguring commitment) alludes to Christ as well as to the caddis fly, whose amphibious shift in life-style between larval and adult stages parallels the fusion of deity and humanity. A precedent for this undemonstrative rather than deictic mode of emblem occurs in Yeats's "Long-legged Fly," though in that poem the refrain is carefully set aside and differently connected with matter in each of the stanzas it clarifies and knits together. In the Wilbur lyric the insect parallel is more intimately braided with the human content, giving rise to what Randall Jarrell has called "an animal-morality poem about St. Paul."[6] The emblematic turn from tenor to vehicle is made at line 5, its monometer supplying the brace rhyme for the second part of the stanza and for its stranded trimeter "afterthought." Indeed the movement of the stanza at line 5 is—in its compressed way—like the volta of an Italian sonnet, springing the material forward to a new thematic path.

But what in sonnets is usually a smooth transition here takes on a startling disjunctness. The unbeliever is like the hero of J. A. Froude's *The Nemesis of Faith* (1849): "Could you see down below his heart's surface, could you count the tears streaming down his cheeks, as out through some church-door into the street come pealing the old familiar notes, and the old psalms which he cannot sing, the chanted creed which is no longer his creed, and yet to part with which was more agony than to lose his dearest friend; ah! you would deal with him in lighter measure."[7] The effect of connecting infidel and caddis fly does not so much equate as dissociate them—the unbeliever persists in his sentimental element of tears, Byronic self-pity at his own damnation, whereas the caddis fly is shifting elements and, in terms of the old Greek hierarchy, aspiring to the nobler one of air. Its "spring-surface" is on one level the hydropneumatic pond-surface and, on another, a reference to the season of spring and the burgeoning life it brings with it. In terms of this discreet emblem of renascence, the caddis fly, given the duality of its nature, hints at the duality of humankind as well—a duality of body and soul that the infidel refuses to acknowledge. None of this is blatantly set forth. The poet's editorial comment is as cryptic and elusive as anything in Frost, his irresolute use of "something" picking up such statements as that at the start of *Mending Wall.* Yet, while the caddis fly might seem to symbolize the evasion of a less-exalted state of being, the poet stresses that its life is cyclical and that it reverts to water to ensure its continuity, a point neatly compounded by the cross-linear assonance of "air" and "heirs." He aligns it now with St. Paul's change from Jewish persecutor to Christian evangelist. The phonetic element that threaded "air" and "heirs" together is paralleled by repeated vowel sounds in the nonce name that compacts separate personalities in a new identity, larva and adult fly are physically discontinuous and yet one and the same thing. There is a subtle reversal, however. Whereas the caddis fly was seen to emerge from water into liberating air, St. Paul walks the point where air blends into water, suggesting the salvific "descent" of intangible God as tangible Incarnation (one would ordinarily expect *water* to mist into *air*), his parturient brooding on the waters, and even the sacrament of baptism.

At this point the poem broaches the topic of regionalism with a bluntness that is not entirely typical of Wilbur. The folksy interior in Virginia invites the poet to root himself comfortably in the local and to surrender the extension and expansion alternative modes of being might secure—as if the caddis fly were to spurn the option of air and live its life in water. It is worth pausing to inquire into the function of disjunctive moments like the one above, which jumps from caddis fly emblem to St. Paul to the poet himself, for Wilbur's transitions are generally so smooth and graceful. The answer, I think, is to be found later on, in the image of the caddis fly's sheath, made from debris of the stream but cemented into unity. Its flat stones momentarily evoke the stone that sealed the sepulcher and so, with the lightest of brush strokes, hint again at the resurrection of the fly, emerging from its three-day sleep in death. But the randomness of its nest materials also indicates the many and various topics the poet has gathered into his poem and sealed into the caddis sheath of stanza form. The angular, disjunct materials therefore have a programmatic function.

After this, we drop from the frequentative present (describing a cycle) to the past tense of another random memory, as folksy and regionalist as the Virginian lamplight, but now rendered with the universal amplitude of Walt Whitman, a debt which Glauco Cambon has also noted.[8] The Whitmanesque feel to this and other moments of the poem derives not only from the recollection of the "cradle endlessly rocking" in the motion of the chair, but also from the prophetic *vidi* that takes all experience into itself. While these observations hardly have the sweep and inclusiveness of Whitman's "omnivorous lines,"[9] they do subsume different experiences in a vigilant, all-embracing consciousness and so bring the *Song of Myself* to mind. The idea is developed later in the geographical coordinates of a northern and southern state and in the antitheses of the material and the spiritual. It is clear, however, that simple annotation, simple passive encompassment, is insufficient in itself, or so at least the question mark of the penultimate stanza would seem to imply.

By returning to the caddis fly at this point, Wilbur suggests that the accumulation of experience is simply a starting point. While a verb of obligation implies that the fly's eggs need to incubate in the passive suspension of the pond, it also has the effect of ordaining the rest—a runway pause, a gathering of the metamorphic energy that will turn Saul to Paul, larva to fly. The poem ends with an application of the emblem made on terms similar to Herbert's, for the pronoun opens the door to anyone sharing the poet's concern about responsibility to region or the world, to the active or contemplative life. Wilbur's solution is to balance them, however tenuous the balance may be, and however often it might involve relapse, return, and reconstruction. The structural reference to *da capo* at the end of the poem makes it over as a rondo extending itself infinitely into the future by renewing its melodic energy in repetition. Bruce Michelson presents a different view by giving the instruction a Sisyphan flavor: "No benedictions here, no consolations; this is one of Wilbur's most affecting poems on the unresolvable dilemma of knowing who one really is, and on the price one pays for affirming anything, within or without, beyond the solid, safe, unsatisfactory places of the world and the mind."[10]

In the lyric that follows "Water Walker," Wilbur looks briefly at the sort of soul that tries to find meaning in action alone, a soul that the choices so delicately adumbrated in the cycle of the caddis fly have never troubled. After fruitlessly trying to identify the subject of this mock-dirge, I wrote to the poet for help and learned that Tywater had been a vigorous Texan corporal who, as a civilian, had performed in rodeos—a fact that gives the poem a sort of acid affinity with e. e. cummings's "Buffalo Bill's defunct." It is typical of Wilbur's bifocal outlook that he should begin his lament for a rodeo artist (NCP, p. 342) as though for a knight in some infinite extension of *The Faerie Queene*. In this way the parallels and differences between rodeo and joust are established in the same breath. Even in the midst of the formality, the suppression of the verb in stanza 1 and of the noun in stanza 2 conveys the laconic, casual toughness of the subject.

The diction veers from an almost Wildean preciousness to the roughspun and energetic idiom of rural America, synthesizing disparate traditions and generating irony all the way. The stress on manly prowess at the rodeo and in the chivalric tradition from which it springs makes Tywater a sort of knight manqué, a knight without spiritual directives. His is a virility hypostatized and divorced from a larger purpose—neither the flowers of chastity nor of comradely faithfulness (lily and hyacinth) can be found on his bier. The skills Wilbur describes are apodictic and futile—whether it be the savage impalement of a swallow on a throwing knife (an act of repulsive brutality) or the virtuoso management of a lasso—Tywater's emotional life is as inorganic as the grin by which, show-business style, he conveys his casualness. In the more conventional idiom of epigraph, Wilbur sums up the life of Tywater in a manner similar to Gray's at the end of the *Elegy Written in a Country Churchyard:* its "alls" obviously resonate with the encompassing "alls" of "He gave to Mis'ry all he had, a tear, / He gain'd from Heav'n ('twas all he wish'd) a friend." But there is not much to add to the précis once it has been made, and the poet bemusedly contemplates his dearth of material, his strong caesura in the final line an image of word-searching hesitation.

"Mined Country" (NCP, p. 343) also at one point invokes Spenser only to revoke him. The title refers to the legacy the Germans have left for the advancing Allies and also hints, as Donald Hill has pointed out,[11] at "mind country" and the reformation of consciousness that the mines will bring about. Wilbur at first creates a sense of respite but, by using the perfect tense, implies that this is only temporary. The absence of soldiers, as he later explains, does not necessarily entail an absence of the war that has permeated the whole landscape. Hills are theologically associated with divine help (as for example in Psalm 121), but here they are as gray and threatening as gun metal. And even the birches, traditionally sinuous and feminine, turn into the panoply of a porcupine. Being and seeming have thus been pulled apart. Wilbur's stanza seems at first to comprise dull, nonrhyming elements, but in a way that represents the delayed detonation of the mines themselves; the rhyme-explosions are suspended until the second stanza, where they are set off line by line. Wilbur is not ordinarily a vehement poet, and his use of vigorous assertions have here an unsettlingly harsh effect. The distress of the speaker emerges in the rawness of the diction, a distress at the loss of innocence and of the Edenic myths that support it.

While cicadas survived the blast of cannon by virtue of being impervious, humans lack this resource of indifference, the more so since the mines have cut to the roots of culture: landscape and civilization are always inter-involved. The American soldiers sweeping the country have potentially differing responses to it, but all are finally subverted and equalized by the presence of death beneath the surface. For those whose sense of Europe extends to the culture it engenders, it is Greek myth or Spenserian fancy whose charm is destroyed; for others more intractably wedded to the native culture, it is the stereotypes of calendar photography that have been undermined. Whatever the cultural projection, it is skewed by the presence of death. *Et in Arcadia ego.* Reconstituting nature in terms of mortality, the Germans have given new force to Augustinian conceptions of the fall.

So it is that the innocent nonsense of "Hey diddle diddle" is at once travestied and literalized in the sky-flung cows while nature at large becomes a sinister Bower of Bliss. Roses, which, as in St. Bernard's *rosa mys-*

tica sine spina, have often been aligned with chastity, are turned into whores. In a word, the pastoral mode is no longer viable, as the wry ambiguity of "quickly" implies. The poem ends by interiorizing the cautious progress of the mine-sweepers, and the poet gingerly retraces his mythic inheritance, revoking, as the mines have forced others to revoke, the axiomatic assumptions of the child who is dumb both in the sense of being an infant (*in-fans*) and unknowing. However, once a field has been swept, its innocence is to some extent restored, and it is toward this restoration, however broken and sorry it might seem, that Wilbur urges his poem.

"Potato" (NCP, p. 345) is also partly about the transmutation of consciousness brought about by war. Its brisk, telegraphic dispatch issues in what we could call lexical apposition, for several of its stanzas are tacked explicatively onto the title. The syntax here is as rough and ready as the outward form of the potato itself. Noun jostles appositively against noun, and a strange aorist verb "got" (or is it a participle?) forcing itself against the grain of the syntax, acts out the tenacity, adaptiveness, and inelegance of the vegetable itself. Wilbur's vision is similarly adaptive. At one point the potato approximates a soldier in his foxhole, dressed in military drab; at another it becomes an icon of the planet earth, paradoxically simple and complex. As well as being an explicable aggregate of chemicals, the vegetable is also a planetary microcosm. At the same time, while "with all" suggests the plenitude of the earth, it can collapse into itself to form "withal" and so take on the the the reluctant, stinted quality of a concessive adverb. These paradoxes are compounded in the following stanzas, which harness the participles of recipe books to fanciful conceits. The oxymoronic tension of its pure stench is almost immediately developed in the idea of a clean-aired grave. Entombed in the flavor of the potato are the primitive civilizations of Europe, civilizations to whose values the soldiers are forced to regress. In the reference to stones we have a hint of the neolithic, in that to the woods a primitive horror of *natura naturans.*

Kenneth Clark has pointed out that permanence is a necessary condition for the development of civilization,[12] but these soldiers, like the marauding tribes who brought about the end of the Roman Empire, leave cinders in their wake. The Dark Ages have returned. And yet, while these sinister data are accumulating, Wilbur is able to present the potato as sustainer and nurturer, its very bleakness the vehicle of salvation. He later invokes the mobility and luxuriousness of postwar society, whose packets of oranges offset the intransigence and minimalism of the potato. By translating the vegetable back from the French, he is able to invest it with mythic nonsignificance— while it might be an apple of sorts, it is neither Hesperidean nor Edenic, but simply an undistinguished source of nourishment. There is something about the poem that invites comparison with an *Intimiste* still life, especially in the way it moves unobtrusively from the object to the clothing ideas and back again. This is how Bonnard described his *modus operandi* to Angèle Lamotte: "The point of departure for a painting being an idea, if the object itself is there at the moment when he is working there is always the danger that the artist will allow himself to be taken in by the specifics of the immediate view of it and in so doing lose the initial idea."[13]

In "Potato" Wilbur withholds all touches of transfigurative glamor to fit it out as an emblem of war and bleak survival; in "First Snow in Alsace" (NCP, p. 347) he does the opposite and presents snow as a benediction in the midst of violence. In the first stanza the moon figures as an enlarged domestic lamp, and the snow disposes cloths across a ravaged landscape, while in the last stanza, the sobering, forced adulthood of war falls away and returns a soldier to the innocence of childhood. Everywhere the evidence of evil is veiled. But whereas nature in "Mined Country" looks like the innocent flower while being the serpent under it, here Wilbur manages a series of double exposures, making us conscious all the time of the machinery of war buried beneath the purifying snow. The *terza rima* chosen to enumerate the details of the scene has faint echoes of the *Commedia Divina* and also perhaps of Shelley's *Ode to the West Wind*, both of them concerned with spiritual renovation. But a much more tangible poetic presence in the poem is that of Robert Frost, especially the rough, peasanty line about the snow's ignorance of change, with its hint of rural animism. Indeed the whole tenor of the poem, in which metaphoric values are half held in reserve, is Frostian. A snow-decked roof has always been a stereotype of Christmas cheer, but here the snow is clasping only a domestic shell—all the family values of the season have been lost to the violence and fission of war.

The same irony pervades the domes by which the snow has transformed ration stacks into basilicas and the semblance of sweetness and light its iced honeycomb has given to heaps of ammunition. Yet all the time we are aware that the snow is transient and that the respite it offers from disruption and chaos is illusory. While the Keatsian aesthetic eye feeds deep, deep upon what it sees displayed about it, we are reminded that snow feeds the eyes of corpses in a very different way.

In the following poem Wilbur also dwells on eyes ostensibly human, yet cold as the snow in the sockets of the dead soldiers. The first two stanzas of "On the Eyes of an SS Officer" (NCP, p. 348) map out climatic and temperamental extremes: polar and torrid zones, the ambition of an antarctic explorer verging on monomania and the self-denial of a fakir that has emptied life of meaning as well as of the self. And yet in the dialectic shift toward the third, which is a sestet in everything but line count, they are absorbed into each other and turn positive in relation to the Nazi ideal. Against its life-denying conception of racial and social "pureness," Wilbur sets the fecundity and inexhaustible fullness of the Creator, improvisatory, various, and unpredictable, encompassing rather than excluding. The poem, slight though it might at first seem, is a little *credo*. As ever, it is fullness of being that Wilbur exalts, a fullness that incorporates the spiritual subject with the object of its desire.

Another poem that, like "Mined Country," explores the derangement in wartime of ordinary decencies and civilized values is "Place Pigalle" (NCP, p. 349). This also brings together mythic types and their debased contemporary equivalents. The first two stanzas begin with the adverb "now," but the parallel phrasing serves only to stress the difference between a bourgeoisie that is returning home and the men and women who embark on a quest for pleasure. The ironic contrast is intensified by the pigeonlike, centripetal motion of the *homing* businesspeople and the centrifugal vigor of bars that *explode* against the night. Commercial thoughts center on improved conditions, implying that the war is over and some sort of restitution is underway, and yet that very stability (forged from references to warehouse, storefront, and nursery) is being guaranteed by soldiers whose values are not those of the citizens. Indeed, a guard-changing quite different from the military one takes place in the inner city each night. The exploding bars are obviously public houses, but they are also figuratively the emblems of discarded restraint, as well as the neon tubes that have become the decor of the urban night. Wilbur seems to be hinting in his own way at that unholy symbiosis of order and indecency that Blake projected in his image of a "marriage hearse." The soldiers' coming to seek their whores furthermore recalls the formula of pilgrimage we find in *The Canterbury Tales* and in Donne's "Twickenham Garden," an irony whose bitterness is compounded by Wilbur's shift from the innocence of boys to the raddlement of age. Indeed the faces are like those of apes, a bestiary emblem of lust. The prostitutes whose company they seek are similarly raddled and ancient—ancient also in the sense of being immemorial, for even in the Homeric epics, war has been the solvent of family life. A jazzy dissonance can be found in failed internal rhymes of "stroll"/"loll" and "glares"/"glass," details that counterpoint the homing scurry of the tradespeople and their protective glass capsules in stanza 1.

The suspended, undirected feelings of the pleasure-seekers register in appositive phrases that bob about without a firm syntactic matrix. Appositions are built on interchangeable foundations, icon of the relations between whore and soldier. These contrasts are underscored by the *inclusio* of the next stanza, where the restless pleasure-seekers are enclosed by references to hounds and puppies (bourgeois citizens) whose static restfulness is also conveyed by the inversion of "snore" and "hounds." The resulting chiasmus projects an image of stability. In the following stanza the poet returns to an insecure, appositive mode of syntax. The electric graces, subverting the idyll of Botticelli's *Primavera* with the feverishness of a cabaret, are picked up again in the reference to ionization. This suggests both the instability of electrically charged particles and the speed with which innocence is subverted by the restlessness of lust. Also in the background of "Ionized" is "Ionic," the softness of the mode subverted by the harsh reality at hand, just as Corinthian curls bring to mind not only the acanthus motif of the capital but also the uncovered hair of the temple prostitutes in Corinth. Further allusions to *As You Like It* and to Shakespeare's twenty-ninth sonnet set their freshness and earnestness against urban corruption. This is the underside of the metropole—a glimpse of its garishness and rootlessness and superficiality.

"Place Pigalle" is a harsh poem, with something of the harshness of Juvenal. Soldier and whore, involved in an unstable union, dramatize the continuity of lust and death. Such a despairing prophetic tone is much less characteristic of Wilbur than of Lowell and, as if to expiate its judgmental solemnity, the poet follows it with "Violet and Jasper" (NCP, p. 350). This dates from Wilbur's postwar sojourn at Harvard and presents a Rabelaisian barmaid as the image of vitality and strength. She is placed in opposition to the students outside, mere epigones of a Puritan tradition. The deictics of the poem align the speaker with the vital life inside the tavern, opposed to the mincing undergraduates, ignorant of the flesh rather than triumphant over it—their sweatlessness suggests that more strenuous confrontations lie before them. While there is something Dantesque about the marl that burns outside, the metronomic click of "pick" against "Pecked," the dainty oxymoron that combines petiteness with damnations, and the uninfernal setting in New England—all these supply a derisory bathos. Neither do Violet and Jasper altogether escape the writer's good-naturedly critical gaze. He gives her an Arcimbaldo profile, a lettuce swarming indiscriminately with both spiritual and carnal concerns. Her paddling fingers similarly confuse those of the lascivious Gertrude—Hamlet uses the identical word—with the wings of the Bethesda angel. The puritanical self-restraint of the students is matched here by the intellectual abnegation of their monkish brains.

In the final verse Wilbur gathers up the traditional opposition of town and gown in an epiphany that might or might not hint at the Atonement, for both the materialistic, semireligious barmaid and the academic puritans are subsumed into another Arcimbaldo form, which is also the sacred form of the mandorla. These ingathering formal distortions result from the refraction of light by a flask of colored water, the dye of which also brings to mind the apocalyptic vision of Faustus—"See, see, where Christ's blood streams in the firmament." Here the poet disarmingly and honestly aligns himself with the scurrying bourgeoisie in the preceding poem.

"The Peace of Cities" (NCP, p. 351) is another of the sober war poems, recording not the thick of battle that Owen and other poets of conflict dwelt on, but the hiatus—blank and discomposing—between armistice and the resumption of ordinary life. "Mined Country" traced the inapplicability of hallowed myths to a countryside refashioned by the violence of war; "The Peace of Cities," while it records the absence of bombs and gunfire, suggests that disjunction and alienation have been internalized in the very texture of urban life. The severance of each couplet from the other almost gives the poem the force of a technopaegnion or shape poem, since it images the barriers that are as much a feature of life in a quiet American town as the barricades in war-ravaged cities. Alienation does not end with war; it persists at the very heart of human affairs. The barriers exclude (and contain) the violence that humankind persists in practicing on itself. Wilbur's couplets, lacking the traditional fixity of rhyme, suggest that within each unit there is no sufficiency. A little room is not an everywhere for people who, far from being members of a community, are merely a congeries of individuals. This sense of being uncentered is then compared with the communities that suffered the blitzes, and which were somehow tempered and unified by the experience. The communality that grew from sharing such horrors is conveyed in the final couplet manqué, where the menace of Waffe (weapon) is lyricized as a wafting—in destroying the cellular, barriered nature of city life, it has allowed sunlight to reclaim shadow and broken down separative and excluding doors.

"The Giaour and the Pacha" (NCP, p. 352) is paradoxical in a different way, being the ecphrasis (or verbal transcript) of a painting that derives in turn from Byron. One cannot be absolutely certain which of Delacroix's fifteen versions of this subject Wilbur had in mind, for he sometimes takes painters rather than paintings as his starting point. Let us assume, though, that the picture in the Art Institute of Chicago is his primary source for the poem.[14]

The poem begins in past tense beyond the frame of the painting (which can present its subject only in the arrested present of plastic form) and then modulates into the tense of contemplation, the tense forever keeping sword and pistol from the pasha in Delacroix's picture. As if further to mark the conversion of time into timeless plasticity, the components of the scene become spatial arabesques and compositional markers: air turns into a two-dimensional bedding agent for materials that the painter has flattened into the pictorial plane. Like the lovers in Keats's "Ode on a Grecian Urn," the Giaour is thwarted of any resolution in time, suspended from its flux in the plastic moment, and so condemned to a state of frustrating evermore-about-to-be. Even an art concerned with things must take stock of semblances. As Delacroix himself noted, "The more literal the imitation, the flatter it is, and the more it shows how impossible it is to rival the original. One can only hope to arrive at some approximate equivalent. It is not the thing itself which must be done, but only its semblance: and there again the effect must be for the soul and not the eye."[15]

While the Delacroix poem ponders the arrestation of the time and the surrender of human to pictorial purpose, "Up, Jack" (NCP, p. 353) deals with the buoyant resurrections that are the property of drama—a form that is ritualistic, and so repeatable *ad infinitum*. The language of stage directions is worked into the very body of the verse and affirms the cyclical nature of an art whose continuity depends in part on its ability to cleanse the souls of those who watch it. The heroism of Hal's combat with Percy would seem a touch strident and even incomplete without the antimasque of Falstaff's cowardice and feigned death. His "resurrection" and the indestructible spirit he embodies accordingly balance the play's heroics and satisfy the viewer's desire for a full, not a stylized, account of experience.

"In a Bird Sanctuary" (NCP, p. 354) shares with "Cicadas" its delicate version of the emblematic mode. Wilbur momentarily catches the tone of Ogden Nash, processing his material briskly through a stanza that brakes sharply on a dimeter—a sort of pulling up and cutting short. The poem's characteristic rhythm and tone are best exemplified by the third stanza. This sprightly verse is from first to last a confession of failure, a linear failure that, by withholding an upper case from each alternate line, suggests that the stanza is tyrannically forcing itself on a decameter that it fractures to secure a fit. At the same time it suggests the failure of the poem to encompass the essence of bird—*quod erat demonstrandum*. All that can be said about the inexpressibility of birds is that it is inexpressible, whether by the naive musical onomatopoeia of such compositions as Leoncavallo's "Stridono lassù" (all trilling flutes), by the line of an artist's composition (Piero di Cosimo's heavy, hurtling birds come to mind), or by the line of the poem in hand, broken like lengths of pasta to fit the box of rhyme. As if to suggest the breathless pursuit by language of the evanescent bird, Wilbur leaves out the syntactic markers, and lets his sentences collide in the scramble after meaning. There is a sense too in which birds signify the immanence of the Holy Ghost, who, in Eastern Orthodox theology at least, is operative "without" (i.e. outside) the Logos of the *Filioque*. Birds offer themselves only in terms of their freedom, making the sanctuary as otiose as the stanza that tries to confine the unconfinable. Hence the need for negative capability, since a thirst for final meanings will simply issue in the pain of frustration.

The point is recapitulated in the final verse, which uses the rough-cast, country idiom that Frost sometimes favors—an idiom that Wilbur himself has termed "his mentor style" ("The Writer's Role," p. 38). The shift to this register after the airy, suave start of the poem marks the arrival of the emblem's knotty moral tag. Here Wilbur balances the humility of accepting things as things against the daring cosmic speculations that could entail their reduction to anythings. The gist of these gnarled Frostian apophthegms is hard to paraphrase, but he seems to suggest that the freedom of birds as they defy containment in pocket-sized sanctuaries is continuous with that of humankind ("becomes" in the nonfactive sense). And if we also take "becomes" to mean "enhances," the very fact that the birds refuse to be confined enriches our own sense of that liberty. Failing to study and respond to the birds as individuals and treating them as a broad category of creatures, our imaginations fail us by betraying the haecceity of the object:

they neutralize "any things" to "anythings." Openness must somehow be balanced against attachment, the unconfined with the locally rooted. It is from the individual that we extrapolate the nature of the genus, from a sense of dwelling that we break loose into the world at large.

Wilbur's ability to move unportentously from experience to anagoge is evident also in "June Light" (NCP, p. 356). This becomes an image of innocence by association with the primal light of summer, and of the early days of the poet's courtship and marriage. The raptness of a Creation as yet untainted by sin is registered by a hint of the *Sursum corda* in the way things raise their seeming. That typical Wilburian balance of matter and soul is caught here in the phonetic melting of "seeming" into "seamless," the uncreate air identical with the Spirit that brooded on the waters, with being itself.

In the next poem, similar ideas come into play. It is "A Song" (NCP, p. 357) about song and derives from a time when, as a child, the poet was taken to a Lieder recital or opera. Wilbur deliberately blurs the allusion, and one is not sure whether the aria is Serena's in *Porgy and Bess* or whether, since the reference to an old man hardly applies to Gershwin, it is Verdi's *Falstaff,* in which Nannetta also sings a summer song. But if that is the case, the imagery of American pastoral will not jibe. One must ascribe the open-endedness to Wilbur's gift for marrying the local with international, the folksy with the formal. In any event, the whispering galleries (which blend the dome of St. Paul's with the structure of an opera house) and the balconies are set in opposition to the child whose sense of suffering is still too immediate to respond to the pattern and distance conferred by art.

In the beginning is the end, for the fall of fruit is implicit in its forming. Only in maturity does the fruit acknowledge its mortality: ripening and declension are one and the same thing. This the child is too young to accept or understand. The epizeuxis in "yearn, / Yearn" creates a suspension (enhanced by the line break), as though the upward impulse of the yearning were countervailing the downward tug of gravity and death, and the use of "groundward" inevitably brings a touch of Frost to summer and recalls the stoic incorporation of "To Earthward." Time is a property of adult consciousness, not of childhood, and it also takes an adult to perceive the order that art can confer on flux. The child might disavow a need for song or rhyme, but at the very moment of disavowal the rhyme is gathered into the pattern of the preceding stanza, where time has been suspended, ready to enter the adolescent consciousness of the child. "A Song" is the first in a series of poems devoted to the vision of childhood and its supersession by adult values. The dualism is one which, in poem after poem, Wilbur tries to resolve in unity.

"The Walgh-vogel" (NCP, p. 358) is also a poem about the transforming properties of art, though its tone is tarter, without the deliquescent nostalgia of "A Song." The first stanza, using material from Sir Thomas Herbert's

Travels,[16] presents the coarse economic motive behind some acts of conservation. Had it proved as succulent as the North American turkey, the implication runs, the dodo would have become a common barnyard bird, but it owes its extinction to inutility. As if in compensation for this sad Benthamite attitude, the poet allows his imagination to supervene extravagantly on the real state of affairs. We have failed to save the dodo, but it can save us by letting our fancies soar in the effort of reconstruction. Yet because the dodo is no longer here to check our imaginative flights with its own intractable reality, these flights can be surreal and capricious. We go out of control for want of sober responsibility—that responsibility to the things of this world that Wilbur offers as a source of health. Anthony Hecht has spoken of the poet's reverence for "the vast alterity, the 'otherness' of the world, that huge corrective to our self-sufficiency."[17] Indeed, remembering that the dodo was a member of the Columbidae (the dove family), one could read the invocation at the end of the poem as a reverent parody of Herbert's and Hopkins's prayers to the Holy Ghost, the creative Spirit by which objects come into being—the poem ends, after all, on a Trinitarian triplet. The wild, almost hysterical quality of an imagination untrammeled by reality, and therefore disordered and exorbitant, needs the corrective reality of the dodo itself. It is not for nothing that Wilbur has reinvoked the archaic Dutch word for the creature, since "walg" means nausea, and much as the "oyliness" of its flesh could not "chuse but quickly cloy and nauseate the stomach" (Phipson, *The Animal-Lore of Shakespeare's Time*, p. 219), so too does the imagination verge on sickness in all its unlicensed reconstructions and rewritings.

"The Melongène" (NCP, p. 359) is as much a companion poem to "The Walgh-vogel" as it is to "Potato." It is ironic about its own extravagance, satirical about the metaphysical arabesques it describes around the vegetable—as though an Intimiste were suddenly to treat his subject with all the formality of a Directoire history painter. There is also the tradition of the mock-heroic encomium in the background of the poem, where hymnic apostrophes collapse into foolishness. According to Denis Donoghue, "William Carlos Williams praised Marianne Moore for ensuring that in her poems apples are apples and nothing more, and they are wiped clean so that no symbolic blur adheres to them."[18] Wilbur on the other hand has no qualms about enriching his objects with a nimbus of ideas—they are firm and focused enough to sustain such treatment.

"Objects" (NCP, p. 360) is perhaps the most important poem of the collection because of its manifesto element, suggesting that poets can arrive at truth as much through periploi of the real world as through the abstract oceanic crossings of philosophy. It offers an apologia—if one were necessary—for the method of almost any Wilbur poem: steady contemplation of the thing, then (and only then) the adduction of the thought. From the very first, Wilbur affirms the graphic immediacy of metaphor, always the vector of concreteness, by weaving abstract geographic coordinates into a net. But because geographers allow them only a notional existence, their version of net can capture only notional data. Remembering the treatment of birds in the sanctuary poem, we can see how the gull opposes the navigator by relying on instinct, instinct so sure that it is fearless in the face of abstract, cross-oceanic flight. But there is also a parable in the navigator's coast-hugging—he represents the poet in his quest for meaning through watchfulness. His reward is the richness of myth, myth so immediate, so shot through with firsthand regionalism, that the golden apples of legend become the coequals of modern hybrids.

Resorting to the epigrammatic, sweeping mode of criticism dictated by the form of the *ars poetica,* Wilbur then presents the would-be artist with a triad of possible positions: the classic that sublimes and smoothes, romantic quaintness that roughens in its search for the picturesque, and neutral observation, embodied here in the art of Pieter de Hoogh. He is a painter well chosen to represent the objectives of Wilbur himself, an Intimiste before his time, concerned with form that canalizes literal truth rather than effacing it, and at the same time, ready to acknowledge the worth and dignity of ordinary experience without being obsessed by Kodachrome fidelities. Here the poem returns to its meridian image, since "feinting" refers not only to the rigor with which the Dutch master transcribed what he saw, but also, perhaps, to the feinting of the stationer. There is a hint that a network of lines, the linear web of the composition, not the geographer's meridians, has been thrown around the subject matter. One could be more literal still, for Kenneth Clark thinks Vermeer (to whom de Hoogh is indebted) "looked through a lens into a box with a piece of ground glass squared up, and painted what he saw" (*Civilization,* p. 212). Such a technique would accord with Wilbur's notion that while in the abstract meridians catch nothing, in the service of observation they do.

The final stanza of "Objects" recalls "On the Eyes of an SS Officer," where Nazi eyes were damned for their sterilizing vision, and the earth embraced in all its multifariousness. Charles Duffy notes that the "eye of the painter and poet is devout because it guards the things of this world as sacred objects which cannot be bought or sold."[19] As its devout guardian, Wilbur reels delightedly through the variousness of the world, his ebullient cross-stanza enjambment supplying a further image of abundance. Only once it has been embraced in all its fullness can the imagination begin its task of modification and recreation, imaged by the phantasm of the Cheshire smile. The imaginative freedom it signifies is one that must be exercised responsibly, and the poet feels fear along with his freedom. Commenting on Emerson's transcendentalism, Harold Bloom has observed that the "ruin and blank that we see when we look at nature, is in our own eye. The axis of vision is not coincident with the axis of things and so they appear not transparent but opaque."[20] This is not the vision of Richard Wilbur, however, for he is concerned to *retain* the opacity of things and at the same time to record their immanent meaning.

De Hoogh also figures in "A Dutch Courtyard" (NCP, p. 362), which, like "The Giaour and the Pacha," is an ecphrasis or painting poem. Unlike the Delacroix lyric, however, in which the transient subject feels himself freeze into the inhumanity of plastic form, "A Dutch Courtyard" concerns the painting as object, unresponsive to the gallery spectators—the denizens of the "Gay-pocked and potsherd world"—but, even so, relevant to them as an icon of fixity in the midst of flux. The poet of "Objects" finds an intractable objectivity in de Hoogh's picture that finally teases us out of thought. Even the owner possesses the painting only in an acquisitive way—its inviolable entirety persists after the purchase—but the eye of the painter, having once registered its materials, is able to recreate them at will.

In no way does Wilbur fetishize reality, however, being Platonist enough to conceive a structure of ideas beyond the surfaces of things. In "My Father Paints the Summer" (NCP, p. 363) he starts with an account of holidaymakers made peevish by the rain and then cuts from this scene (full of shrewd, Tatiesque observations) to a man who paints a picture by artificial light. While that light is artificial in the sense of being electric, it is also the immanent light of artifice: art can generate its own radiance, so long as it is served by the accurate memory of the artist. Wilbur père is able in fact to paint *the* summer, the definite article turning summer into a Platonic idea. Even so, because the summer is evoked and not observed, it is a summer encased in myth, much like the dodo in "The Walgh-vogel," and hence without a local habitation and a name. The transcriptive energies of the poem have all gone into creating the frustrations of holiday-makers in rainy weather, while the alternative, ideal summer of the father seems as remote and mysterious and visionary as the granting of grace. While the rain falls unrelentingly outside the hotel, the painter's canvas dissolves into a series of mythical appositives, each standing in for the idea of summer itself—the improbable oxymoron of "luxuriant Sahara," the innocence of Eden, the immersion of Pyrochles (who is tormented by burning armor in book 2, canto 7 of *The Faerie Queene*), the romance-like translocation of Roman citizens to Anzio.

From the polarities of the real and the ideal, the regional and the international, Wilbur forges a dialectic resolution. It is not a case of either/or—it never is with Wilbur. In the very act of arresting what is the otherwise imperceptible (time itself), art imposes on reality and captures otherwise elusive entities for our inspection. Inserting a nonparticular epithet into a proverbial expression ("time out of mind" is embellished with an "any"), Wilbur suggests that his father is simply painting out of a collective memory and that the alertness of his observation has primed the creative act—i.e., readied it for the igniting imagination. The heart has recapitulated the macrocosm of the seasons, its own spring that nurtured and conceived the life of the painting a guarantee of the summer that comes behind. ("Prime" inevitably brings the Italian *primavera* to mind.)

In "Folk Tune" (NCP, p. 364) the imagination has a more imposing, prophetic task to discharge. Its point of departure is the American folk imagination which, by a sort of euhemerism, has turned people into demigods. Wilbur is culturally rooted but at the same time open and versatile, for in his poetry, as Francis Warlow points out, "Folk creations like Paul Bunyan and John Henry appear along with esoteric creators like Gerard Manley Hopkins and Hölderlin."[21] On the occasions when he needs a racy frontier idiom, the poet is equal to the challenge. Wilbur intensifies the roughness of his diction and the brutality of the subject by alluding to "Orpheus with his lute made trees," a poem whose quatrains are altogether more finished and which celebrates the civilizing effects of art. The swaggering jauntiness soon loses momentum, however, and the parade of Anglo-American folk heroes gives way to the African-American figure of John Henry, whom Constance Rourke describes as having a "hammer that rang like silver, shone like gold, [and] who blew down mountains."[22] He exemplifies the forces soon to issue in the civil rights movement, forces that haunt the sleep of white suburbia. The drill that his massive hammer challenges is as much the implicit violence of military drill as it is the inhumane industrial equivalent of his pastoral tool. This is a more obviously regionalist poem than others, for Wilbur has constructed its statement from the materials of folk culture. Indeed its very point, the displacement of one mythic figure by another, draws our attention to the injustices and cultural displacements that have given Paul Bunyan hegemony in the first place.

A poet such as Wilbur, mesmerized by the infinite variety of the world about him, is sometimes content simply to evoke an aspect of its multifariousness. One such evocation is "Sun and Air" (NCP, p. 365). Poems like this can be traced back to Leigh Hunt and Keats, who in sonnet after sonnet refashioned the form as a descriptive instrument. The old sonnetary dialectic, the shift from a first to a second position either complementary or antithetical, simply becomes descriptive contrast. "Sun and Air" is written in *terza rima,* but its thirteen lines make it a curtal sonnet—a descriptive sonnet, moreover, of the Huntian kind. The first two tercets present summer heat as a stasis so insistent that it can even swallow intransitive verbs and quench their movement in its own inactivity. They are followed by two contrasting tercets that chart the violence of a hurricane, unleashed upon the sonnet with the same sort of energy that breaks into "The Windhover" at its volta. As if to acknowledge a lack of dialectical tension in his poem, Wilbur avoids a stabilizing couplet and thus falls one line short of the traditional fourteen. No synthesis, no development occurs: the contrast is simply restated. Often a regionalist is content simply to evoke his region as comprehensively and as vividly as he can, whether it be Hampstead Heath spread before Keats as he stands tiptoe upon a little hill or Wilbur giving us the drama of a New England thunderstorm.

"Two Songs in a Stanza of Beddoes'" (NCP, pp. 366–67) are also, like "Sun and Air," *evocations poétiques*. The debt extends beyond the stanza pattern of the earlier poet, however, for the songs are also touched with that slightly hopeless, Beddovian melancholy we find, say, in "Wolfram's Dirge," the poem from which the pattern has been taken.[23] Wilbur's versatility is demonstrated by the contrast between this poem and the rhythms of "Folk Tune," between rough-cast balladry and languor. He is a poet open to what seem to be irreconcilable alternatives, bent on making his poetry common ground for both. While his own stanzaic inventiveness shows how skillful he is in the province of design, he seems to have chosen the Beddoes pattern as an act of homage to that strange Romantic, annexing him as an integral part of his heritage along with the Paul Bunyans and the John Henrys.

The quality of the first song is slightly precious, with extravagant synesthesia and syntactic inversion. It is a poem that pivots on the *ubi sunt* topos, and Wilbur makes the dimeter (coming as it does after four-stress lines) function as an image of loss. While the poem starts in Beddoes, it ends in the Shelley of the *Ode to the West Wind*—but with this difference: If the poet invokes the energy of autumn to cleanse his insentience and heaviness, he is equally ready to have winter match that insentience with its own gripping night. Being half in love with easeful death is not a habitual Wilburian stance, and one senses that the cletic hymn to winter forms part of an exercise in thinking Romantically.

The companion song is about a gull, a diptych viewing its subject from the different perspectives of day and night, of the beautiful and the sublime, of a reason that deals with mirrors and balances, and an imagination trafficking in monstrosity and atavistic fear. Here in diagrammatic form is that tension between the object perceived in its quiddity, a New England gull observed by a regionalist, and a surreal imagination that enriches the datum by distorting it. Wilbur pays homage to Tennyson rather than to Beddoes or Shelley in the first stanza. "Ringed with the azure world he stands. / The wrinkled sea beneath him crawls" has been reworked in the first stanza.

"The Waters" (NCP, p. 368) is a much more detailed, subtler reworking of the gull song, empowered by the same contrast between the bland and the terrible. Wilbur has the sea symbolize the effacements of "cormorant devouring Time," starting with Aurelian's sack of Palmyra as recorded by Flavius Vopiscus. He counterpoints the disintegration of Zenobia's *genus purpureae, quod postea nec ulla gens detulit nec Romanus orbis vidit*[24] with the loss of Atlantis, though of course he also has the Atlantic coast of America in mind and wants to convey the passage of time by commingling its sands with those of the Syrian desert. But while the poet-seer records and acknowledges these images of *sic transit gloria*, modern humanity conceives the sea only in terms of the recreation it offers, reducing it, as in some Primitive painting or sub-Primitive travel poster, to flat pictorial bands. Since the same formula applies as much to New York and to the Riviera, Wilbur no doubt intends this abolition of space to match the earlier abolition of time. Such interchangeability is antiregional, a comment on the bathers' disconnection from space as from time. On the beach, in the superficial milieu of the holiday resort—Juan-les-Pins and Coney Island—people are brought into unregarding contact with the sea, whose dark symbolic menace they cannot appreciate. Yet, since it has engulfed monuments of human civilization, it promises to engulf humankind as well. While it is clear that children are amusing themselves with mock burials on the beach, their games are darkened by the allusion to an epitaph by Crinagoras,[25] one that records the beach burial of an infant. The sea is soothing us into lotos-eater oblivion, whereas we ought to be hearing its *memento mori*.

This frail oblivion is made more poignant by Wilbur's use of the homiletic "we," by which he admits his own seduction by the holiday warmth of a beach. It contrasts with more heroic visions of water, those of Thomas Mann, of Leonardo, of Adam, and of Hölderlin. In quick succession come the yearning and anguish of Aschenbach at the end of *Der Tod in Venedig*— "he pointed outward as he hovered on before into an immensity of richest expectation"[26]—and the vision of Leonardo, fascinated by water;[27] a fascination that Walter Pater detected in the tonality of the *Mona Lisa*—"some faint light under the sea."[28] No sooner have these allusions swept by than more crowd upon us, too fast, perhaps, for comfort. We are confronted with Adam's *contes* and the impassioned classical nostalgia of Hölderlin, in whose vision, to quote Rolf Deneke, "die Kluft zwischen der Welt seiner erhabenen Gedanken und den Forderungen des Alltags vertiefte sich immer mehr."[29] Because of this "ever-deepening chasm between the sublime world of his ideas and the demands of everyday life," the swan in the waters in "Hälfte des Lebens" inhabits a world of perfection inaccessible to the poet in his suffering.[30]

"Superiorities" (NCP, p. 370) distinguishes, like "The Waters," between the vision of ordinary people and that of reckless prophets. Malachy and Phipps, immersed in the destructive element above board, are in a metaphysical and physical sense superior to those huddled beneath. This lightweight poem shows yet again how Wilbur can vary his diction when occasion calls. Here it is nautical invective that salts his formality. The companion poem of "Superiorities" is "A Simplification" (NCP, p. 371), where the Branns and the Bryans figure as equivalents of the reckless seafarers and are themselves presented as variants of Tywater—crude and impassioned and invigorating. The poems seem to present these values in an act of negative capability, for they do not really lie close to Wilbur's heart. An Episcopalian by profession and by temperament, he generally prefers balance and synthesis to dogmatism. Since neither the theology nor the homiletic practice of his church harmonizes with those of the ranters, one must assume that the poem is essentially a rhetorical outburst, read to praise energy of any kind (no matter how rough) rather than none at all. It is as if the poem were a ventriloquial exercise in the sort of rhetorical vehemence that Yeats, for example, has made his own but that seldom figures in Wilbur's output. By calling the poem "A Simplification," he confesses its rhetorical expediency, for he more usually entertains a complex vision of things. Even so, he is able to make its vehemence an instrument of criticism, and the phonetic congestion is almost apoplectic in its explosiveness.

"A Dubious Night" (NCP, p. 372) following as it does on the heels of a poem that praises vigorous reductiveness, is ironically placed. It is as close as Wilbur ever comes to a poem of doubt, though it is more strictly a record of the spiritual aridity called the "dark night of the soul." Using the *terza rima* of "Sun and Air" and, like that poem, falling one line short of the statutory fourteen, it might even have its starting point in famous lines from Dante's *Purgatorio: "se ode squilla di lontano, / che paia il giorno pianger che si muore."* Be that as it may, Wilbur's choice of the meter of faith for a poem of doubt is not without its irony. The slurring bell in the first stanza is one of several images of instability, the slide of the glissando contrasted with the stability of vowels. Insecurity and indecisiveness are compounded by the clamor of the echoes, which Wilbur mimics in the internal rhyme and assonance of "summons" and "some" and "Down" and "town." This scumbling of sound and certainty is semantic as well as phonetic. Wilbur twists *eleison* to "elision," supplanting mercy with absence, and mocks the untuning of the spheres in *A Song for St. Cecilia's Day* by unstringing the senses in the third verse.

The star that stabilizes and focuses the blur of the preceding tercets is superficially like the steadfast stars of Shakespeare or Keats, but the affirmation is muffled, almost cynical. Its expression brings it much closer to the smirking moon in Cole Porter's "Love for Sale." By stranding his resolution in the final line, Wilbur makes it seem perfunctory and irresolute. Acknowledging the impassible perfection of divinity is not always sufficient to reconcile one to the confusion of life on earth. Though he is generally able to reconcile the celestial and sublunary realms, Wilbur here confesses his failure to do so. The poem, to use an expression of his own coinage, is one of "those moments of homage to the word 'or.' "[31]

Another sonnet in everything but length is "L'Etoile" (NCP, p. 373). Like "A Dubious Night," it ends in lassitude, even though it begins in elation and energy. Availing himself of the dynamic that language can bring to static painting—a privilege of ecphrasis—Wilbur takes a danseuse of Degas through the quick preparation, freeze, and resolution of an arabesque, an arabesque forming part of an allegro enchaînement, not a contemplative adagio. It is a moment supremely natural, supremely artless, or so we think, until Wilbur draws our attention to the fixity of the teacher's feet as he stands in the wings. The dancer's spontaneity, governed by the strictest of all art forms, is illusion; her lightness a trick of technique. The last stanza is given over to divestment—the literal undressing of the dancer and the undressing of our perceptions as we are forced to view the physical exhaustion, even the mindlessness of the girl, the corset that has given form to her flesh, and the crone supervising her toilette. She is a *memento mori*, reminding us of the fate that time has in reserve for the impalpable brilliance of the star. The synecdochic star of "A Dubious Night" has become nothing more than a rank in the hierarchy of the Opéra, a rank that few can hold for any length of time. The moment the poet takes us beyond the fragile suspension of the Degas painting, he dooms the star to fall.

It is not unusual for Wilbur to make aphoristic claims in his titles and then present the poems they announce as logico-poetic "proofs" of them. Such a procedure can be seen in "Sunlight Is Imagination" (NCP, p. 374), the rhetorical *quaestio* from which the poem devolves, reasoned premise by premise. The topography of the poem reinforces the effect, for it "hangs" its amplifications on prefatory sentences. Literal dependence matches logical. The poem is one of Wilbur's epistemological reveries and demonstrates the way in which the imagination shuffles its sense data. Our perceptions of reality depend as much on its configurations as the retina on the radiant energy of the sun. Of course there is nothing new in this, for Wordsworth says as much in *Tintern Abbey,* but the poem remains a fine enactment of its premises, its syntactic meetings and reformations like the play of the sunlight it describes and like the improvisations of the imagination. By syncopating his sentence structure against his stanza, Wilbur creates an effect of hide-and-seek, of meaning that eludes its would-be capsulator, of significances that flare and vanish and baffle.

Wilbur then invokes Juan Ponce—not the distressing, violent figure of William Carlos Williams's essay[32]—but a man who, in searching for the well of youth, perceives the world in terms of his quest. Imagination thus reconstitutes Florida as another Eden. An ordinary Floridian spring becomes mythic well, the "reflaire" of which portmanteaus the French words for "sniff" (*flairer*) and "renovate" (*refaire*) and compounds these in turn with *savoir faire*—a virtuoso effort of *refaire* in itself. Enticing though these mythic visions and projections might be, they are not the province of the regionalist, of the realist who honors and loves the unadorned realities of the earth. Earlier in the poem, Wilbur has mimicked Shakespeare's "Shall I compare thee to a summer's day?" but opts for a different resolution. Whereas Shakespeare makes the comparison a point of departure, eclipsing the summer's day in mythic hyberbole, Wilbur knows that Petrarchism, apart from being untenable in the twentieth century, is finally untrue to the experience of the world. Its objective beauty does *not* concenter on the subjective experience of the lover; the beloved's loveliness is simply the transient instance of more permanent, Platonic forms. The answer lies in a wise, not a godless, version of *carpe florem.*

In the last stanzas the poet moves to an unanxious sense that all things are mortal. Ponce's desire for eternal youth is a sterilizing one, since, like the mechanical bird in Yeats's "Sailing to Byzantium," its mythic permanence is hostile to flux, the flux in which life itself subsists. Wilbur further recalls the end of Catullus' *Mea Lesbia vivamus atque amemus* only to make it a point of departure. The *nox una dormienda* that awaits the end of the sun's wasting is not a foil for reckless hedonism, but rather a call to quietude and restfulness. Any attempt at freezing that fugitive beauty would be a blight, a source of infertility. There can be no shutting the regionalist eye that lingers on the world and would not wish it changed. As Frances Bixler puts it, " 'thirsting' too much for the unattainable is destructive."[33]

Whereas "Sunlight Is Imagination" faintly resembles the Italian *canzone* with its elaborate shifts and swings about the *chiavi* (the monometer key lines), the poems which follow it ("&" and "O"—NCP, pp. 376–77) are much less dynamic, less interested in dialectic play and resolution. They strive rather for the stasis of contemplation, using that appositional slow motion that Herbert exploited to the full in "Prayer (I)." The syntax of equivalences immobilizes the poem and turns it into a rapt exercise in attention. "O" enjoys the additional gravity of sonnet form, a variant that Wilbur has hybridized from the Italian and English traditions. The Petrarchan chiasmus (abba), always a slowing and stabilizing pattern, persists into the sestet and so exerts its sway more forcefully than usual. No better parable could be found for the way abstractions like "O" become replete and hermetic in their perfection. For Wilbur, Platonic forms, once divorced from their transient and accidental embodiment, tease the mind out of thought. He can grasp the circularity of "O" only in the wheel and flight path in which it is incarnate. This sonnet presents a corollary of "Sunlight Is Imagination," viz., abstraction (which, dealing with essences, has the properties of myth) can be derived only from its particular instances.

If "O" moves from abstraction to concrete embodiment, then "The Regatta" (NCP, p. 378) begins with glimpses of country club life only to take off toward the realm of parable and leave its satirical proem behind. The result is fascinating but uneven, as though some delicious ingredient had survived the mixing and lodged in the dish as an alien flavor. Mrs. Vane, a society matron, watches a yacht race and fusses over her sickly husband to the visible amusement of the speaker. Wilbur mocks her description of the race (as though it were some swashbuckling spectacle), as well as her interest in personalities rather than events. But it is almost incidental, there only as a launching pad for a meditation on freedom. From the trivial specifics of East Coast society, we move without preparation into the language of abstract discourse. William Carlos Williams's yachts are as yacht-like as it is possible for an object poet to make them; Wilbur's, while they retain their sensuous reality, in some respects are transformed into Shelleyan essences— free things and blithe spirits are surely close relations. The way in which the craft in all their frailty can triumph over the sea in all its power becomes a parable for the triumph of a comic over a tragic vision. Even if the effect is partly illusion, like the symmetrical marriages in the fifth act of a comedy, it is nonetheless liberating.

Constraint can serve to measure liberty, a paradox that opens the final section. Its neat, assured aphorism is left stranded, however, and the poem loses its pattern at this point, an irresolute sestet supplanting the smooth run of quatrains that has gone before. The poet seems to be confessing in the same breath that patterns do not always fit, material cannot always be contained. He himself feels a loss of purpose, and it is on the frail, untriumphant figure of Mr. Vane that the lyric comes uneasily to rest. Bruce Michelson notes that for "all the skill of the artist as a conjuror, moments of real imaginative engagement come quickly when they will, and pass as quickly away."[34] The watery shades that the yachts have spurned reassert themselves in this quizzical *memento mori.*

"Bell Speech" (NCP, p. 380) is also a poem that states the inescapability of death, though, as always in Wilbur, it emerges from a balanced awareness of transience and eternity—the poem shows neither Manichean contempt for the physical nor giddy hedonism. Its starting point, perhaps, is Donne's *Devotions Upon Emergent Occasions,* for the bells are presented as bearers of a meaning beyond that of time, as their music is beyond the range of linear, expository prose. By substituting dark for doctrine, they come close to offering the sort of mysticism practiced by Dionysius the Areopagite. They are oracles, purveyors of dark speech, their shape matched and inverted by the trees, each mediating the darkness of ineffable experience to the world. Their deltoid forms also recall the archetypal delta of the Nile, and so the Nile itself, the archetype of flooding. Local details are gathered up and placed within a larger, anagogical framework, the bell tower of an Ivy League town assimilated to the well in which, according to Democritus, Truth has made her home.

"Poplar, Sycamore" (NCP, p. 381), coming as it does after "Bell Speech," repeats the *chiaroscuro* of "A Dubious Night," which is a poem's throw away from "Sunlight Is Imagination." It is an effortless impressionist lyric of a kind Wilbur has made his own. He sets down two trees of differing character with as much panache as if he were Monet or Bonnard, and his words pigment on the brush, before offering an unportentous reflection to point and direct his virtuosity. The absence of a coordinating conjunction in the title ("Poplar, Sycamore") suggests that the poet is throwing down his material before shaping it—like two squiggles of paint straight from the tube. Moreover, the imperative verbs in both stanzas are like the cries of a painter to his models, begging them to hold their characteristic postures. Recollecting the poplar's etiology as the nymph Leuce, Wilbur presents her as a *prima ballerina assoluta,* while the sycamore seems by contrast to have been dredged up from chthonian depths. The *sententia* that caps the poem claims the right of the spirit to augment the seen with the visionary, to mythologize its regionalism. Since dry rot is a tree-threatening disease, it almost seems as if their continued life depended on the poet's own immunity from mental dryness.

In "Winter Spring" (NCP, p. 382) a thaw is depicted with an atmospheric precision that recalls the lyrics of *Love's Labour's Lost,* but all the time the atmospherics are being shaped to a thematic end. Winter stands for an analytic response to experience, one that defensively observes boundaries and categories. The premature spring breaches these defenses, mining domes, and crisscrossing the isolate kingdom with navigable canals. Its somersault inverts and fuses traditional hierarchies and separations, for which reason Wilbur (poet of fusion and reconciliation) takes it to his heart. Such credal endings occur quite frequently, antitypes of the impersonal *sententiae* the poet uses on other occasions.

No less typical is the credal point of departure we find at the start of "Attention Makes Infinity" (NCP, p. 383). Wilbur posits two worlds, that of earth and that of air, the elements associated with body and soul respectively. At first, playfully using the jussive associated with prayer, he attempts to separate them out and keep them distinct. Later, however, he charts the invasion of the real world by the world of the spirit. Both ultimately intersect, for while the air descends and disembodies the inertia and weightedness of matter, the spirit also rises from the earth in great parabolas of aspiration. Wilbur uses hypallage to give a noun force to the verbs of sinking and springing. It is in the realm of the spirit that imagination has its being, a realm that creates the world afresh in every effort of attention. The creative Spirit that brooded on the waters of chaos is glimpsed in the sigh with which the relenting air (relenting as in *rallentando*) withdraws from a world the fancy has refashioned. Of course Wilbur has enough respect for the laws of physics and for the intractability of things to admit that the variety is adamant and therefore physically indestructible—all that the imagination has done is to resort, aerate, and spiritualize that variety.

The poem ends by adapting one of Blake's *Auguries of Innocence* in a characteristic aphorism. Wilbur conceives the infinite as being partly immanent, there to be discovered as much by the attentive regionalist as by any visionary. Here "Prove" retains its archaic sense of "experience" along with its more modern one of "test empirically" and suggests once again that synthesis of immanence and transcendence for which Wilbur regularly strives. That is why the poem ends with another prayerful jussive—not for the separation of realms presented in stanza 1, but for their mutual contagion, their balanced contiguity. Only thus can asphalt become an allegorical pathway of love and skyscrapers turn to pillars of the universe as in some Judaic cosmology.

If air and earth have to be married for a proper sense of their significance, so do judgment and instinct. It is to the integration of these that Wilbur turns his attention in "Grace" (NCP, p. 384), where the argument is conducted by dialectical steps. Images of instinctive grace are set up, investigated, and then not so much discarded as extended and modified. (Wilbur is not a wasteful poet but chooses rather to build on his initial images, making corrections and adjustments as he moves toward a definitive synthesis.) Whereas the creative Logos descends to humankind in the Incarnation, Wilbur suggests that there are moments when, like scales in contrary motion, the flesh ascends to the godliness of pure physical grace. A triad of images illustrates the claim: gamboling lambs from Wordsworth's *Intimations Ode*, Nijinsky's famous *jeté* at the end of *Le Spectre de la Rose*, and a waiter dexterous enough to balance a tray in a moving train. Because these exemplify grace's revenue, or coming again, they have an almost theological charge, as if innocence of Eden were in these instances restored to fallen instinct by a sort of Parousia or second coming. Even so, they are deficient because they are purely physical. Nijinsky's "merely," while it presents itself as the "merely" of *sprezzatura*, is also "merely" in the Latin sense, for as John Ciardi has noted, "the Latin root sense . . . shines through so much of Wilbur's diction."[35] What is wanting is synergism, the collaboration of divinity with instinct in the procurement of grace. Wilbur might have come across Karsavina's account of her first encounter with Nijinsky,[36] in which she contrasts Nijinsky's verbal clumsiness with his perfect technique. The flesh might be made word in his dancing, but his flesh cannot make the word.

Because the waiter is at the service of the physical appetite, his skill is similarly incomplete, itself only the linear skeleton of Nijinsky's physical prowess. It is possible that by "Hebetude" Wilbur intends a pun on Hebe, the waitress of the gods. The antithesis is a waiter in another sense—Hamlet. Hamlet delays because he senses the complexity of things and feels reluctant to privilege instinct above judgment. Grace here is not an instinctual jump but a reticulum of nerves, indecipherably mediating thought into action. As usual, Wilbur has focused on that elusive moment in which the physical and the spiritual intersect. The tentativeness of a man confronting complexity has a grace of its own: the *aplombe* of the danseur yields to the mental balance of Renaissance "man." Wilbur enacts the sobering drag of intellect on instinct by the traction of an internal rhyme and then balances energy and poise in a pithy, proverbial finish. F. C. Golffing has elegantly summed up the poem as "a set of variations on a theme by Hopkins, where the discourse shifts from the notion of naive animal grace to that of routine nimbleness, bordering on legerdemain, thence to the scholar's halting grace-in-awkwardness and alights, finally, on the paradox of graceful reserve—the minimum holding back—in rapid action."[37]

Given Wilbur's attachment to the things of this world in all their variety and detail, one might imagine him to feel a certain anguish at the thought of leaving them in death and that any poems he might write on the topic would paraphrase Gray's "longing ling'ring look." This is not however the case in "Lightness" (NCP, p. 386). The poem is an expanded conceit that links the fall of a nest from a forty-foot elm to the dying of a saintly woman. Lightness hinges the two dissimilars, for just as the unattached nest is able to breast the air currents, so Aunt Virginia, resigned to her death and therefore lightened of any grief, can open herself to what remains of life. The intactness that Wilbur cites at the end of the poem is the intactness of integrity as well as the intactness of preservation. Death has not been able to touch the woman's essential being, just as the violent winds have been unable to break the eggs borne down in the nest. Lightness is above all evident in the lightness of Wilbur's touch, for the poem is in fact a scherzo—not a bitter or mordant scherzo such as Mahler might have written, but nearer to the spirited ripostes of St. Lawrence on his gridiron. The nest is present as a cuplet/couplet that falls down a chute of thirty-odd lines, threatening to spill its eggs and break its capsularity all the while, but able somehow to keep form in the face of the enjambment that tries to pull it out of shape. The dip and flurry of the nest are also realized in the in-and-out of the tetrameter and pentameter lines, while *ad hoc* Hopkinsian compounds suggest an improvisatory flair, a making of fragile, transient nonce words that will vanish the moment their purpose has been served.

While Aunt Virginia has achieved a childlike simplicity and trust in the face of death, the little girl in "For Ellen" (NCP, p. 388) has yet to learn its meaning. She is absorbed, like all children, in the present but will one day have to synthesize the experiences that at the moment she is perceiving as simple, serial alternatives. Her name, which is Greek for "bright," places the poem in the tradition of such meditative lyrics as Donne's "Nocturnal Upon St. Lucy's Day," where the name of the subject is put to similar use. In the first stanza the child falls asleep and stands on the threshold of nightmares that will threaten the security of her daylight experience. The sun shines in the second stanza by way of contrast, and her eyes become the focal point of the heavens' blue. In a light-hearted parody of pastoral exaggerations, like those of Pope's *Summer,* Ellen virtually causes heal-all to break from the paving stones with a blueness to match her eyes. However, in this monocular, sunshiny vision, the antitype of nightmare, a cripple becomes an object of mirth. Tragedy is imperceptible to the child, and that is why the future will bring the anagnorisis of adulthood. Opposites will fuse in a Miltonic blend of darkness and vision.

Much the same thing is said, with the same dialectic balance but with different images, in "Caserta Garden" (NCP, p. 389). This garden owes its provenance to the wall that has framed and separated it from the life outside. The poem could be viewed as a parable about the aesthetics of the Decadent poets and even, perhaps, the aesthetics of Wallace Stevens. The temptation to obtain decorative poise and elegance by exclusion is one that Wilbur has obviously to exorcise. The rewards of order and tranquillity seem sirenically attractive ones, a fact acknowledged even while it is being rejected. Like Spenser's Bower of Bliss, the Caserta garden depends on dangerous illusion, and its richness and fecundity have obscured its origins in a kind of apartheid, a fission of real and the recreated. It takes the eye of a stranger to recognize this—the eye of the combatant, perhaps, who knows that Caserta was bombarded in the Second World War, even though the garden bears no scar to tell of the suffering outside its walls.

The poem is full of unspecified pronouns, "theys" and "theirs" that obviously refer to the Casertesi but that serve also to give them a more widely representative status. They are regionalists who have become so accustomed to their garden as to have lost all sense of its origin in separateness. And, viewed allegorically, they are also regionalists of the world of art, so acclimatized to its ordering form that they have forgotten all that form has failed to encompass. It is a world like the Platonic meta-universe, where haecceity has given way to smooth geometric form. Wilbur puts us on the alert by referring to untested childhood and by using subjunctives that point to the reality they cannot fit against. As things reduce themselves to pattern, so they are emptied of human content, and a twisted trunk, while it is linked appositively to human pain, has become nothing more than a twisted column like those that support Bernini's baldacchino. By the same token, the grapevine, no longer yielding fruit for human need, has turned into a seductive filigree. Wilbur's regionalism is altogether richer and more various than these garden-dwellers', however. It acknowledges mutability and suffering and a sense of pattern more subtle and elusive than that of the Euclidean diagram.

"Praise in Summer" (NCP, p. 391) also confronts the fact that art is guilty of distorting its material, sacrificing essence to the exigencies of form. But, as in Herbert's "Jordan," it is not so much art as the extravagance of the artist that comes under fire, a fact borne out by the obsessive use of *verba dicendi*. These are like the endless "she saids" of Tennyson's "Marianna," a poem concerned with saying, not with doing. It is not metaphor that must be blamed for the distortion but rather the poet's extravagant employment of the trope. Craig Abbott remarks how the "praise that the speaker in 'Praise in Summer' recounts creates a *mundus inversus* in which, through metaphor, up becomes down and solid becomes nonsolid."[38] The poem is in fact an indictment of Clevelandism, of self-indulgent wit.

This becomes apparent the moment we turn to the eponymous poem of the collection. In "The Beautiful Changes" (NCP, p. 392) it is not the chattering "I" that imposes its deranging metaphors on experience, it is the impersonal "one" that tentatively and gradually feels its way toward an aptness of language, a language that serves its material instead of obscuring it. Wading involves moving with difficulty—often (but not exclusively) through water—and by this delicate transition, the poet begins to convert the meadow to a lake. We are far removed from the egotistical exuberance of

"Praise in Summer." The reader assents to comparison because the data have been assembled with a careful eye and the connections documented in such a way as to make them seem inevitable. So delicately and persuasively are they managed that they even make plausible such artifice as pastoral hyperbole, as when Charlotte Wilbur turns the poet's mind into a Swiss valley. This is plausible because it returns us to the meadow image at the same time as it takes flight for Europe—lucerne, another name for alfalfa pasturage, has blue-mauve flowers. Metaphor is not the static, antimeric inversion of the previous poem, but a coming and going, a traffic of possibilities. In contrast with the lotos-eater changelessness of "Caserta Garden," "The Beautiful Changes" locates the ideal in mutability itself, in the turn of the kaleidoscope tube as much as in the patterns its turning brings to birth. The chameleon, which we could view as the type of the regionalist, adapts itself to its setting and, in so adapting, reconstitutes it. His tuning is an image of art, since tuning produces concord, and chordal structures are the raw material for symphonies. Likewise the mantis, *arranged* both transitively and intransitively, as the beautiful itself changes both transitively and intransitively. Aesthetics center on perception and on the frames that perception creates for its data, and perception itself is an acknowledgment of the essential thing, its "kindness" or typicality.

Yet it is kind also in the sense of being good-natured, for it blesses the percipient. Without the rhetorical forcings of the conceit, the prodigious technique of the virtuoso blinded to all else by the glare of its brilliance, it recreates simply by renovating the essence of things and reaffirms a thisness that was always there for the finding.

I have dwelt on this first collection at considerable length because I consider it a remarkable performance. Much of the essential Wilbur is here, sprung forth with a Minerva-like maturity. Even some apparent shortcomings can seem, when viewed from a different perspective, to take on the stature of virtues. It is true that the poet has spoken rather scathingly about the aural qualities of some items: "when I look back at my earliest poems I notice how, quite often in them, there are clots of consonants that make some lines unpronounceable" (Robert Frank and Stephen Mitchell, "Richard Wilbur: An Interview," in *Conversations*, p. 29). However, Wilbur makes this judgment with the hindsight of a performer. We have only to recall the poetry of Donne and other "hard-liners" to realize that phonetic struggle can generate toughness and energy. Commandeering Wilbur's own parable image, I would say that it is sometimes better for the voice to clamber through a window than to glide through a door. The career of Mendelssohn proves that facility can sometimes issue in the attendant vice of blandness.

two

c e r e m o n y
and
o t h e r
p o e m s
(1 9 5 0)

fourteen years after the publication of *Ceremony and Other Poems,* Wilbur gave a public address on the nature of ceremony, describing it, among other things, as a known route to the unknown (cf. *Responses,* p. 71). Viewed in this light, ceremony helps to place the contingent in the context of the eternal and, through its sacraments, to offer visible signs for inward and invisible graces. And because it gathers individual experience into immutable and absolute forms, it accords with the program of a poet concerned to register both the hard reality of his world and the numinous aura that the spirit confers upon it.

The 1950 collection begins where Wilbur left off in the lyric "For Ellen" and once more contemplates that crucial shift of vision that accompanies a consciousness of death. "Then" (NCP, p. 281) is a song lyric, which Wilbur himself has defined as "a shortish poem of personal feeling or perception, characterized at its best by intensity and by felicity of phrasing and form."[1] But whereas in "For Ellen" the poet had contemplated the innocence of the child with some of the grave, "parental" foresight of Gray's Eton College ode, the speaker of "Then" is more fully caught up in the transition *from* innocence *to* experience. The exact status of its pronouns is hard to establish—either the speaker could be reminiscing on behalf of another individual, or he could be construed as a spokesperson for us all. It is by its intensity that the song lyric breaks from a personal to a universal application. Wordsworth's "Intimations Ode" also lies somewhere behind the temporal shift of a poem whose soberness derives from retrospection rather than from prolepsis. "Then," after all, is a conjunction associated with narrative, not only marking off phases of time, but also serving to hinge the phases of plot and argument. Both functions apply. In the community of childhood there is no recollection of the past or anticipation of the future, the whole being is surrendered to the present moment, and it is time (in the guise of summer) that pervades stanza one—the childlike "before" that precedes the adult "after."

It seems possible that in the alliterative verbs of line two Wilbur is recollecting the brisk tabulation of arrival, sighting, and conquest in Caesar's "Veni, vidi, vici," which some classicists pronounce with a "w" sound. For even as it is tending us, the season is asserting its power. Our infantile helplessness is matched by our failure to perceive the passage of time and, with that, to respond attentively and lovingly to the material universe it governs. Immutability, properly an attribute of God, is misapplied to sublunary experience. The descent of line six implies both descent to the realm of death and descent as the lineage of generations, neither of which commands the attention of the child. With the consciousness of time comes the consciousness of history, and so memory is brought to birth. Lapsarian fall coincides with seasonal fall when the notion of mortality strikes home for the first time, and the simple lyric finds further enrichment in echoes of Shakespeare's Sonnet 73, a sonnet that also meditates on death through images of choiring birds and falling leaves.

The title of "Conjuration" (NCP, p. 282) contains a preposition crucial to Wilbur's vision, the preposition *cum*. This is another "Jordan" poem, concerned as always with unifying rich evolutionary minutiae with the simplifying forms of myth, the bric-a-brac of the real and the tidiness of the ideal. It is one of the many allotropic forms taken by Wilbur's recurring theme, viz., how to unify disparate visions and materials. He begins by taking us to the New England coast, where the sea shows forth various organisms as though it were reversing the sweep of evolution. The description is the work of a regionalist who is documenting the sea drift as he picks it over, but underneath the love there is also a sense of disquiet. The sunlight and the air are disnaturing the sea harvest, dehydrating the sea lettuce and mollusks. The backtrack of the sea is clearly not only a recession along the beach, but also a reneging, a revocation of promises, as when one backtracks on one's word.

Those promises have been projected by the poet in his dreams, however, not made by the sea itself, and the movement of the waters symbolizes a transition from hypnagogic state to waking reality. The symbolic perception of the sea in cultures predating Darwin has had the effect of stylizing and falsifying it, as in some medieval illumination where blue pigment is a mere adjunct of the design, and the sea is presented not as the matrix of evolution but rather as treasure trove, both literal and symbolic. But at the same time he confronts these unreal symbolic values, the poet holds a hermit crab and feels as entranced by the creativity of evolution as he is by stylized blueness and pearliness—the repeated "see" gives a prophetic urgency to the act of looking. It also rhymes in a flat, homophonic way with "sea" itself, suggesting that the continuity is there for the finding. The search is much harder for the twentieth-century poet than for some of his New England predecessors, however. We have only to recall the glib allegorizations of Longfellow to sense the difference. As Dennis Welland points out, in a poem such as "Seaweed" "we are aware of the almost mechanical way in which the sea is being consciously used for allegory, much as Holmes, confronted by a chambered nautilus, has to draw a moral lesson from it."[2]

But while Wilbur cannot assent to a "nature so instructive as William Cullen Bryant's" (Joan Hutton, "Richard Wilbur," in *Conversations*, p. 51), he senses that meaning *is* there and must be found. Even as he holds a Darwinian crab in hand, he invokes a pearl as talisman to bring together the local, evolutionary abundance scattered before him (which he cannot comprehend), and the formality of art that by its conscious choices and heightenings seems far removed from the random "pa*ludal*" jouissance (*ludus* = "game") of an evolutionary swamp (*palus*). Perhaps he means us to think of the anonymous fourteenth-century poem in which a child called Pearl, taken in infancy, appears to her father in a vision and expounds the mystery of grace. She symbolizes the gift of wisdom and more besides, for, as E. V. Gordon points out, "the pearl . . . becomes a symbol of her immaculate spirit and the blessedness of her heavenly state."[3] All this doubtless impinges on us as we read Wilbur's poem, but he himself makes an important addition to the freight of meanings—the pearl marries the spheres of sea and sky and so recalls the mediating image of "Water Walker." In effect it becomes the moon and governs the tides and the disclosures they make in stanza 1. No longer will the sea be a stylized surface in an illuminated manuscript, but rather a more faithful blue that incorporates the life within it instead of patterning it out of existence. At the same time, evolution, far from disquieting the poet with its aleatoric mutations, takes on the trustfulness of friendship. So it is that the mutual hostility of dualism gives way to a vision of monistic peace.

The ocean might disturb Wilbur with its mysterious fecundity, but being a source of objects, it is also a source of delight—as he tells us in "A World without Objects Is a Sensible Emptiness" (NCP, p. 283). This follows a procedure, familiar from such poems as "Attention Makes Infinity," of leading to and from a proposition in a sort of *QED*. Traherne's meaning for "sensible" is "sensory," but it is not unlikely that Wilbur means us to bear in mind its modern signification and associate the "pure" rationality of the sensible person with the deserts that the poem so firmly renounces. Rationality, then, is to be tempered with imagination, abstraction founded on the concrete—and what better image for this synthesis than the Nativity. The camels of the first stanza might well have been suggested by the presence of these animals in some Flemish Nativities, for this is Wilbur's version of the journey of the Magi, internalized, as in a spiritual exercise, and applied to his own condition and temperament.

Christianity has since its inception been bound up with ascesis, from the very moment, indeed, that St. John the Baptist retired to the desert to prepare for the coming of Christ. His diet of locusts and honey seems hinted in the imagery of the oasis, which marks the last contact of the camels with the amenable green of human experience. Wilbur can understand the attractiveness of these renunciations and of those the Desert Fathers made after St. John, but they are not for him. They damage the balance of matter and spirit and threaten death, for the desert is pure vacuity, abstraction without body, and its water simply vibrations of the air. As Prospero's island is eventually dismantled as the stuff dreams are made of, so too are the prosperous islands of the abstract a visionary baseless fabric. A magus who seeks divinity in nothingness is bent on a suicidal quest. Here Wilbur returns from vacancy to the crowded, gay, and multifarious pictures of the quattro- and cinquecento, for it is in literal, dimensioned images, not in blankness, that painters have expressed their vision of the divine, even to the extent of giving the radiance of aureoles the solidity of plates. Art is a process of incarnation and blending, not of disembodiment and separation. They need to be carried in all the fullness of their weight and so brought to birth.

This provides the cue for a palinode. With the plangent tones of a Hebrew prophet, Wilbur urges himself to turn from the desert, depicted with the linguistic sterility of traductio (the repeated use of "flame"), because it represents an experience undifferentiated and barren. Against the flatness of its horizon he sets the majestic verticality of trees as brilliant in the New England sunshine as Yahweh's burning bush. He remembers too the way in which the painters literalized the divine by turning aureoles to plates, and so he divinizes the literal by contemplating the aureoles of the waves. As a finger describes arcs in the process of dialing numbers, so do they catch arcs of light and forge them momentarily into nimbi. Virginia Levey has written well on the poetry of Wilbur, but I cannot help feeling that she goes awry in her reading of this particular stanza, in which she sees the transfigurement of ugliness and sorrow:

> Here, however, Wilbur gives expression to a celebration based not only upon blooming radiance but also upon the anguish of human life. The river that is transformed to a "halo-dialling run" is the dark river of time that ferries life away. The "bracken tiaras" are, after all, bracken, an unpleasant image in itself, composed of disagreeable sounds. The tiaras are drops of water (dew) with the sun shining upon them. They could be called salty tears. The word "bracken" calls to mind another word of nearly the same sounds: "broken." The first two syllables of "tiaras" contain the diphthong of the word "tears" broken into its separate sounds.[4]

Bracken is not an unpleasant image for me, and I would imagine it were even less for a regionalist wedded to his milieu. It is there in all the rusty intricacy of its pinnules, and as the setting sun catches it, the metaphor translates its inherent value into other terms and offers it as a copper filigree for the brow of the hill. (Levey's dew seems premature, for the sun is still in the sky.) The exultation is not to be traced to the fact that something ugly has been made beautiful, but that something potentially absent (as it would be in the desert of pure form and pure reason) is gratefully and happily acknowledged to be there. It is not Christ in the abstract alphabetic guise of Alpha and Omega but Christ as God incarnate that the poem hymns in its concluding stanza.

This is a particularly happy invention, for whereas Wilbur could have returned to his Italian and Flemish canvases and given us the jeweled and lustrous images of an Adoration tableau by Botticelli, say, he keeps the poem on the farm of his childhood. The stable has become a barn, a barn like that in Whitman's "Farm Picture," and a supernova has displaced a stylized five-point star. I cannot understand how, after a conclusion so poised and certain of its direction, Charles Altieri can say that "the poem seeks to reverse Christian notions of the incarnation: the sensible world is source of value and the true home of spirit with light replacing the word as the principle by which natural process generates meaning and hence value."[5] Perhaps he has forgotten that one of the definitions of the Word in the Nicene Creed is *lumen de lumine*. Wilbur is not reversing the Christian notion; he is reminding us of its subtle integrations, integrations that all too often we allow to unravel.

"The Pardon" (NCP, p. 285) returns us to that New Jersey farm and returns us also to the line of thought begun in the lyric "For Ellen" and continued through "Then," once again setting child and adult views in opposition. Although it is placed in a volume called "Ceremony," "The Pardon" is a poem about ceremonial failure, about a child's refusal to take cognizance of death and so give his pet the rites of passage. Having found the rotten corpse, the ten-year-old Wilbur recoils and leaves his father to bury it. In his closed pastoral vision, the child conceives providence as the persistence of things as they are and as they are known. Hence he loves the dog (living as though by its own volition) and rejects it once it "fails" in this task. The moment of loss appears to have remained unresolved for about twenty years, until a dream vision of the adult rectifies the attitude of the child who would not conceive of death. In a setting ostensibly the same as that of the original discovery, the greenness (once thought the attribute of an inextinguishable summer) now seems so vivid that it draws attention to its transience. And in the midst of its mortality, the dog resurrects not as living but as a dead thing. One is reminded of Owen's *Strange Meeting*, with its phantasm that reproaches and clarifies and its setting half recognizable, half apocalyptic and distorted. A vision that failed to take account of mortality has been balanced and adjusted by the ceremonial acknowledgment of death, and so the poem ends in reparation. For Wilbur, the fullness of the physical world can be apprehended only when the spirit puts that fullness *sub specie aeternitatis*—the regionalist of earth inevitably loves that well which he must leave ere long.

"Part of a Letter" (NCP, p. 286), removed as it is from "The Pardon" both in spirit and execution, also ends with an earthing, the earthing of a verbal electricity that has surged and flashed so beautifully throughout the poem. I have earlier had occasion to compare some of Wilbur's "genre" poems with the painting of the Intimistes, and it is to this set that "Part of a Letter" belongs. Its title alone is proof of intimacy, as though the correspondent were letting us glimpse a paragraph or two so neutral as not to create a breach of confidence. We are worlds away, however, from the verse epistle as the Augustans practiced it.

The poet at first takes us to the shore of a New England cove, evoking the sound and motion of waves by vowels that also flatten and recede in the mouth. But even as we thrill to this vividness, we realize that it is only the datum of a metaphor and that the actual motion and energy belong to tables in some Provençal garden, painted with the alfresco vitality so typical of Bonnard. The headiness is sustained by the use of past continuous verbs and gerunds, many of whose suffixes ripple in the rhyme, and by daring enjambments, one of which literally drains the shower into the thirsty earth. This *perpetuum mobile* depends on virtuosic blurring and scumbling and even suggests a certain tipsiness in the viewer, who, unlike the speaker of "Praise in Summer," is not wantonly inverting and deranging his subject matter, but is helplessly caught up in the intoxication of the moment. All *perpetua mobilia* must eventually come aground on a tonic chord, and in this instance it is a regional one. The trees that have up till now been a pointillist tremble of green and gold ("minting" both in the sense of coining spangles and refreshing like the herb) suddenly take root in soil. Then the sun catches the tongue of a woman as she utters a real tree name, and the word itself becomes the gold of afternoon sunlight and the gold of the acacia flower. The poem ends like a medieval macaronic, interleaving English and French. In contrast to the dazzling technique of the preceding three stanzas Wilbur offers us limpid simplicity—so simple as to take on a profound, baffling pathos.

In "Part of a Letter," the French language acts as a rooting agent, but in "La Rose des Vents" (NCP, p. 287) it functions rather as the sirenical voice of myth, tempting the poet away from his "periploi" of objects. The rose in question is the elaborate, many-pointed compass design that old cartographers set in their maps to give direction to the viewer, and the poet decides to set sail for one, inviting his lady to join him on the voyage. Since real continents suffer the attrition of the sea, he offers an island of the mind as happier venue for their love. But the diction as much as the reasoning is designed to alert us to the Romantic falseness of the option. In the last line of stanza one we hear the naive chant of Stevenson's "Travel" ("I should like to rise and go / Where the golden apples grow"),[6] and the seductive but unsatisfactory resolve of "The Lake Isle of Innisfree."[7] Departure poems that base themselves merely on wish-fulfillment are bound to lose their way.

That is why the Lady interjects with a caution much like that in " 'A World without Objects.' " She reminds the man that no rosette of compass directions floats in the sea, recollecting that substantive "rose" only as the transient past tense of "rise." Wilbur also hints at the instability of erotic as opposed to agapaic love by invoking "roving wave" of William Collins's poem on Phoebe, the wave that bore Venus Anadyomene. Only on what Keats has called "earth's human shores" do real roses grow, their reality appositively linked to the fact of their fading. Just as in "The Pardon," the poet suggests that the real can be grasped only through knowledge of its transience.

"Epistemology" (NCP, p. 288) comprises two couplets that encapsulate two old problems of philosophy with all the niftiness of proverbs. Proverbs, however, have a reputation for canceling each other out: the many hands that make light work, for example, can also spoil the broth. It is this inconsistency that Wilbur seems to have in mind when in the first couplet he scorns the crudity of Dr. Johnson and, by implication, of the Scots commonsense philosophers, while in the second he sides with them and points out the disconnection between idealist epistemology and the ordinary course of human affairs. But out of the cancellation some sort of implicit synthesis emerges, and the poet affirms the importance of the mind and of the senses by his dual allegiance to different epistemological traditions. The epigrams are lighthearted, but taken together in paradoxical tension, they say something quite important about Wilbur's art. His judgment of I. A. Richards's verse applies as fully to his own: "What we do *not* have in I. A. Richards's poems is rhymed and metered philosophic wisdom. Rather we have the mind in full speculative action, its behavior not separable from moods, affections, scenes, situations, persons, and a respect for mystery."[8]

"Castles and Distances" (NCP, p. 289) is one of Wilbur's longer poems, and while it has passages of great beauty, it is not without wobbles and discomposures, especially in the first section. The castles in the title are something of a red herring, for it is with distance above all that the poet is concerned—aesthetic, moral, and spatial distance. First he sets up a contrast between spectators to whom experience is ferried by camera and hunters who pursue that experience at first hand. Seeing walruses on the cinema screen, we laugh uncomprehendingly and uncompassionately—or so the poet claims—because we have not closed the distance between the animal and ourselves. Only hunters are capable of sympathy with the hunted prey. This is sheer sophistry of course, the decadent and fruitless sophistry of a Karen Blixen who in *Out of Africa* claims to love the things she kills,[9] or an

Oscar Wilde who talks of killing the thing he loves.[10] Hunters cannot *regret* the pain; they have voluntarily and premeditatedly been its cause. Nor do people necessarily laugh at walruses in documentary films but rather delight in the experience vicariously recorded for them. (The slippery aphorisms that Wilbur constructs in this poem in order to oil the passage of his argument would be unacceptable at any time, but they are more especially so in the nineties than in the fifties, now that the rhinoceros and the African elephant are on the verge of extinction.)

Cutting to a relief of St. Hubert, converted during the hunt by a crucifer stag, the poet suggests that beatitude comes from a suspension of will, in this case the will to destruction—*En la sua volontade e nostra pace.* However, the sculpture at Amboise does not depict the beatific sequel to this moment—the saint's renunciation of the world and of the violence within it. Nor does it record the legend of St. Giles, who intercepted with his own body the arrow directed at his hind. This would have given Wilbur a perfect entrée into the renunciations of section 2, but it is one he chose not to use. Instead he applauds the circlet of real antlers amid the flamboyant architecture of Amboise, whose extravagant tracery and crockets they no doubt partly inspired. They have assisted the designer in his hunt for God, we are told, though why this should be so is never explained. The elision of spiritual search and hunting strikes me as nothing more than a flippant Clevelandism.

It is a relief to turn to the second half of the poem in which Wilbur wrestles with the old polar contrasts of his temperament, regional dwelling and abstract aspiration. Distance is associated with renunciation, with the ascesis Wilbur rejected at the start of " 'A World without Objects.' " Here, though, it is not so much sensory deprivation that the poet deplores, as irresponsibility, the cultivation of a fugitive and cloistered virtue at the expense of the world from which the sensibility withdraws. Prospero, already glimpsed in an earlier reference to islands, returns as the paradigm of the desert saint, recovering a Golden Age by imaginative abdication and exile. Retreats such as his might restore the wounded soul, but castles and *turres eburneae* must be breached and distance reduced by returning to the real world. The poem ends loudly and tendentiously on a hunting song that reminds Prospero of his return to polity. Would that it had been a madrigal instead.

The piece in "Museum Piece" (NCP, p. 292) is both an artifact worthy of display and a piece in the musical sense of *pezzo*, in this case a *pezzo capricioso*. It provides a witty and spirited footnote to the ivory tower mentality rejected in "Castles and Distances" by presenting a gallery custodian in all his everyday ordinariness. Among the works he guards in his stolid and honorable way is a painting by Degas, an artist whose interest in pure form led him to the stylizations of ballet. But Degas painted ordinary scenes as well—women ironing or washing their hair—and this double allegiance to the ideal and the quotidian relates him to Wilbur in turn. The poet attempts his own integration of polar opposites (though the effect is a touch too anecdotal and Rockwellian) by having the dancer pirouette on the guardian's head. The point is made again in the final stanza, a Clerihew in spirit if not in form, where an El Greco (all febrile ecstasy) does service as a clothes horse. Degas owned two works by this painter, both of them sacred—"St. Ildefonso Writing at the Virgin's Dictation" and "St. Benedict Praying."[11]

"In the Elegy Season" (NCP, p. 295), though less iconoclastic than Degas' trouser rack, also takes a sacred object and adapts it to secular ends. Here it is not an El Greco but the aspects of the Requiem Mass that serve the poet's evocation of autumn. Our first clue comes from the reference to All Souls', a feast that commemorates the dead, and cues the reference to the "hellish" bonfires of autumn. Although the allusion is nowhere explicitly made, I feel certain that when Wilbur describes the leaves that gather in gulleys and wells, he is recalling the autumnal leaves that in *Paradise Lost* "strow the Brooks / Of Vallombrosa."[12] There the fallen angels on the sea of flame were metaphorically assimilated to leaves; here the leaves are metaphorically assimilated to souls in purgatory. It is the very absence of summer that makes it present to senses no longer dazzled by its sensuous abundance, and like his father in an earlier poem, Wilbur begins to paint the vanished season. The elegy commemorates its death, as the feast of All Souls' the death of people—and just as the introit of the Requiem begs that *lux perpetua luceat eis* so Wilbur paraphrases that *lux perpetua* in the light of his noetic summer. His mental lakes, morever, while they are clearly the amniotic fluids of conception and creativity, seem also to transfigure the *profundus lacus* of the Requiem offertory.

All the while, of course, Wilbur's central tenets about the mind and the real are being borne out. Imagination is supplanting with concrete leaves the great vacant abstraction in line 2. Even in his summer dazzlement, Wilbur has been attending to his world and is able to supply the missing details. There are little heightening touches, as there were in the father's summer picture. Proserpine's spring rising receives a blurry, synecdochal treatment that recalls the feminine presences of early Keats, and the delicate Latinism of "cordial" conjures up the heart-shaped lilac leaves in Whitman's elegy for Lincoln.

After the rather queasy celebration of the hunt in "Castles and Distances," it is refreshing to see Wilbur's native compassion and empathy flare forth in the anger of "Marché aux Oiseaux" (NCP, p. 296), which reads like an amplified Augury of Innocence. The minor calls of the captive birds imply both the notion of a minor tonality as well as readiness and the burden of the crowd, its obsessive refrain as much as its encumbered spirit. The regionalist in Wilbur loathes the confinement of the birds whose natural habitat is air and also deplores their disnaturing transposition from Africa into France. This is movingly caught in the stanza about the travailleur, lost to its native Sudan. While the self-obsessed buyers project joy upon the Rorschach blot of its music, the poet's quiet addendum, only a line long, cancels out that sentimental lie. The love that the bird-fanciers profess for the birds is of course nothing of the kind, since it substitutes mere dependence for reciprocity. Recalling Burke's distinction between the sublime and the beautiful, Wilbur angrily notes how in confining birds, we disallow the sublimity of their aspiring flight.

Aspiring flight is also projected in "Juggler" (NCP, p. 297), the poem that follows. There is—to use a Wilburian word—a distinct revenance of "Grace" here, but the poet has changed his mind to some extent and is altogether less dismissive of instinct and hebetude in this celebration of a pointless art. We have seen how he conveyed the fall of a nest in the kinesthetic contour of "Lightness"; he also captures the fragile balance of the juggler with a legerdemain worthy of its subject. There are the familiar terrifying swoops of enjambment and a syncopation of syntax against stanza that gives the poem its precarious, teetering motion. Also worth noting are the expletives that parents might utter in the presence of a child to indicate that they too are participating in the excitement. The thematic burden beneath this ebullient virtuosity is not unlike that of the "Intimations Ode"— the loss of visionary gleam. Juggling has the effect of restoring things that have fallen foul of stolidity and indifference. By placing them momentarily out of context, rather like a Cubist painter, the juggler invites us to reassemble them in their proper weight and sequence, and so to invest our perceptions with new energy now that both Newtonian gravity and our own grave temperaments have received a jolt. What we take for granted has momentarily been deranged, so that even the unscrutinized convention of applause turns into an absurd battering of hands in the last stanza.

Although an allegorical level is never disclosed, it is hard not to read "Juggler" in precisely the same terms as those invited by "Parable" (NCP, p. 298). This, like "Praise in Summer," criticizes poetic renovation by derangement and validates barns at the expense of uncentered levity. By electing a regionalist bourne, the horse gives anchorage and purpose to the unbridled fantasy of its rider. It is likely that the poems grouped here were written at roughly the same time, for they all have recourse to a reckless, allegorical type of metaphor more characteristic of Auden and Lowell than of Wilbur, who otherwise favors precision in his marquetries of image and experience.

Such uncharacteristic looseness comes to a climax in "The Good Servant" (NCP, p. 299), in which conceit supervenes extravagantly on conceit in the description of the servant's hands. Wilbur's title is ironical, of course, for the poem is not about service so much as servitude, and although it seems to recall the "good and faithful servant" of Matthew 25:21, the omission of "faithful" helps point to the irony. At first the hands are a harborage for the vessels of the world, slimy and dark and barnacled; then they are barren trees limed by a fowler to betray the wings of love; and then they are simply hands such as Blake might have described (the archaic pronoun "mine" is strategic) gloving themselves in velvet enmity. The point is that the hands, ostensibly engaged in tasks of service, like the selfish hands in Herbert's "Collar," are in fact being directed by a resentful and treacherous mind.

Further hints of rottenness occur in the following stanza. Far from having inner strength, the speaker confesses to divided, schizophrenic selves placed in "soft" contiguity with each other, while the outer face, ignoble and hardened, becomes a sort of exoskeleton for an invertebrate being. Stanza 3, a record of the servant's dreams, likewise reveals the inadequacy of his spirit, for it surrealistically takes elements of scripture—James and John mending their nets by the Sea of Galilee, Christ asleep in the midst of the storm, the disciples asleep in Gethsemane—and distorts them out of recognition. In this vision, Christ sleeps on in spiteful indifference to his disciples, who, with the dreary futility of a Sisyphus, are fishing with broken nets. Christian service has become a tyrannical and arbitrary servitude. Wilbur supplies the key to the malaise in the phrasing of the final line, for it is not by the "could" of capacity but the "would" of volition that the servant fails.

Psychological derangement is also the subject of "Pity" (NCP, p. 300). One is not certain whether the murder in question is a *crime passionel,* or whether, like that in "Porphyria's Lover," it is prompted by some psychopathic possessiveness. The fact that the speaker uses an affectionate epithet to describe his victim's face suggests an intimacy between them. He feels no remorse, however, and the memory of this strange, faceless being—like the shadow on the wall of some de Chirico nightmare—centers entirely on the caged bird, which once set free, exits like a psychotic phantasm from the brain. This simile surrealistically takes the slang epithet "cracked" and presents it as a fissure from which obsessions emerge in concrete form. Wilbur's detractors sometimes patronize him for his "safeness," but poems like "The Good Servant" and "Pity" show that he can render dark materials with a chilling acuity, the more chilling for the finesse of the form in which they have been encased.

"The Sirens" (NCP, p. 301), a manifesto poem like Frost's "The Road Not Taken," exorcises the loreleis of false choice and deflection that the poet has triumphed over in the course of his life. The vision is much less austerely allegorical than that of "The Good Servant," for details like the wild birds seem to derive from experience rather from than allegorical design, but it is no more a regionalist poem than "Parable" before it. It does tell us, however, that Wilbur's commitment to the real and the immediate have not been cyclopean and that the very awareness of the sirens' call has enriched the ambience of his art and given it a complex texture. The lands he has never encountered represent on the one hand the internationalism he synthesizes with his Americanness and, on the other, the lands of the spirit contiguous with the perceptible world.

While "The Sirens" marches doggedly forward, rather like the trudging song that opens Schubert's *Winterreise,* "Year's End" (NCP, p. 302) is a poem of freezings and fixtures. It acknowledges that pattern is best perceived by overview, not in the thick of things, and tries to gain perspective by looking back. That is why, even though it is written on 1 January, Wilbur has called it "Year's End." Following the great mystic contemplatives who, in the words of St. François de Sales, "lock up our spirit as it were within the closet of the mysterie which we meane to meditate,"[13] Wilbur gathers up images of perfect composure (all of them significantly nonhuman) and sets them against the mindlessness and violence of human beings who hurtle forward without pause. He is a poet who clearly loves the ballet, as the various Degas poems and the meditation on "Grace" make plain, and it is possible that his opening image was suggested by Fokine's famous *pas seul, The Dying Swan,* in which the danseuse is downed in the sense of folding her body over itself against the floor, and downed also by her snowy costume. It marks a return to a tangible milieu after the surreal and allegorical landscapes of the poems that go before. The poet has noted the activity of whitefish and lake trout beneath the ice of a New England lake and forged his metaphor from this notation.

But it is not the movement of fish that arrests him—it is rather the leaves frozen into ice, their random fall now converted into pattern. The crucial word is *perfection*—finish and poise, but also completedness, as in the Latin *perficere.* Whether it be in the ice of a New England Lake or of Siberian plains or the ash and lava of volcanoes that fossilize ferns and encase the perfect circle of a dog asleep, nature is shapely by virtue of being immemorial, unconditioned by the "before" and "after" of human time. Giving itself eternally to the present moment, it is perfected through that endless moment of submission. The human content of the poem is characterized instead by imperfection, partiality, intermittence and discord. Snow that at the start of the poem was settling with the permanence and tenure of settlement is, in the noisiness of the New Year, now contesting the proclamation of the bells, affecting the air waves in a way that emphasizes the discontent so close to the surface of human gaiety. It is nature that creates ceremony in this poem—humankind simply approximates or fails.

"The Puritans" (NCP, p. 303) also explores the disconnection of ritual from the reality it purports to serve. Although the title leads us to expect a Lowell-like indictment of the *Mayflower* and all it brought with it, it is not the Charles so much as the Mississippi that the poem brings to mind, if only because the event it describes would be familiar to most readers of *Huckleberry Finn.* Although the imagery is not as stark and extravagant as the conceits of, say, "The Good Servant," it is another of Wilbur's allegorical poems, asking us to give an emblematic value to each of its details as they come into focus. The whiteness of the ship, for example, is the whiteness of a whited sepulcher but, if we stay in the South, it might signify also an oppressive society that lynches by night and makes a token effort to expose the crime by day. The quest for justice has become hollow ceremony, for the victim, in emblematically umber waters (the dark of the unconscious that the day seeks to censor and nightfall unleashes), has been carefully weighted to escape the ritual search.

"Grasse: The Olive Trees" (NCP, p. 304) whisks us across the Atlantic to a Europe that Wilbur has revisited in peacetime. Rooting himself there for the moment, he gives us a Midi landscape with an eye as loving and as sharp as that he turns on his New England settings. However, there is also a faint unease at the *luxe, calme et volupté* of Baudelaire, which suggests that one's puritan heritage cannot be easily sloughed. The poem begins with *natura naturans*, its fecundity and abundance caught in the sticky, clogged enjambment that recalls the viscous trickle of jelly at the same time as it points to heavy stasis of being jammed. The landscape is similarly static. Light does not clarify and illuminate but is concretized into hanks of passive wool, and the sky is soft and receptive enough to receive the impress of a palm. In fact, the landscape resembles the bedding medium of paint that in "The Giaour and the Pacha" converted human drama into formal arabesque. Since everything is quiescent and heavy and content, it falls to the olive trees to represent aspiration, the world of the spirit otherwise blocked off by an indolent satiety. In " 'A World without Objects,' " Wilbur reached his balance of body and soul by renouncing the opposite extreme—ascesis. In "Grasse" the procedure is reversed. Here the thirstiness of the olive redresses the complacency of the South and teaches it that it is not paradisal.

The next poem also seems to stay in the south of France, for its title recalls canvases by Picasso and Matisse. There is nothing voyeuristic or even sensual about "Five Women Bathing in Moonlight," however, since the poem is about their dissolution into abstract form and then into pure color. The landscape is first set up in readiness for the figures that will eventually be painted in and cryptically dissolves the poet out of the frame to leave the night to its own devices. Solid land and water then begin to establish an accord not unlike the "interchange of favours" that Keats depicts between the "bowery green" and "ripples" in "I stood tip-toe,"[14] except that here the actual boundary between liquid and solid is effaced, anticipating the liquescence of flesh into color and form. First the women turn into mermaids, their hair like seaweed, and a definite article gives to their shoulders the impersonality of pure form. Their human speech turns to wordless melody, and then they themselves become pictorial elements. While they imagine themselves to be exercising their freedom as they swim at will through the water, their every movement is governed, having a spatial line and purpose in the aesthetic consciousness of night (or of the poet ventriloquially speaking on behalf of night). While a prima ballerina might project an effortless grace and spontaneity, her every movement has been dictated by the choreographer and by her technique. That is the point of the compulsions to which the five women, resembling the danseuse Alexandra Danilova, have been subjected.

In "Five Women," darkness is the medium of fusion and disintegration, but in "The Terrace" (NCP, p. 309) it has precisely the opposite function. If we are still in France, we appear to have moved northeastward toward Chamounix, for there is no other way to account for the snowy peaks in stanza 3. The poet and his wife, eating a meal on a terrace, soon take to eating the view itself, as it were to illustrate the epigraph from Baudelaire— *De la vaporisation et de la centralisation du Moi. Tout est là.* It is a vivid and spirited evocation, with touches of the Swift of Brobdingnag and Lilliput, and bits of Arcimbaldo too. Usually the invention of a chef is taxed by finding edible equivalents for inedible items (e.g., green-tinted coconut for grass). Wilbur's challenge is precisely the opposite, and he meets it splendidly by turning towers to cheese, and bells to melons. But the extravagance and headiness of the analogies have a touch of the Clevelandism criticized in "Praise in Summer," and we feel no surprise when the *vaporisation et centralisation du Moi* become solid and marginal with the onset of night. Where an exorbitant egoism organized the world concentrically about the self, subordinating human industry to leisure and making washerwomen into sauce, now the ego loses its reality before the irresistible onset of things. The poem has an antimeric structure, and although it ends on a chastened downbeat, there is no doubt that Wilbur expects us to apply to the epistemological balance of perceiver and perceived to give the poem its offstage resolution. *Moi* must be titrated against *Elle* for the salt of reality to form.

"A Problem from Milton" (NCP, p. 311) is obliquely related to "The Terrace" insofar as it also turns on the clarifying and classifying impulses of the mind. The problem is said to come from Milton because, cast in imagery from the creation myth, it is one that any theodicy must strive to address. If knowledge is the avenue to sin, then why should humankind have been made *capax rationis?* Of course, such a problem is insoluble outside the framework of faith—almost all the problems of theodicy are—but Wilbur fashions a splendid poem out of the paradox. He begins with the simple Euclidean forms of nature—the symmetries of palm and conifer and vine whose forms are simple enough to yield their meaning without difficulty, but whose beauty is slightly impoverished as a result.

But implicit in the act of creation is the inscrutable complexity of God's own mind: streams follow incomputably random courses, flowers yield intangible scents, and the taxonomy of plants eventually proves more tricky than at first it seemed. It is a human habit to perceive new problems at the very moment of solving the old, so that Alps on Alps arise. Wilbur conveys this by a sort of anadiplosis between stanzas 2 and 3 and between 3 and 4, the last line of the preceding verse picked up and elaborated at the start of the next. As the mass of trees converges in an unsortable wave, so Wilbur cuts to an actual wave as it tears toward the seashore, an image of instinctual, irrational freedom. In the old classification of matter, it is mineral, the least complex of forms, and in that lies its apparent salvation. The poem sets its freedom against the rockbound dwelling of whelk and limpet, considerably higher up the great chain of being. And yet even the configurations of a humble shell are so subtle and intricate that the whelk reference, hinged by anadiplosis, leads Swedenborg straight to the *Deus artifex* in stanza 3. The type of Swedenborg and Emerson is Adam himself, demonized by his thirst for knowledge and so forfeiting the vegetative paradise that was rejected in "Grasse: The Olive Trees." Wilbur might be drawn to the pacifying mindlessness of this condition, but he knows that it is subhuman. While he chaffs Adam about the tides and their ignorance of what controls them, there can be no doubting he would sooner contemplate the spiral of a whelk (whatever the cost) than carry it unreflectingly on his back.

"A Glance from the Bridge" (NCP, p. 312) takes us back to New England, not to its rural loveliness, but to one of its industrial towns. The title might suggest an inattentive, random act of looking, but Wilbur's glance is every other person's stare, and a great deal comes of it. The bridge from which it is taken hints perhaps at Wordsworth's sonnet on Westminster, where an ugly industrial sprawl is also transfigured for the moment, while the canalized river recalls Blake's "chartered Thames." The twentieth century has learned to adapt to industrial ugliness only by escaping it at every opportunity, and it takes the steadiness of the regional eye to detect potential loveliness in its disarray. Wilbur's vision of the city, one ought to stress, lacks the affectation of W. H. Auden, who claimed to prefer a stroll along the Oxford Canal to one in Christchurch Meadow. Wilbur acknowledges the ugliness for what it is, and even as the reclamation of squalor occurs, he has the tact and the honesty to insert an adverb of degree that separates the bodies of girl and whore. Wilbur has accepted this kind of enterprise as part of his poetic task, observing that the "urge of poetry is not, of course to whoop it up for the automobile, the plane, the computer, and the spaceship, but only to bring them and their like into the felt world, where they may be variously taken, and to establish their names in the vocabulary of the imagination."[15]

"Clearness" (NCP, p. 313) is to some extent a palimpsest of "A Problem from Milton," stressing as it does the impossibility and, worse, the inhumanity of pure reason. Wilbur has already acknowledged the cloudiness of the simplest matter in "Epistemology" and not for nothing calls his poem "Clearness" rather than "Clarity." The two are not commensurate. Phenomenologists believe that by a process of *epoche*, framing and inspecting the act of perception, one can arrive at the reality outside the mind. So too do "objectivists" like William Carlos Williams. Wilbur himself, as we have seen again and again, is more than ready to point to a noumenal world, but he knows that the very irreducibility of objects is itself ineffable and mysterious. The more simple a lyric poem, for example, the more it defies explication of its power. So in the opening catalog of the poem, the bucket of water seems to offer itself as the cousin of a certain red wheelbarrow on which, as on the shoulders of Atlas, so much depends. Perhaps Wilbur also means us to think that it has been drawn from the well in which, according to Democritus, Truth has made her dwelling.

But of course the honesties we imagine it to signify are simply that— imaginings. Our perceptions of snowflakes are no less awry. While seeking unfounded solace in the fact that snow is ultimately crystalline (not opaque, as it appears), we see them in dynastic terms. Dynasties, however, endure through time, heirs succeed in time, and types define themselves by time, and any projection of the timelessness of snow in these terms is faulty. It is timeless rather in the fact of having no duration. By the same token, the replicable pattern of pine needles, far from leading to a great anagnorisis, amazes the mind of the poet and lulls him into a visionary sleep that lifts the veil of which Shelley forbade the lifting. In an *Ultima Thule*, as unreal as the prosperous islands of " 'A World without Objects,' " he finds a final realization of clearness, utterly unclear because it is inhuman and therefore unintelligible. The vision that strives for that sort of exactness is guilty of coercion. Wilbur always shuns the polar extremes of thesis and antithesis, always drives forward to the middle ground. The clearness of materialism, which attempts to get matter into focus at the expense of the soul, is the sort of clearness from which this haunting dream poem recoils.

"Games One" and "Games Two" (NCP, pp. 314-15) are not happily named, recalling as they do the mechanically numbered titles with which George Herbert prefaced some otherwise wonderful poems—"Affliction I– V," "Love I–III," and so on. A title like "Games," moreover, invites the reader to treat the poems lightly, even though they are poems of substance and, it goes without saying, perfect craft. Artists have always delighted in the imposition of impossible limits, forging something defiantly complex within them. The sonnet form, among others, testifies to the persistence of this challenge. So too does Wilbur's poem about the asterisk, which picks up where "&" and "O" left off. In a poem about vertical descent and ascent, he has written in quatrains of dimeter and trimeter, which constrict and funnel the flow of the verse and give it its columnar form. He has also taken a chiastic rhyme scheme (abba) to create an icon of reflection and inversion, also thematic concerns of the poem. As the asterisk alerts us to a footnote at the bottom of the page, so do we footnote the astronomical stars in a rhythm of reciprocal clarification. The stars might signify the eternal and unchangeable and otherworldly, but we perceive them in anecdotal frameworks—the constellations that have come down to us from antiquity (Ursa; Canis) and the even more prosaic imagery from daily life, as in the Big Dipper, which the *OED* traces to the nineteenth century.

Thus does Wilbur return to an old preoccupation, viz., how to connect transcendence and the real—and so gives the lie to Reed Whittemore's claim that he proposes "an immanent, as opposed to a transcendental, principle of being."[16] With a happy, almost chattersome inconsequence, Wilbur goes on to mention starfish as if they were the analogues of stars, honoring, like Marvell's "The Garden," the old belief that the ocean contains parallels for everything on land. And where most poets would conceive the sea as the looking glass of the heavens, he turns the notion around and has the heavens reflect the sea, preparing us, with a natty use of the preposition "up," to supply a gloss—not an oceanic gloss or sheen, but the gloss of a footnote, which, be it remembered, comes from the Greek word for tongue.

"Games Two" contemplates the colon, the symbol of pause and therefore of silence. Mystics are not the only ones who have complained about the inadequacy of language. Even rhetoricians, dedicated as they are to linguistic expertise, have invented the trope of aposiopesis, which stylizes a failure of language, and so conveys emotion too large for speech. It would not be entirely accurate to describe Wilbur as a mystic poet, since he lacks the mystic's impatience with the flesh, but his spirituality is evident in poem after poem, and it is entirely fitting that, as a religious man, he should join T. S. Eliot in berating words for failing the spirit. He does so by establishing the right-hand margin as an emblematic East, a place of pilgrimage to which all words move, but which typographic convention prevents them from reaching. And of course it is not only the physical constraint of the page that prevents the words from arriving at the "sweet golden clime / Where the traveller's journey is done"—the meter also governs the tide of words with a pull akin to the moon's.

As John Thompson has observed, in "verse the language turns from time to time and forms a new line. It turns at a point determined by the meter."[17] The dimeters and trimeters sharpen that tyranny, reining words in and forcing them to return to the capital (demarcating the left-hand margin) from which they set out. And since "capital" derives from the Latin *caput* ("head"), it is to the mouth that they return, having failed in the task of expressing the ineffable. They fall and are granted, in the silence of their falling, a Pisgah view of the promised land whose occupation they are denied. This is a type of heavenly nominalism, in which things need no words, being contained in the Word, and the breach between stating and being is closed in contemplative silence. Here the colon becomes a gate of pearl, separating, with a moat of pure space, the failed words and the heaven their failure will secure. Raymond Benoit has gone so far as to claim that Wilbur has indeed come close to achieving this paradisal equation: "His poetry in theme and technique more and more rests upon truth as this hypostasis . . . rather than concept or judgment or proposition."[18]

"Beowulf" (NCP, p. 316) is another poem that plays with conventions— generic conventions in this instance, not typographic ones. It does two things. First, it compresses epic into lyric and then it brings a modern sensibility to bear on heroic Anglo-Saxon attitudes. The result is a brilliant précis—quizzical, skeptical, and elegantly listless—commenting as much on the cynical mindset of the twentieth-century reader as on the ruder temperament of the Old English listener. If it does not quite prove that genres cannot marry, it shows that when they do, the offspring does not resemble the parents. The effect is not unlike one of Liszt's operatic "paraphrases."

Wilbur starts the poem in the mode of Douanier Rousseau and Grandma Moses. The epic landscape is flat, overemphatic, and gaudy. Indeed the Roman road registers as an extension of the Yellow Brick Road garishly conceived by MGM artists. The laws of physics do not apply in a heightened and simplified mode: reflection persists after the object has vanished, stone withstands attrition. Bruce Michelson connects this sort of distortion with dreaming: "How are we to understand this place, no quality of which we recognize from the text of the original epic, except as a world of excessive and perverse dream, a world where imagination trusted too blindly has led the inhabitants into dreams which have turned toward nightmare?"[19] The people also live under the constraint of their narrative design and function, having no real spontaneity and purpose beyond that which the epic poet gives them. Epic ritualism is reconceived in twentieth-century terms as mental disorder, as compulsiveness: the people endlessly repeat themselves. As though to convey his uneasiness about the epic Danes, Wilbur twice uses epanorthosis, suggesting that he needs more than a first impression of warmth or coldness to put his finger on their oddity. This repetition, like the repetition of the opening line, offers token homage to the repetitions of the epic mode. It does not make for plangency, however, and strikes the reader rather as a bemused, exhausted failure of language to grasp inscrutable ideas, ideas no less inscrutable to the original bards.

"Still, Citizen Sparrow" (NCP, p. 318) is a beast fable, and therefore somewhat open-ended. It has been taken to present the contrast between bourgeois and visionary, ordinary person and politician, and although these levels are undoubtedly there, there is room for other readings. Given the long tradition of poetic self-address, one could assume that it is Wilbur who self-deprecatingly conceives himself as a sparrow, in contrast to prophetic poets like Lowell. These, while they might feast on carrion, are capable of magisterial flights that orchard aisles by their very narrowness make impossible. A precedent can be found in Thomas Gray's "Progress of Poesy":

Though he inherit
Nor the pride nor ample pinion,
That the Theban eagle bear
Sailing with supreme dominion
Through the azure deep of air.[20]

Although he does not say it in so many words, Gray also conceives himself as a sparrow in relation to Pindar. Modesty is most becoming in poets, but their critics need feel no inhibition in pointing out that Wilbur and Gray are both of them great poets, even if their greatness differs from the greatness of Lowell or Pindar. Chastity and sobriety are the characteristic notes they strike instead.

Wilbur moreover likes by his own admission to move toward the unknown by short stages, while the Lowells of the world take in experience in great rough hunks, a quality conveyed by the asyndeton, both abrupt and comprehensive, in stanza 3. There is a certain heartlessness in distance, however, and Wilbur makes us aware of the cost of prophethood and the serenity with which Noah is able to contemplate the destruction of others. For someone called by love to the things of this world, such detachment is difficult, and so the poem argues through the alternatives of regional weddedness and prophetic conspectus in a way that leaves no doubt as to the validity of each in turn.

As if to extend the imagery of engulfment in "Citizen Sparrow," Wilbur uses a sustained oceanic metaphor in the regional poem that follows. "Wellfleet: The House" (NCP, p. 319) bears comparison with the "Time Passes" interlude in Virginia Woolf's *To the Lighthouse*. Like that interlude, it has the Berkeleyan property of suggesting the perception of things without a human percipient, of mediating the consciousness of God himself. Not surprisingly, since experience is passing through the mind of God, time itself eventually abolishes itself *sub specie aeternitatis*. If, in the words of Isaac Watts, "Time like an ever-rolling stream / Bears all its sons away," that ephemerality is nonetheless fixed in the vision of God: "A thousand ages in thy sight / Are like an evening gone."[21]

At first Wilbur presents the house as the castle of the Sleeping Beauty, caught up out of time in a bower of shadow and leaf, unnaturally fixed in the amber of history. But the spell is broken by the light that floods it every afternoon from the seaboard and brings with it an oceanic dissolution of fixities. All of a sudden the chiming clock becomes a clanging buoy, and the rooms are ground into sand. And at the very moment that the house is atomized, the poet paradoxically stresses its regional attachment, since in being mutable it is suited to the sea. Hence the oxymoron melding blight and recovery, which also imparts preternatural stillness to the movement of time.

Time is said to pass rapidly before the eyes of a dying person and to disclose, by the touch of a fast-forward button, the entire compass of his or her life. "The Death of a Toad" (NCP, p. 320) does more; it recapitulates whole hunks of evolutionary history, so that the creature, in dying, returns to a paradise conceived not in the past of Eden, but in the geological past when amphibians and reptiles dominated the earth. It is a moving poem and belongs to a tradition of animal elegy founded by Cowper, a tradition that forgoes the mock-heroic inflation that Catullus, Ovid, and even Gray have brought to bear on the death of animals, as if embarrassed by a subject too slight to warrant real tears of pity. Even Dickens, a great-hearted man if ever there were one, is embarrassed enough by the notion to include the satirical "Ode to an Expiring Frog" in *The Pickwick Papers*.

Wilbur starts his poem in the twentieth century, in a garden kept trim by technology. He has told Joan Hutton that, as a boy at least, he was less than fond of gardens ("Richard Wilbur," in *Conversations*, pp. 46–55), and this one, as tidy and as exorbitant as any in the suburbs, is not presented sympathetically. The brutal mower is recalled in the castrate lawn of the conclusion, where the civilizing order (that made possible by the barrier of "Caserta Garden") has emasculated nature and given the sun the stressful pallor of an urbanite. Even though, as Spangenberg and Beukes point out, "castrate" here has its archaic horticultural meaning,[22] a castrate lawn is still a lawn deprived of seed and its disfigurement made by a death-dealing machine. The verge the gardener has obsessively maintained blends in the eyes of the dying animal with other, more meaningful verges, the shores of Amphibia.

The diction has been heightened, intensified in the manner of Keats, and is not, as Randall Jarrell ungenerously suggests, "an excuse for some Poetry."[23] Wilbur himself acknowledges its role as a transition marker: "I may have found the word ['emperies'] in Donne in the first place, but I think I wanted to use it here as a kind of confession that I'm doing rather a lot with that toad. I'm turning him into the primal energies of the world in the course of this poem. And so I get a little bombastic as a way of acknowledging that I'm going rather far."[24] The language must thus be viewed as language vesting itself for an apotheosis, one in which the creature that the garden has marginalized and killed reclaims its inheritance of time, so much nobler than that arbitrary maintenance of pattern which has caused its death.

In "Driftwood" (NCP, p. 321) the poet also takes us back in time, away from present debasement, and, in the course of tracing that graph of history, transmutes slag into gold. The poem is a sublime version of a genre familiar to composition pupils in Grade School—"The History of a Penny," or "The Story of Piece of Chalk"—compositions that trace the origins of the subject in a copper mine or in the white cliffs of Dover. Wilbur's starting point is not the Paleozoic time of "The Death of a Toad," though, but a mythic golden age, when greenwoods made the earth into a vast *locus amoenus*. Here the trees, rooted by their regional concern with growth and continuity, add ring to ring and in that growth find their own limited fulfillment. Wars and cities require the felling of trees, however, and they are sent out into global waters, which in their formlessness and shapelessness present the very negation of a racinée life on earth. Yet even through this purgatorial reshaping, in which their outer shapes are conformed to the invisible contours of current, wave, and tide, they retain their essential substance and, in so doing, honor their birthright. This comes close to being a parable of regionalists who retain their identity even while they are forced into receptivity of outside influences. Indeed, the tight circular grain and the random attrition together present a Wilburian synthesis of opposing forces, a synthesis acclaimed by the alchemical shift in the imagery, which takes the slag of the opening stanza and by a series of graded metallic transitions, reconceives it as crowns and scepters.

The driftwood retains a redemptive identity throughout its trial by water, but in "A Courtyard Thaw" (NCP, p. 323), the droplets are dismissed because of their dissociation from the world. The poem might be read as an answer to Marvell's "On a Drop of Dew," where the intactness of the drop (*gemmula* in Marvell's Latin version) is celebrated for its "Trembling lest it grow impure."[25] The droplets of "The Courtyard Thaw" are by contrast false. Their gemmation, intended in the organic sense of "budding," is also meant to pick up the hard mineral impassivity of "gem" and the soft vegetable impassivity of *gemmula*. While dew serves Marvell as a sacramental species ("Such did the Manna's sacred Dew destil"), for Wilbur the droplets are unworthy of the office, a tinkling travesty of the magisterial rhythms of the year.

The water of "Driftwood" and the air into which the droplets dissipate in "A Courtyard Thaw" make an elemental return in "Lament" (NCP, p. 324), where they are dismissed for their want of corporateness. Nashe's "Litany in Time of Plague" rather than Marvell's dew is the point of departure here. His queens are young in a poem that has given them longevity, old by the passage of time that flows outside the frame of art—hence the witty and improbable paradoxes of the opening stanza. It is almost as if, having arrived at an avaricious old age, they are trading in lightweight coronets for ones more heavily embossed with rubies and sapphires and emeralds—but we have known all along that the stones in question are headstones and that there can be no bargaining with death. Even so, Wilbur confirms their lyric timelessness through the zeppelin conceit, and through bony allusions which manage at the same time to evoke the intricacy of X-ray photographs and the confusion of the charnel house. The passing of the queens has been rendered material by the corporealizing fullness of art.

The perception of the beloved is a product both of her essential being and of the poet's recipient soul, her spirit corporate in the sense of incorporating more than one spirit and corporate also in the sense of being embodied in his art, as Donald Hill has pointed out (*Richard Wilbur*, pp. 65–66). Water and air evade decay by being incorporeal, art by means of its *monumentum aere perennius,* which remains visible. While the poet laments the inevitable passing of his wife's loveliness, that loveliness is being preserved by his art, even as Nashe's queens endure through the ages in the permanence of *his* art. Wilbur laments the short term of grace, but as he laments it in verse, he extends that term and forges a radiant future for it.

The same quiet futurity consoles the speaker in "Flumen Tenebrarum" (NCP, p. 325), since acquiescence is the only dignified response that can be made to the transience of things. The title obviously alludes to the Styx, but the river begins life in the American countryside before being dilated to the level of symbol. By the end of the poem it has come to represent the principle of extinction. Most apocalypses breed anguish and terror and have done so ever since the alarming oracles of the prophet Zephaniah. Wilbur's, by contrast, is calm and accepting, despite the qualms of its start. Here we are presented with a landscape of disconcerting flux and unsteadiness, measured by what seem to be the unchangeable constellations above. In the old Ptolemaic cosmology, the earth, being closest to the sphere of the moon, is governed by its mutability. The reference to earth accordingly suggests both the planet and the transience of human clay.

Two lovers are caught up in the unarrestable flow of the past, which they see streaming away toward death. Rising in apparent contrast to this flux is the constellation of Orion, who quested for his vision in the ultimate river of Oceanus. Whereas the man and woman have come together in union, he is perpetually frustrated in his pursuit of the Pleiades, and their virginity is ensured in turn by his frustration. But even if, according to the old belief (familiar from Donne's *Songs and Sonets*), consummation entails a shortening of life, that curtailment is preferable to the cold stellar permanence of the skies, for they have no permanence *sub specie aeternitatis* and will be engulfed by the river of time. The freezing (friezing) of desire into pattern is therefore no guarantee of immortality. Wilbur takes a line from a dirge by Shakespeare ("All follow this, and come to dust") and, substituting "life" for "dust," suggests the coextensiveness of life and death, even at the moment of vivification. Marvell is also present along with Donne and Shakespeare— the Marvell of "To His Coy Mistress." In that poem another river, the Humber, is likewise placed in the context of eternity, and another "long preserv'd Virginity" lost in the consummation of the grave.

"From the Lookout Rock" (NCP, p. 327) also moves from the local to the allegorical, from the specific to the universal, from the regional to the international. Like "Flumen Tenebrarum," it has a touch of Marvell, Marvell as mediated by Archibald MacLeish. In "You, Andrew Marvell" MacLeish, standing on American ground, projects the onset of darkness in far-flung corners of the globe and weaves an allegory of death and extinction as he does so. Wilbur, standing on a rock on the Atlantic seaboard, notices not the onset of night but a failing of the wind and projects a picture of universal becalmment, a becalmment close to death. The poem does not have the inexorable, mesmeric insistence of MacLeish's, but there are moments of comparable intensity, such as the account of a Western landscape in which the tumbleweed has ceased to tumble. This Sleeping Beauty-like arrest is life-in-death, brought about by an exhalation of the Spirit, the withdrawal of the Ruach from its creation. Since the peace of heaven is not to be found in stagnation of the earth, and since stasis is the quiet of the tomb—Cardinal Newman always insisted that growth was the only token of life—the poem ends with a Shelleyan invocation of the wind to return and vivify what, in a strange visionary instant, has turned to stone. The wind, like the olives in an earlier poem, signifies the creative principle of spirit.

Wilbur is not a poet whom we ordinarily associate with satire, perhaps because he lacks that essential nasty streak, as Cowper lacked it before him. The result is amiable, but a touch bland, since the satiric blade always seems to be sheathed in the charity of the poet. "To an American Poet Just Dead" (NCP, p. 329) is, all the same, a well-turned mock-dirge, two-pronged in its attack. There is the mismatch of the unnamed poet's Anacreontic fervor and the squalor of his addiction; and there is the indifference of the suburbs, so caught up in their own consumption that heaven itself is conceived in monetary terms. Neither commands Wilbur's loyalty, but then neither evokes his savage loathing, and *saeva indignatio* gives way to playfulness. This is best illustrated by the stanza that parodies the syntactic and thematic rhythm of deprivation in Gray's *Elegy:* "For them no more the blazing hearth shall burn, / Or busy housewife ply her evening care." Deep-freeze units and Studebakers replace these domestic details in Wilbur's version.

Clearly, then, it is not through satire that Wilbur expresses his urgent sense of values awry and purpose lost, but rather through meditative and essayistic poems like "Giacometti" (NCP, p. 330), one of the most profound in the collection. While he acknowledges the greatness of the sculptor, Wilbur cannot help noting the human diminishment his art records. Sartre, with all the enthusiasm of an existential humanist, exults in the way the figures of Giacometti "shoot up into existence,"[26] but Wilbur, who puts the statues in the context of those by Michelangelo, Bernini, and even, perhaps, Thorvaldsen,[27] detects no such energy—only weariness and lassitude. The sculpture of rock is heroic and combative: it challenges the will and embodies it, and it belongs to an era of human culture in which art and life were purposive. Making a gypsum maquette does not require the same degree of strenuousness, whether of body or spirit, and yet the attenuation of Giacometti's form fits it for the twentieth century.

Again, as in "Conjuration," the waters of evolution seem to have run backward, but instead of the multifarious life they offer there, here they present only a reduced form, spare and mean enough (in both senses) for us to grasp. The heroisms of public sculpture have become both physically and spiritually inaccessible to our impoverished sensibility—indeed the whiteness and infertility of chalk provide a metaphor for twentieth-century humankind, especially if we contrast it with the life-giving clay in the dirge that follows it on p. 332. Where in more resourceful and heroic cultures we were challenged to feats of Promethean creativity, now we meekly follow, like parodic pilgrims, in the footsteps of Giacometti's statue.

The pastoral elegy of "He Was" (NCP, p. 332) redresses the sourness and barrenness of "Giacometti," and breathes a restorative love of the New Jersey countryside. Wilbur commemorates a laborer native and endued unto his element, regionally rooted—everything, in fact, that Giacometti's image fails to be. He is a sort of *genius loci,* not so much a man as an aggregate of sounds and activities, of nurturement and loving cultivation. In the cycle of nature he finally finds his meaning and fulfillment and at last speaks with the surrogate voices of leaves and birds that rejoice in the fruits of his silent labor. As so often in Wilbur, dogma is rendered in fact, not in abstraction, the facts of apple trees and sparrows, and even the apparently unpastoral minutiae of spray-carts.

"A Simile for Her Smile" (NCP, p. 333) is another brief lyric, not like its predecessor inspired by Frost, but rather by the Herrick who pauses to record some aspect of Julia's loveliness. Again, as in "A Glance from the Bridge," we are placed in an industrial landscape, transfigured for a moment by the passage of a boat, which gives a ceremonious alternative to the rhythm of the traffic it interrupts. From this contrast Wilbur fashions a conceit for his wife's smile, which is simply the phonetic compression of his simile.

The ceremony of the boat pacifies and orders the raw energy of an industrial city; the ceremony of the final poem (NCP, p. 334) ostensibly tames a forest—ostensibly, because the form has the effect not so much of ordering what it contains and harmonizes, but of emphasizing all the energies that escape it. It is important to note that the setting in stanza 1 is not a real but a painted one; the clearing is not the work of a forester but of a painter. And the subject herself is more a decorative metonym than a personality. Wilbur seems to have chosen Bazille because his brand of Impressionism has a marked quality of artifice and sometimes plays neo-Primitive tricks with conventional perspective. The geometric pattern of the blouse might at first sight seem far removed from the organic contours of nature and render the woman in her Second Empire outfit much more the patroness of bows than of boughs. But a hint at Hamlet's riposte to Claudius ("A little more than kin, and less than kind") shows that seeming is not being and that the formality of the costume serves rather to intensify our sense of nature because it heightens the discontinuity of figure and setting.

Stanza 2 evokes the sort of painting that the Académie would have had no qualms in accepting, a voluptuous idyll like Ingres's *La Source,* where the naked nymph (ironically lifted from Milton) blends into her surroundings. The effect is altogether less bracing, because less ceremonious. That is why the final stanza begins with a stylized yawn, as if to suggest the ennui of the poet, more engaged by exhilarating differences than by creamy transitions. He returns to the canvas and, tracing its formal values and balances, notes how *natura naturans* is evoked by that very formality. A social square dance cannot encompass the variety that a temperate forest yields, and the value of the painting is like that of a measuring cup placed beneath a waterfall, proving by its perpetual overflow that the forces of nature cannot be measured. But even at the moment the poet suggests that ceremony cannot contain, he has recourse to the ceremony of metaphor. There are of course no tigers in the temperate forests of France, even those painted by Rousseau. They owe their provenance to Blake's poem about the inconceivability of God and ceremoniously displace the real fauna of terror (boars and adders) with a symbolic one, matching the formal stripes of the lady's blouse with a formal poetic allusion.

Having thus accounted for the pleasures of form, Wilbur refocuses on the exigency of things, the things of this world that feature so happily in the title of his next collection. At the same time, *Ceremony and Other Poems* makes an interesting pendant to the volume that precedes it. The points of continuity can be found in the common denominator of reflective lyrics set in the New England countryside, those of contrast in its vision of Europe viewed through the eyes of a noncombatant rather than a soldier's. The accent accordingly falls less on images of transience and passage and fragmentation than on landscapes of peace into which, by means of a sort of provisional regionalism, the poet is able to root himself for a space.

three

t h i n g s

of

t h i s

w o r l d

(1 9 5 6)

In the traditional Christian view, the world has always been a place of spiritual danger and temptation, and some of its injunctions, like that of St. John—"Love not the world, nor the things that are in the world"—issued in such austerities as the catacombs and the pillar of St. Simeon. But the world in this sense is largely the social world of luxury and vice, and great Christian teachers—St. Augustine, say, from whom Wilbur takes his title, or St. Francis of Assisi—have tried throughout the ages to redress the balance, to distinguish between the things of the world that are worldly and those that are divine. Wilbur, it goes without saying, is a celebrant of terrestriality rather than worldliness, not so much because "the spiritual exists only when clothed with flesh" as Virginia Levey suggests ("The World of Objects," p. 41), but because it is only *through* the flesh the spirit can be apprehended.

"Altitudes" (NCP, p. 231) makes this plain. The title seems to allude to a famous exclamation in *Religio Medici,* in which Sir Thomas Browne revels in the abstractness and intangibility of religious thought:

> As for those wingy mysteries in divinity, and airy subtleties in religion, which have unhinged the brains of better heads, they never stretched the pia mater of mine. Methinks there be not impossibilities enough in religion for active faith; the deepest mysteries ours contains have not only been illustrated, but maintained by syllogism and the rule of reason: I love to lose myself in a mystery, to pursue my reason to an *O altitudo.* 'Tis my solitary recreation to pose

my apprehension with those involved enigmas and riddles of the Trinity, with Incarnation and Resurrection.[1]

Browne's "solitary recreation" is to some extent like Emily Dickinson's, and the altitudes to which they aspire, the heroic altitudes of the spirit. Yet Browne lived in Norwich and Dickinson in Amherst, provincial towns—and even though Norwich has its cathedral, it cannot quite match the grandeurs of St. Peter's or St. Paul's, the basilicas with which the poem begins. Wilbur is concerned with relative altitudes and with the inner and outer coordinates for their measurement. Emily Dickinson, confined to a New England town and discovering the unknown by the known, is a regionalist of the spirit; the architects of Renaissance and Baroque cathedrals are cosmopolitan. Each pursues the sublime by a different route.

Like many of Wilbur's poems, the structure of "Altitudes" is antimeric, an hourglass pattern of parallel inversions. Section 1 examines the way in which God has conventionally (and successfully) been imaged by vast architectural space, aspiring curves, and perfected circles and spheres. But what for the human being is vast and awe-inspiring, for an angel is simply cosy. In the grand cupolas of Bramante and Wren, the angels come and go, not talking of Michelangelo exactly, but certainly conducting a salon and casting appreciative glances at the decor. They are angels conceived in human terms, civilized, sedentary, and domesticated, not the apocalyptic angels of *Macbeth,* say, or *Paradise Lost.* "Dome," indeed, comes close to recovering its Latin sense of "home." Being immaterial, the angels cannot take part in the world, but they can mediate the prayers of the believing, massing in numbers and in sacramental reverence down below. The angels chat (Wilbur's relaxed version of a *sacra conversazione*) and even live in premises. These premises, however, at the same time as they give prayer the concreteness of floorboards, are also the premises of theological argument. The spiritual is conceived as existing through the concrete.

In the second section, the line of direction is reversed. Here it is not the angels who come down from the transcendent world to the physical, but the regional poet who, "seeing New Englandly" from the confines of a suburban belvedere, is reaching upward through the accidents of the world to a transcendent Being that, as in the medieval *Cloud of Unknowing,* remains ineffable. Even as the experience is felt in its inexpressibility, Wilbur relates it to the ordinary life of a town, to dormer windows, to a neighbor in his garden. That belvedere, a reduced cupola, is not only the place of Dickinson's meditations, it is in a sense Dickinson herself—its panes are the homophone of her pains, its chamber the cranium in which her mystical poems come to birth. In a different dome, working to a different rhythm, she too does the work of an *angelos,* mediating her vision of the other through percepts of the world, rising as it were by levitation. Hers in a compound vision, like that of the flies that she sees *in articulo mortis* as they buzz against the window. Donald Hill has noted how the poem presents "the geographical and the cultural distance of Puritan New England from Catholic Italy" (*Richard Wilbur*, p. 96). Extending this notion, one could say that it also dramatizes the efficacy of two opposed dogmas (external authority and inner light) as avenues to the same experience of grace.

One senses the presence of Herbert behind a poem like "Altitudes," with its divinizing of the ordinary and its familiar treatment of the transcendent other. The mood persists into "Love Calls Us to the Things of This World" (NCP, p. 233), where angels take up residence on a suburban washing line, a pleasant enough venue, I dare say, after the schoolmen's needle. Here they represent an ideal that is yearned for, but which cannot be divorced from life in the world. In its hypnopompic state the soul perceives the repleteness and perfection of paradise, but the body, as it comes to consciousness, calls it back to the purgatory of being. Calling is perhaps the operative word, for the title suggests that some sort of vocation is involved, the dedication of the self to a principle of service.

Wilbur starts the poem not with a subjective "I," but with an impersonal eye, the sight of someone who has not yet connected perception with response. The frictive scream of the pulleys is doing more than stringing out the washline, it is pulling the eye toward its load. The most famous pulley in poetry is of course George Herbert's, where God denies rest to the world at the moment of creation for fear that humankind would "adore my gifts instead of me, / And rest in Nature, not the God of Nature."[2] Peace for Herbert is thus a pulley drawing our gaze to the perfect stasis of paradise, whereas for Wilbur it is the principle of action that draws the soul from serene ataraxia to engagement with the world. While paradise will eventually dawn in all the reality of its peace, this kind of suspension is presented as a false dawn, false because it is premature. Moreover, like ghostly sunlight reflected off cosmic dust, it is only a pale type of the reality to come, bounced off the dust of human transience.

The form of the poem reflects its hypnopompic uncertainty, as when the suspension of the soul drops by a vertical lapse of the line into the real world. Such programmatic effects of lineation show how astutely Wilbur can command the resources of free verse. His more usual preference for definitive form must be viewed as an issue of temperament, having nothing to do with incompetence in the looser measures. The lines of "Love Calls Us" attempt to cluster and regulate themselves into a five-limbed stanza, but their sleepy efforts at convergence have not quite come off, and many unraveled threads and uncropped edges remain. What we have is, in effect, an old-fashioned Pindarique—the kind practiced by Cowley in which the irregularity provides an index of rhapsody and abandon. Keats's "Ode to Psyche" also belongs to this tradition, and it is just possible that this ode also prompted the image of the open window. But while Keats "leaves a case-ment ope at night, / To let the warm Love in" (*Poetical Works,* p. 212), Wil-bur displaces the figure of Eros with the winged beings of Agape. His soul, suspended above his body, is in the same irresolute state as the stanza that is trying to form, but with the heightened senses that are a hallmark of ecstasy, it perceives angelic presences in the most humdrum articles of clothing.

At first this seems like mock-heroic reduction, but if we pause to recollect biblical accounts of transfigurement, many of them center on imagery of spotless clothes. Mark 9:3, for example, describes Christ's Transfiguration in terms of a fabric "exceeding white as snow; so as no fuller on earth can white," while in Revelation 3:5, white raiment is promised to the person "that overcometh." Wilbur is simply domesticating and regionalizing an es-tablished train of biblical images. In almost the same breath that he speaks of bedsheets and blouses, he is able also to meditate on the apocalyptic gran-deur of angels, modulating through the humble imagery of white water (white with suds) to the sublime white water of a cataract. Pinned to the line, the creatures seem to be restricting movement to a specified area (as in the ballet directive *sur place*), a feat of virtuosity that also includes the idea of flying in formation. Both meanings are subsumed, however, to one de-rived from Einsteinian physics—movement at such inconceivable speed that it collapses the notions of time and space and creates a kind of paradisal immobility. But, like a garment in hot water, the soul shrinks from this un-sustainable beatitude and falls like something ill-fitting to the line below. This shrinkage marks the supervention of time upon the timeless, and time finds its vehicle in memory, a memory that violates the peace of morning. Also at the etymological root of the rape is the idea of snatching (*rapere*)—snatching the soul back from its exaltation.

Notice how subtly and suavely Wilbur superimposes a vexed profanity (as uttered by the reluctant soul) on the idea of benediction—the things of this world, being loved, are blessèd. The Homeric epithet for the dawn—*rhodo-daktylos*—is now reconceived as the reddened hand of a washerwoman and the mists that are dissipated at sunrise as steam rising from a tub of laundry. At the same time as Homer comes to mind, so too does Sappho, who in her poem to Atthis describes love as being *glukupikros* (bittersweet). After all, the soul is surrendering to a divine summons to love the sublunary, and so the love is bitter, bitter with all the sin it has to encompass and forgive. As purification is followed by defilement, so do angelic presences convert back to items of washing, washing that, in the endless ceremonial cycle of reso-lution and lapse, will be polluted by the sin of the world. Nuns exemplify this tension, their heavy, sin-prone bodies enhaloed by the linen habits of their calling and by the spiritual habits of prayer and contemplation. The poem provides an instance of Wilbur's terrestrial regionalism and insists on the notion of dwelling instead of escape. Frank Littler has noted in this regard how "In contrast to St. John's plea, to avoid the world and the things of it, Wilbur would have us accept them, though we should also retain the capacity to perceive the world of the spirit in the everyday."[3]

Wilbur reuses a clothes image in the following "Sonnet" (NCP, p. 235). Other elements of balance and correspondence also connect the two poems, which at first sight seem very different. In contrast to the dawn of "Love Calls Us," we encounter a sunset, instead of a body's coming to consciousness, a body on the verge of sleep, and a final note of upward aspiration rather than of reluctant descent. The octave begins with a series of participial and adjectival phrases that read like the "ablative absolutes" of a Latin crib. They convey the inertia of completedness, for their verblessness points to a stopping of time. This is the mood of Frost's "After Apple-Picking." Eidetic images of labor trouble the exhausted body and cause it half to grudge the peace that comes with an end to winter tasks. Likewise the oxymoronic yoking of rigor and repleteness, which suggests a continuity of the working and recreative selves.

But while the body of the farmer is earthbound, muscular and weary, and sealed up in the hibernal warmth of his kitchen, outside his clothes, like those on the washing line in "Love Calls," strain upwards in an effort of aspiration. They approximate the movements of spiritual fire and, like a scarecrow, try to keep at bay the extinction of night and winter, imaged as the descent of a vast bird. Even as the body is acquiescing (however reluctantly) in its rest, the soul is restlessly escaping the constraints of the flesh. There is a particular daring in Wilbur's conceits of the crowlike night and the scarecrowlike soul (imaged as a cast-off vestment)—Yeats's alignment of scarecrow with decrepit body in "Among School Children" and "Sailing to Byzantium" seems almost conventional by contrast. More arresting still is the way the sonnet makes its syntax a symbolic rather than a merely functional adjunct of its meaning. The inward collapse of the octave's "ablative absolutes," verbless and heavy, toward a point of closure contrasts "choreographically" with the fierce adversarial energy of the sestet and the resistant preposition "against."

"Piazza di Spagna, Early Morning" (NCP, p. 236) derives from the poet's Italian sojourn and shows him as eager to capture the spirit of the place in Rome as in his native New England. Regionalists are often obsessed with the idea of a *genius loci*, a spirit transfused through a landscape and somehow personifying it. The man in "He Was" seemed qualified for the role by his very anonymity and impersonality, and the anonymous and impersonal woman serves much the same purpose on the Piazza di Spagna. Although the poem presents an event in Charlotte Wilbur's life, Wilbur takes care to suppress biographical elements that might otherwise compromise the impersonal tone, so impersonal indeed that G. S. Fraser has compared the poem to "La Figlia Che Piange."[4] It certainly deserves to be prefaced with the epigraph Eliot prefixed to that lyric, for like Aeneas, Wilbur seems to be wondering *o—quam te memorem, virgo?*[5]. The subject loses her human identity, being as it were dreamed by the place. Her descent of the staircase seems not to entail a voluntary movement, but rather something passive and elemental—a fall of water over a terraced fountain. Furthermore, she is contained by the mind of the *genius loci,* a noetic phantasm rather than a creature of flesh and blood. And by her movements Wilbur, like Aeneas, perceives her for what she is—*et vera incessu patuit dea* (Virgil, p. 268). Her steps are choreographed by an ordonnance existing beyond herself, by aesthetic necessity.

The poet himself proceeds with an impersonality and open-endedness that matches the woman's. The multiple-choice format of his simile emphasizes the fact that it is not the agent but the action that is the issue. So too the irregular lineation of the stanzas, foursquare to suggest the constraint of the staircase, but variable enough to evoke the promptings of mood. This dreamy fluidity creates a sort of hesitant slow motion, for the voice has to proceed cautiously when dimeters, trimeters, and even hexameters turn up at unexpected junctures, impairing any confidence of tempo. Yet, like the motions of the woman, the line lengths are far from arbitrary. They move rather at the behest of the meaning beyond themselves, as when the long line is programmatically resolved into a short at the moment of descent. This limpid, perfectly turned poem is too ample, perhaps, to be called Imagist, but it has a faint affinity to Pound's lines about the Paris Metro. Its meaning is secured by an appositional shift, not by statement, and it is all the more fascinating for its obliquity.

Wilbur is a poet of inclusions rather than restrictions, and many of his lyrics ask us to reconsider and revise our stock responses to toadstools, say, or to vultures. Perhaps because he gave deserts a bad press in " 'A World Without Objects,' " he redresses the slight in "John Chrysostom" (NCP, p. 237) and shows how even their heat and vacuity can be pressed into the service of eloquence. St. John's soubriquet means "golden mouthed," and Wilbur traces this quality back to the saint's retreat in the desert mountains of Antioch. Here the sun burns his skin to a metallic gold, anticipating his golden rhetoric, and the whistling sandstorm likewise inspires him to eloquence. St. John's penitential posture in stanza 1 becomes an act of regionalist empathy, fitting him for his homiletic task in stanza 2, where his desert experiences have enabled him even to make a poem out of the tortures in hell. Dwelling has issued in mental and spiritual order; regionalist retirement has groomed the cosmopolitan homilist.

By now it will have become apparent that the art of Richard Wilbur, not unlike the art of Henry James, has a palimpsestic element. Certain preoccupations recur in variant forms, each successive statement ringing subtle changes on what has gone before, and at the same time, altering the landscape that lies ahead. "A Black November Turkey" (NCP, p. 238) is one of the poet's bird apologues and takes us back to "Still, Citizen Sparrow" and, beyond that, to poems like "The Walgh-vogel." As in "Superiorities," "Still, Citizen Sparrow," and "To an American Poet Just Dead," Wilbur sets up two categories of people: the contented, massed bourgeoisie and the solitary prophets who move in their midst, arraigning them and judging their futile obsessions, but all the time ignored. The chickens represent the first and the turkey the second. One need not be numerologically solemn about the nineness of the hens: what is important is that, in contrast to the solitary turkey, they form a community, a community caught up in getting and spending. Their whiteness, brilliant in the sun, is likewise there to offset the mourning black of the centerpiece; as in another poem by another poet hens supply a white foil to the redness of a wheelbarrow.

Because chickens are not associated in any special way with any special feast, they enjoy a destiny much less final than the turkey's. He, by contrast, is able to foresee his death, recalling his cousin in *Bleak House*, "always troubled with a class grievance (probably Christmas)."[6] But, unlike Dickens's morose turkey, Wilbur's has given his life over to contemplation of the four last things and reached the beatitude of timelessness, while the hens, as in a conflation of two Haydn symphonies, are clucking and clocking. They are hopelessly entrammeled in the fuss and temporality of life, incapable of regarding death in their obsession with the moment. As usual in Wilbur, nothing is dismissed without a charitable grace note or two, and nothing hymned without a touch of sobriety. The hens, after all, are an unassuming lot and have even had their brief moments of illumination, while the self-importance of the turkey brings Donne's unflattering portrait of death to mind in "Death be not proud." There is also a touch of bathos in the fatality of the card image, with its theatrical memories of *Carmen* and *Pique Dame*.

"Mind" (NCP, p. 240) belongs to the line of meditative poems and couplets about the imagination, reality, and epistemology, and like them, it couches its thoughts in the form of a parable. Pure mentality is for Wilbur a sterile thing and aptly imaged by spelean darkness. The bat's maneuvers, governed by the vibrations of sonar, are senseless to the extent that they are dictated by instinct, and also the senseless arabesques of a mind in an experiential vacuum—sophistry, in a word. A certain kind of philosophy (the schoolmen's, say) ignores the exigencies of the real world, and so too, in Wilbur's opinion does the thought of some French intellectuals: "We are all kickers of stones, you know, and we are not as likely to get enchanted with abstract thought systems as some Europeans, especially the French, are" (quoted in Peter Stitt, Elessa Clay High, and Helen McCloy Ellison, "The Art of Poetry: Richard Wilbur," in *Conversations*, p. 189). Forever avoiding the solid walls of the cave (experience), the mind's movement remains indeterminate and inconclusive; unbloodied by collision. Even so, the adverb "darkly" recalls St. Paul's famous statement about the inklings of knowledge that faith can furnish, and this suggests an element of epistemological trust in even the most austere rationalist, whose mind, however perfect its courses, cannot in the last resort illuminate itself.

The final stanza, while at first endorsing the sufficiency of its simile, is ready to break it open and release new meanings, thus offering it as a kind of *Vade, et tu fac similiter* to the rationalist. By paraphrasing St. Augustine's notion of the *felix culpa*, Wilbur suggests that a grace not of body but of soul would result from the visibly ungraceful impact of bat against cave wall, since it would represent the mind's encounter with all it had hitherto circumnavigated. Its solipsism would be fractured by an avenue into the real. The stuff of stones might be cloudy to the speculative intellect, but that does not mean it cannot be investigated in its tactile reality. Plato's cave, after all, was not in itself an *ignis fatuus*—it was simply the solid screen on which the unreal phantasms came and went.

"After the Last Bulletins" (NCP, p. 241) is a baffling poem, even if its heritage is easily enough established. It owes something to the Augustan night piece, a poem in which a vigilant poet meditates in darkness upon the four last things, lineaments that we can trace even in such updated versions as MacNeice's "London Rain." Another generic influence to bear in mind is that of the atmospheric nocturne, best represented by Robert Bridges's "London Snow." In addition to these elements, Wilbur also supplies a touch of parody. Whereas Bridges had seen the snow as a nocturnal purifier and transfigurer, Wilbur describes the ways in which litter disperses through a derelict urban landscape, the sort of landscape familiar from Eliot's "Preludes." The chief component is day-old newspapers, which rustle and cavort in a *danse macabre*. All the ideas and attitudes that we control only as long as we have the newspapers in hand are demonically inverted in the dance of the litter.

Since the wind rises as the city sinks into slumber, one could view the urban parks and streets as the subject matter of its collective dreams, and its feast of misrule the gambolings of the id, sleep-freed of its censor. To some extent Wilbur has duplicated the rhythm of the winter sonnet, where a slumped human form is also counterpointed by an inanimate soaring beyond itself, and where we also sense the alert presence of a speaker who, like some Berkeleyan deity, documents details that would otherwise be lost in human oblivion.

The poet later develops his opening image of immersion into a mass-drowning. By doubling the prepositional phrase "in x," the poet seems to collapse literal into metaphoric space, so that the lots, while they exist as tangibly as the vacant lots in the Eliot poem, also signify a collective human destiny from which verbal dictates have vanished. Casting aside the high-mindedness of editors and the acumen of political analysts, our worse selves disfigure the ideals that in daylight we assent to and vandalize and spurn the solid citizenly virtues that public statutes and police force attest.

Out of this dark night of the soul, the reassuring voice of the radio announcer who sent us to sleep registers in the morning light as a blasphemous version of the Archangel Gabriel's. Bulletins and editorials once again trim the chaos of world affairs into manageable packages, and we return to a landscape of certainties and niceties in which refuse collectors take on the semblance of saints, bent as they are on removing the evidence of our sin.

"Lamarck Elaborated" (NCP, p. 243) is a throwback to the spry improbabilities of such works as Donne's "Problems and Paradoxes," a brilliant response to the *quaestio* "*The environment creates the organ.*" Poems such as these turn on logical rather than epistemic truth: the question is not "Is this so?" but "Is this persuasively argued?" One can have no doubt as to how the Inns of Court would have responded to Wilbur's *coup d'esprit* and a congener like "Never Again Would Bird's Song Be the Same," where Frost presents Eve as singing instructress rather than progenetrix. In "Lamarck Elaborated," the poet's mischievousness becomes evident from the moment he dismisses the faulty ancient notion of eyes as lights (*lumina* can mean both) only to supplant it with a much less tenable notion. Having set up this momentum of mischief, Wilbur continues to pile up extravagance on extravagance until, in the last two stanzas, the poem takes fire as poetry of the first order, suggestive and mysterious in a way that the buoyant start belies. This sudden amplitude enters the lyric as a shift from literal to metaphoric statement, where improbability becomes the vehicle for, not the obstruction of, meaning. What Helen Peters has said of Donne's *Paradoxes and Problems* is no less applicable to "Lamarck Elaborated," since it is "neither entirely serious nor merely intellectual jugglery."[7] Wilbur is playful about the etiology of our sense experience, but altogether more reverent and awestruck about the origin of mind, since it is in its effort at grasping the infinite and ineffable that reason has come to birth. Taking the snail-like spiral of the cochlea as a starting point, he sets it afloat in a mental sea, a portable and compendious ocean that, flooding out from the confines of the skull, is itself whelmed in the infinite universe. The numbers he mentions are the numbers of calculus, but they are also the classical numbers of meter and song, and the image therefore weds reason with imagination, Pythagorean "music of the spheres" with eighteenth-century rationalism, and marries human aspiration with fantastic loreleis bent on drowning their victims. In this way, even in the semblance of a jest, Wilbur affirms his old creed: the things of this world and the spirit that perceives them are locked in an eternal interchange. The final end of evolution is the spirit, and it is the spirit that, by retrospect, tries to account for the body that enshrines it.

While the opening stanzas of "Lamarck Elaborated" flash with the brilliance of the Inns of Court, a gentler seventeenth-century influence— George Herbert's—can be detected in "A Plain Song for Comadre" (NCP, p. 244). The poem that most obviously comes to mind is "The Elixir," where housework, provided it is done in the right spirit, is canonized as a saintly pursuit:

> A servant with this clause
> Makes drudgerie divine:
> Who sweeps a room, as for thy laws,
> Makes that and th' action fine.   (Herbert, *Works*, p. 185)

This ennoblement of the ordinary is implicit even in the title of Wilbur's poem, for, taken together as plainsong, it has a celebratory, liturgical force, and pulled apart as plain song, it refers to a song unpretentious and simple. The comadre (a charwoman/verger) has found an elixir in the simplicity of her chores and transmutes their leaden ordinariness into the gold of praise. In the opening stanzas, Wilbur generalizes his theme to include all honest labor, hinting, perhaps, at the carpenter's shop in Nazareth, or St. Paul's proficiency with the tenting needle. While the visionaries might feel more bitterness than love when their souls descend, the less exalted, never having reached those levels of transcendence, maintain their steady commitment to the world of things, which as Wilbur never tires of telling us, is not only compatible with spiritual pursuits, but essential to their success. The fly's buzzing seems to have come from Emily Dickinson's poem about the threshold of death, a detail of poignant domesticity supervening on the first of the four last things.

The movement from flies and itches to the workplace is easily made, and here the devotion to craft represents a loss of self in creation, an end identical with the saints' but effected by different means. Simple artifacts like bowls and furrows are tested by the dark that concludes a day of labor— tested and found to be good. Even the vastness of the universe seems to concenter applaudingly on workers who stand back to appraise their handiwork. Spheres and studs point to the craft of the *Deus artifex*, the divine type of all human labor. One of Patrick White's visionary characters in *The Vivisector* (published fourteen years after *Things of This World*) also applauds the honesty of simple artifacts, an honesty that is almost mystic in its elusiveness: "But take an honest-to-God kitchen table, a kitchen chair. What could be more real? I've had immense difficulty reaching the core of that reality, in I don't know how many attempts, but I think I may have done it at last."[8] Nor in reading "A Plain Song for Comadre" should we forget Wordsworth and the "spot of time" that gives the skater his mystic centeredness in a reeling universe—"yet still the solitary cliffs / Wheeled by me—even as if the earth had rolled / With visible motion her diurnal round!"[9]

Having set up his generalizing proem, Wilbur now focuses on the comadre herself, a woman whose vision is not the less visionary for being centered on the job well done. In an emblematic fashion that once more brings George Herbert to mind, her tasks encompass the clay porch and the sacramental altar, liminal mortality and final transfiguration. Wilbur dramatizes the gulf between them by means of stanzaic enjambment. It comes as no surprise, then, that angel feathers should flash in the dirty water of her pail.

While "A Plain Song" hymns a simple purpose that has been sanctified by the agent's attitude, "Merlin Enthralled" (NCP, p. 245) does the reverse. The obvious antecedent for the lyric is "Beowulf," for something of that poem's ennui and listlessness pervades the first stanza, where a slovenly still-life of cups on a table is presented with comparably careless syntax. Hyperbaton turns the sacramental adjective of the Round Table into an adverb of scattered placement. Wilbur gathers up the knights into an unceremonious, unspecific "they" and sets them moving without purpose. Their quest no longer has a goal, for its *raison d'être*, the imagination, has vanished from their world. Merlin, who, in the words of Tennyson, "knew the range of all their arts, / Had built the King his havens, ships, and halls, / Was also Bard, and knew the starry heavens,"[10] exemplifies that imaginative principle. It has underpinned the forms and functions of Camelot, and without it, a rift occurs between the perceiving and the creating properties of the mind. Sensibility dissociates into inert materialism on the one hand and inert formalism on the other.

So it is that on their journey the knights stop in the hope of recovering an imaginative response to experience. What they find is not the graceful and extravagant fauna of romance—no hart with golden horns, or unicorn, or yale—but a New England pondscape. Elements in the diction are calculated to disrupt the Arthurian spell here—the bugs (applied to water insects) have an anachronistically American ring and algae (in preference to "slime") supply a note of dispassionate botanizing. The antitype of this stanza is to be found in the diction of the last two lines, where as John Farrell has pointed out, the knights fade away into "mere fabulous characters."[11] Here form dwindles into ornament, the incredible blue of "Conjuration." The moment a work of art becomes quaint, it invites condescension. We respond patronizingly to its charm, since its outmoded conventions connect it too closely with its era to allow it much universal force.

In stanza 3 the spirit was seen to have departed from things; in the last, things from the spirit. Their interface was in the imagination of the poet, now impotent in the toils of Niniane. In the actual legend, Merlin does indeed speak to Gawen beneath the whitethorn where first he was enthralled; in a post-Merlinic era, the event is demythologized as mere projection. Howard Nemerov compares this defancifying to the closure of the golden age and, by implication, to a fall from grace:

> I think I experience this appeal whenever—and it isn't so often—a modern poet returns to legendary figures and themes not for decoration but in order that we shall see deeply into their present truth. When this happens, when, as here, the poet has heard the very footsteps of Astraea leaving the earth, I feel

that literary criticism is scarcely to the point, and I answer with love and sorrow to his thought, as well as with that impersonal gladness, that elation, that comes when beautiful and accurate saying seems to overcome the sorrow of what is said.[12]

"A Voice from under the Table" (NCP, p. 247) is a dramatic monologue, one that might have been spoken by the American poet just dead, whose passing Wilbur recorded in *Ceremony*. It is an apologia for excess, excess as a side effect of idealism. While it clearly does not enjoy the poet's whole-hearted support (what dramatic monologue ever did?), it is nonetheless argued with inwardness and conviction (and what dramatic monologue worth its salt ever lacked these?). The speaker has failed to marry the real with the ideal and, scorning the things of this world, has short-circuited their reality.

We are alerted to this faulty vision in the first line, for it is not individual women and wines but their archetypal absolutes that concern the speaker. The marriage vow in line 2, with its promise of fidelity through unequal, up-and-down experience, is at once violated by a yearning for things beyond this world—an indulgence disguising itself as intensity. A typical *poète maudit*, the speaker flaunts his visionary transports that others of greater moral fixity cannot achieve, but he makes his Decadent claims while lying drunkenly on the floor. In such circumstances, the solid citizens, for all their bourgeois stuffiness, would seem more properly to deserve the epithet *homo erectus*. Like most egoists, the drunkard projects his own exorbitant appetites upon his audience (as if it were common practice to go to the woods in search of love) but then discards the pretense and reverts more honestly to the first person. Having made the indeterminate wind his erotic ideal, he finds that all his subsequent experience fails to measure up, and an endless round of promiscuity results.

All ideals, he proceeds to argue, justify the physical excesses that accompany their search, a sophistry that belongs rather to the paradoxical world of "Lamarck Elaborated" than to the real one it turns upside down. Without the myth of Venus Anadyomene, he claims, he would have forfeited a Joycean epiphany in which he perceived a real woman bathing in the real Aegean as an incarnation of the goddess. She is magnified out of all proportion with pastoral hyperbole and, as in Macbeth's image of cosmic guilt, becomes an erotic center, making the green one red. The same unreal heightening is present in the following stanza, where a translation of Archilochus à la Dowson disregards the mock-heroic context in which the fragment has been preserved (Synesius' *Laudatio Calvitii*). According to Synesius, the poet praised a harlot's hair because it gave her protection from the sun,[13] whereas Wilbur's speaker magniloquently reconceives the whore as Aphrodite herself, investing her with an emblematic myrtle wand. His is the vision of Don Quixote, a vision that makes Dulcineas out of waitresses.

The drunkard then goes on to scorn academic sobriety that undervalues the flesh and disconnects mythology from its embodiment, punning nicely on the symposia that, once literal drinking parties, have now become temperate discussion groups. Because he has neglected to synthesize the world of the spirit with that of the flesh, he fails on both counts—his life is physically squalid and his dreams perfervid and unreal. An aphorism underlines this discontinuity, since failure is inevitable if one is conceived in divorce from the other. Making the necessary connection demands an act of will of which he is incapable, so instead he glamorizes his life as a purposeful search, whereas it has actually been nothing more than a rondo of futility. Horace Gregory appears to think that Wilbur uses this poem to speak *in propria persona* and is led to the conclusion that "his phrase, 'God keep me a damned fool,' rings false," because "one gains no other evidence from Wilbur's writing that he is foolish."[14] Arguing in the same vein, one could say that *My Last Duchess* fails to convince because there is no evidence in the rest of Browning's work that he did Elizabeth in!

"The Beacon" (NCP, p. 249), like "Mind," is an epistemological meditation, except that it works more conventionally with the light-of-reason topos, whereas the earlier poem turned on a bat, an image that more properly belongs to Goya's *El sueño de la razon*. Ordinarily a beacon advertises danger; this one takes paradoxical pride in its rocky foundation, and its flashes are intermitted with blinks testifying more to dazzlement than illumination. Although it is impossible to exclude the idea of pollution altogether, I think Wilbur means us to take the fouling as entanglement, the better to prepare for the conceit about the Gordian knot. Alexander's solution was not really a solution, but rather a shortcut; and much the same could be said of the mind that confidently trains its faculties on the mystery of experience, but is able at best to give a fitful account of what it encounters. The sea in this parable is the noumenon, the unknowable *Ding-an-sich* upon which we comfortably project the phantom order of sea-roads, or picturesque myths about Tritons and Nereids. These seem immemorial but are not the less mental constructs for seeming so—a fact beautifully registered in the syntactic delay between attribute (hair) and owner (nymph). We sense that the mind is furiously similizing its materials during the pause.

However, each familiarizing image is followed by occlusion, and what we project vanishes repeatedly in a Wilburian version of "darkness visible." Remembering the desolate tidal roar of "Dover Beach," and still sustaining his beacon image with a hint of land's end, Wilbur reminds us that we have reached the limits of our mental strength, the mind's end described in "Lamarck Elaborated." Most poets would despair, but Wilbur manages instead a tempered, stoic optimism. The sea in all its formlessness cannot be beaten—which is to say that it is invincible *and* unscannable. Furthermore, the tears the poet sheds are tears of an impotent metric order (Alexandrine = a hexameter) as much as those of the Greek leader on the banks of the Hyphasis.[15]

These setbacks nothwithstanding, the light of reason continues to flash, and in its systematic efforts lies some hope. It might be stretching things—but not wholly beyond the bounds of reason—to claim that "Alexandrine" alludes also to Alexandria, and so to the famous lighthouse at Pharos: despair and solace thus come together in a single adjective. The dark sea, shapeless and vast, is another version of the deserts in " 'A World Without Objects,' " and as in the case of those deserts, its abstraction is better comprehended by the human markers that measure its void. Nereids are a humble version of the Incarnation that makes infinity accessible, and the ship, like a compositional pointer, gives concentric form to what would otherwise be a blank. The world can properly be conceived only by regionalist location, and the consequent sighting of its *genii loci*.

While the beacon scans its truths from the fixity of rock, the children in "Statues" (NCP, p. 251) introduce corrective images of flux to a garden disnatured by its symmetry. The formless sea needed the redressing presence of myths and signs, the garden in its sterile order, a sense of mutability and indefiniteness. This the children provide and, doing so, present an epiphany of change to the strollers otherwise caught up in their static habits. The stylized chaos of the game images the primordial chaos out of which order emerged, the chaos of perpetual displacements, where as Ovid puts it, "Nothing had any lasting shape, but everything got in the way of everything else."[16] What we would like to conceive as the permanence of art and nurture endures no longer than the caesuras that represent the fleeting postures of the children, and the momentary attention of the world. But a healthful disorder radiates out from the game into the lives of the people who pause to watch and even allows nature itself to recover its essential vitality. The maples of the grove, surrender their stiffness and disperse into the cloudy indefiniteness. ("Cloudy" is an adjective Wilbur has already used in "Epistemology" to characterize the inscrutable nature of things.)

But in the midst of this pageant of exhilarating change and bustle, there is a figure inhuman in its static blankness—a vagrant who at an earlier stage of his life might well have spoken the monologue beneath the table. Humankind has adjusted to mutability in the confidence that its discomfort is cyclical and that any unpleasant change will, in the order of things, be followed by another. No such comfort attends the man who, having failed to make a stand, has himself become a stative chaos, his formlessness an unalterable version of the children's grotesque postures. Their passing playfulness has frozen for him into an apocalyptic eternity.

The ficelles of time and fixity link the idyll of "Statues" (like Mussorgsky's "Children Quarrelling in the Tuilleries Garden") with the more strenuous meditations of "Looking into History" (NCP, p. 252). Indeed the form of the poem resembles not a Mussorgskian sketch, but a grand, monothematic sonata by Liszt: it takes a theme and an image and refracts them through different harmonies and at different tempi. The title suggests both

investigation and peering, as though history were some sort of camera ob-
scura or well. The investigator is the poet himself, who, in stanza 1, is puz-
zling over a sepia photograph from the time of the American Civil War. It
is an image of soldiers on the verge of battle, but owing to accidents of focus
and fading, it at first denies the speaker any idea of a context. The men
caught in the amber atmosphere of the picture, have the atemporal, deific
quality of an icon, much as the miniature of Hamlet's father invests him
with the stature of a god (Hyperion) rather than of a man. At the same time
they are like insects petrified in resin, their suffocating preservation no
guarantee of life. Wilbur accordingly finds it difficult to make any sort of
emotional contact with these unregioned, unrooted figures, in a land all but
effaced by the fading of the photograph and at the same time preternaturally
silent, like a film from which the sound track has been subtracted. However,
as soon as he notices an avenue of trees and, more important, is able to give
them a habitation and a name, the whole static photograph swings into aural
life, a transition dramatically flagged by the halving and pulling apart of the
pentameter. This gives the first two feet the effect of a *chiave* from an Italian
canzone, and a *chiave* those sycamores indeed prove to be, since they supply the regionalist key of empathy. They are recognizable trees and so help
confer the reality of a natural continuum on the discontinuities of human
history.

Section 2 contemplates the mythic trees of *Macbeth* and the *Iliad,* trees
that have been carved and cut out of recognition by the collective mind. As
by a process of euhemerism an actual man turns into Hyperion and a real
woman into Aphrodite, so these trees testify to the transfiguring power of
art. Art and history, as Aristotle tells us, are not commensurate: "Poetry,
therefore, is a more philosophical and higher thing than history: for poetry
tends to express the universal, history the particular."[17] Instead of sycamores
in section 1, we have driftwood draped in weed. As the sea has engulfed and
stylized living wood, so history itself suffers the sea-change of myth and
poetry. While John Farrell is no doubt right to claim that the driftwood is
"still inherently more appropriate as historical records than the photo-
graphic memorabilia of the first stanza" ("The Beautiful Changes," p. 195),
its lost identity cannot properly furnish Wilbur with an ideal, and so he
gathers these two alternatives in the energetic third section, a coda in which
the trimeters charge forward to a resolution. He acknowledges that history
remains inactive without the energizing imagination; if the sycamores had
not caused the regionalist in him to respond, the Brady photograph would
have continued to seem inscrutable. A sense of the past is bound up with
imaginative engagement, even if that engagement itself runs riot in the form
of myth. That is why Proteus in all his multiformity is invoked as patron, for
his impostures and changeability are proof of the living and universal force
of myth, as opposed to the potentially dead records of history. But much as
Wilbur is attracted to protean impostures, he is more taken with his old

solution of synthesis, one which combines the recognizable form and root-edness of the sycamore with the extravagant formalism of driftwood; we accept history as one of several springs nurturing our composite experience.

"Digging for China" (NCP, p. 256) also resolves into synthesis of the other and the known, the international and the local. Its first stanza astutely renders the speaking voice in meter and bears comparison with Frost's skill in this field. An adult mock-solemnly tells a child to dig a hole from New Jersey to China, and it is on this task that the (strategically) flat second stanza focuses. When in the third, the boy leaves his task and stands up, a combination of sunstroke and rushing blood disorients him entirely. The New Jersey landscape becomes a locus for a Wordsworthian "spot of time," with a comparable sense of earth's diurnal course and sacramental images of patens and palls. The delirium that construes this regional transfiguration was suggested perhaps by a similarly delirious moment in Elizabeth Bishop's "The Fish"—her threefold repetition of "rainbow"[18] seems to have been reworked in the "China" triplet of the last line.

It is hard to see why the following lyric should be entitled "Apology" (NCP, p. 261), for most people would be more than delighted to be the sub-ject of such accomplished verse. It connects the poet's wife with a landscape of apples and rye and wind so intimately that she becomes its presiding deity, a Pomona composed like Keats's Autumn from the constituent parts of the scene and greeted in a run of honorific phrases that bring the clauses of a Marian litany to mind.

"Beasts" (NCP, p. 263), a dream poem like "After the Last Bulletins," is difficult to construe. Since such poems have an oneiric rather than a rational logic, Wilbur seems to have kept their mysteriousness intact, knowing that it would escape from a more deliberate, thought-through mode of statement. His title takes us back to the important Latin distinction between *bestia* (an animal without reason) and *animal* (any living creature, humankind in-cluded). In the first two stanzas a strange, uneasy nocturne gives us the beasts' consciousness of self not as self but as environment. A gull dreams its setting into reality and, even more oddly, the water transitively sleeps a sunfish, as though its being were predicated on its element not in a zoo-logical but in a Berkeleyan way. The waters of this oceanic creature are then elided with those of an inland stream, in which the splashes made by the spotless deer (blameless as well as unmottled) concord with the blood splashing from the mouse in an owl's claws. There is something very random and uncoordinated about this catalog (it reads like a transcribed dream), and its natural history is suspect in the extreme.

However, the connections between the various animals, arbitrary as they are, are meant to convey a life peacefully exempt from consciousness of time, and so from past and future. Wilbur does not censor elements of disquiet—the deer are at risk from predators and hunters, after all, and the mouse is bleeding to death—but he certainly downgrades them. The phrasing that effects the transition to the werewolf suggests that dark and harm *are* there, but not to the degree that they are for lycanthropic creature, whose senses shift from a human to a bestial key. That is why I find I cannot wholeheartedly agree with Anne Williams when she claims that the animal world is "suffused with harmony, a completeness and interdependence between the beasts and nature."[19] Wilbur is not deleting harm and darkness from that world, he is simply muting them.

Lycanthropists, at least as Webster defines them in *The Duchess of Malfi*, are

> those that are possess'st with . . .
> Such melancholy humour, they imagine
> Themselves to be transformed into wolves,
> Steal forth to church-yards in the dead of night
> And dig dead bodies up.[20]

In keeping with the uneasy, dreamlike mode of the opening stanzas, Wilbur adds the folkloric details of actual change, so that human gives way to feral judgment, what was fierce becomes soft, and what once was rounded and insensitive becomes pointed and alert—sharper in both senses. The werewolf experiences with dual consciousness only at the moment of change; once transformed, he feels and responds to his environment as beasts do. He can even sense the stepped formation of the rock beneath the streams. That portion of humanity that is not subject to the change continues in its rational pursuits, allegorically imaged by the searches of the astronomer.

But, *capax rationis* though it might be, humankind nonetheless sublimates the bestial instincts of competition and survival. Science enslaves itself to war and brings about the devastation of cities. That, at any rate, is how I read the reference to monsters and crows. Compare Isaiah's oracle on Idumea:

> 11 But the cormorant and the bittern shall possess it; the owl also and the raven shall dwell in it: and he shall stretch out upon it the line of confusion, and the stones of emptiness.
>
> 12 They shall call the nobles thereof to the kingdom, but none shall be there, and all her princes shall be nothing.
>
> 13 And the thorns shall come up in her palaces, nettles and brambles in the fortresses thereof: and it shall be an habitation of dragons and a court for owls. (Isaiah 12)

What Wilbur presents is an urban landscape reclaimed by the beasts, projecting the frailty of civilization by this standard archetype of transience and decay. Ideals, generated from the mind, are corrupted by instinct the moment they are applied.

"Exeunt" (NCP, p. 265), a descriptive poem in the Chinese manner, records comparable extinctions and eclipses in nature's cycle. Wilbur sets down its quiet, precise notations piecemeal in mimicry of the piecemeal death of the season. Usually he redacts his nature poems, but this one is unusual in having no thematic focus beyond its immediate data. In "Marginalia" (NCP, p. 266), on the other hand, the poet reverts to his more usual procedure of description and inference or, in this case, proposition and image-argued support. In ordinary circumstances, marginalia are relatively unimportant side issues, backwaters to an onflowing argument or essay. Here, though, they prove central to a theme of concentration—concentration in the sense of distilling more intensely into the things they are and also in the sense of gathering density as a result of centrifugal force. Water in the abstract is comparatively bland, but the margin of a pond presents the aesthetic sense with a tapestry of flotsam altogether richer than the diagram of H_2O.

From this literal margin we move to liminal states of consciousness, as in the transitions to and from sleep that, as "Love Calls Us" has already shown, fleetingly disclose a spiritual value in things that to the waking eye are otherwise opaque. Wilbur images the demarcation as a circumference of cricket chirps, a round to be construed musically as a superimposed canon of song and also as a girdle of sound that vanishes each time the listener approaches and reassembles in his or her wake. The final boundary in these variations on a theme is the edge of a vortex that signifies extinction and prompts us to the consummation of Wagner's *Liebestod,* the music of loving that well which we must leave ere long. As so often in Wilbur, material things become most fully themselves when they are set to merge with the infinitude of spirit.

"Boy at the Window" (NCP, p. 267) brings us back to childhood, to an incident not unlike that of "The Pardon." The snowman in the garden is content—satisfied with and contained by the icy winds that ensure its continued definition; the child, in a burst of misplaced sympathy, would have it share his claustral world of warmth and protection. Just as the young Wilbur refused to admit Death into Arcadia, so here the child will not admit to the sufficiency of the natural order, his innocent love approximating that of the bird fanciers in "Marché aux Oiseaux." It is a charming lyric, its anthropomorphic fantasy seeming to challenge the cold deletions and sterilities of Wallace Stevens's snow man poem—but, like the whimsical efforts of other great poets, it comes close to sentimentality. The danger zones are the description of the boy's eye (which brings the dilated eyes of cuddly toys to mind) and the measurement of the single tear (with its effect of squeezed-out emotion).

"Speech for the Repeal of the McCarran Act" (NCP, p. 268) is oddly named, and one feels compelled to smile at the effect of such an oblique and allusive poem on the members of Congress. Nonetheless, it relies as heavily on rhetorical tactics as any political utterance you might care to name. Wilbur takes up the debate where Wulfstan left off in the eleventh century as serenely as if he had spoken only days or weeks before, and he furthermore resorts to the trope of *occupatio* to draw attention to Allied ravages in Eastern Europe while pretending that they are of no account. Donald Hill has pointed out that the "MacCarran Act of 1952 limited the opportunity for immigration into the United States at a time when distressed European refugees needed it most" (*Richard Wilbur*, p. 165), and it must be borne in mind that legislation of this kind is often posited on fear of cultural domination, and even on racial prejudice. Wilbur on the other hand points out that a culture insular enough to view enrichment as invasion is a culture as insecure as a faulty spiderweb. Taking the web as the type of other reticula, he uses synecdoche to note the impoverishing effect of Allied action in Europe. There is the destruction of the leaden web that holds the stained glass of a rose window in position (spiritual institutions) and of the metal web of railway lines (commercial infrastructure). The damage to both is reparable. Even the destruction of rose windows, horrifying though it might be, reminds us that the church ought not to be identified with its physical structures. Should any fall, their fall ought by rights to fertilize a growth of churches to replace them. (The regeneration of Coventry Cathedral, arguably more impressive than the Perpendicular church it replaced, was already underway when Wilbur wrote this poem.) These concessions notwithstanding, he implies that the victors in Europe, having made the place uninhabitable, should show greater generosity to those who wish to leave and should welcome the opportunity to enrich and fertilize their native culture with influences from abroad. Such influences would help forge a composite web (both regional and international), a web of the spirit.

"All These Birds" (NCP, p. 269) should be taken in conjunction with "The Walgh-vogel" of *The Beautiful Changes*, for together they form a diptych of opposite responses. The earlier poem urged discipline on an imagination running riot in the absence of an object; this one is about the extinction of the fancy for reverse reasons. Each position, extreme in itself, needs the synthesizing balance of its antitype. The title is meant to sound as offhand and collective as possible and bundles together in one perfunctory line the birds that have been hymned *inter alia* by Hopkins, Shelley, and Keats. This effect is compounded also by the telegraphic way in which the poet agrees with the reader, as though premises were being got out of the way to let the argument proceed unimpeded, and by the *adjunctio* that strings verse after verse on to the (suppressed) main verb. The topography of the stanza also has the effect of losing pitch, as when the second member of the fifth line sags away from its partner, like a broken limb or a string that has lost its tension.

The natural historians that haunt Wilbur's poems as protagonists of an unspirited, materialist investigation of the natural world—Fabre and Lamarck—are represented here by Hébert. He observed how birds (traditionally images of vulnerability) are armored by the air bubble that surrounds them when they dive. This bubble Wilbur connects with the bubble of earth's atmosphere to show how birds (traditionally images of freedom) are shut in by a vast skylight that in planetary terms is as claustrophobic as an oyster shell. Having thus wearily listed the reversals that science has brought about in our perception of, and response to, birds, Wilbur envisages a time when the spirit will rise in revolt and forge myths to supplement what on another occasion he termed the "dryness" of materialism. His jussive verbs (that up till now have signaled his submission to the dominant mode) suddenly modulate into the jussive of creativity, of *Fiat lux*. The exfoliating imagination will shelter the spirit and its percepts from the reductiveness of science; it will resemble a creeper to which birds are naturally drawn. By substituting the adjectival form of "natural" for the expected adverb, Wilbur creates an appositive tension between noun and epithet, so that birds become most truly and unartificially birds when they enter consciousness this way. But the substitution also permits the sense of an instinctive, ungovernable upwelling of the spirit, as in the slang phrase "it comes natural." Like "The Walgh-vogel," "All These Birds" ends like a cletic hymn, though the emphases have been reversed. In this version of *Veni Creator Spiritus,* Wilbur invokes the Holy Ghost by the image of a bird and asks him to reconnect our observations to our souls, severed from our sight by the imperatives of science. As John Reibetanz has noted, "the imagination will out and must" ("What Love Sees," p. 75).

"A Baroque Wall-Fountain in the Villa Sciarra" (NCP, p. 271) is an emblem poem, but one of such prodigal descriptive power that its affinity with emblem poems of the sixteenth and seventeenth centuries can easily be overlooked. We have seen Wilbur's virtuosity displayed in the contrapuntal weave of "Lightness" and "Juggler," but the achievement here outshines even those dazzling efforts. The programmatic effects of the enjambment are well adapted to the depiction of falling water, as Wilbur himself has noted, "the length in this poem—a lot of the length of sentence—has to do with an effort to imitate the trickling down of the water."[21] However, even though the poem has had many admirers, few have paused to consider the iconography of the fountain. Its actual sculptor, swept along by his Baroque exuberance, might well have strung the elements together in an unconsidered way, but it is not wholly improbable that he had a statement in mind, a statement that Wilbur cannot help relaying as he ecphrases the design. Could not the suspended crown represent the topmost link in the chain of being, empty because godhead is ineffable, as in some Northern Hebrew sculptures that present Yahweh by means of a riderless bull? And does not the cherub, mysteriously assailed by the serpent-tempter, represent the angelic orders below the throne of God. The fauns, in this graded hierarchy, are like the werewolf of "Beasts," mediate beings between the *ratio* of humankind and the *appetitus* of the animal kingdom. Fauns are notoriously sensual, and the ménage that they form represents the loose play of instinct above duty. Even the goose is not without a phallic charge and possibly invites the sinister, bestial inversion of "goose familiar."

Whatever the case, Wilbur does not present them in a judgmental way, though various adjectives do hint at their deficiency of spirit. He also takes care to spell "saecular" in the Latin way to touch off the idea of generation as well as of worldliness. The descent of this fountain is all that the viewer sees, for the pipes that lead the water back are presumably concealed in the masonry. In Maderna's Vatican fountain, by contrast, the effort of ascent and aspiration is visible, even if gravity, like the flesh that entrammels the ascetic saint, dictates a return to the things of this world. Obviously such a program constitutes a higher level of being than the hedonism exemplified by the fauns, but it has its own attendant danger. There lurks in this strenuousness a shadow of self-congratulation, a fault of which the bestially indifferent would never be guilty. Wilbur resolves this crisis of choice by reapplying the emblem altogether. Neither fountain satisfactorily images the nature of humankind, but the resignation of the fauns, odd as it might seem, does approximate the perfect resignation of heaven, that pacific state *en la sua volontade* for which St. Francis yearned. The wall fountain remains a shade, nothing more than a vague approximation, but its dynamic stasis hints at a central aspect of paradise, a place where the amaranth replaces the fragile *flos* of *carpe florem*. It can be encountered only after the dissolution of the flesh which is grass, in the dimension (projected by "Games Two") where Cartesian divisions are healed in a seamless continuity of datum and experience. The worthy hand suggests a hand cupped for the rite of baptism, recapitulating but at the same time sublimating the basins of the wall fountain, and the caesura in the middle of the final line, a line of leaping and falling, is like the weightlessness effected by a certain kind of flight path. It is the still center to which all human movement tends. In many Wilbur poems there is a pattern of contrary motion—of descent met by aspiration, of aspiration countered by descent. Here a resolution is effected by a kind of heavenly stasis.

"An Event" (NCP, p. 274) is a metafictive poem and therefore tells us a great deal about the poet's compositional practice. Since Ted Hughes wrote his "Thought-Fox" the year after *Things of This World* was published, it is even possible that he found his inspiration here. Wilbur draws our attention to the "how" of poetry by stating his "what" with an uncharacteristic neutrality and baldness. That is not how regionalists usually set about their task. Where is the landscape, and what are the birds? Are they swallows? Are they starlings? Both fit and do not fit the bill. The poem's title is also as neutral and unspecific as a title could possibly be, though there is a faint chance that Wilbur intended a pun—while "event" actually derives from *ex* and *venire*, he might have wanted us to cobble a folk etymology from *ex* and *ventus*, since it is with spirit and breath and air that creativity has traditionally been coupled. An event has seized the poet's attention and moved him to record it. Somehow he must do it justice, and since metaphor is his primary resource, it is with metaphor that he begins.

His image, drawn from reverse filming, betrays his urge to recapture and grasp a fleeting experience as much as it describes the experience itself. What follows has something of the excitedness and disjunction of rough notes: a question is thrown down without an answer (or half-answered by an image), and then a reservation is voiced about that image in turn. At the moment of its formulation, it has been outmoded by the changing nature of the subject. The singular vision is the vision that fails to render the multeity of its object, but it is also the singular (extravagant) vision of a Cleveland-ism, which, even at the pitch of its inventiveness, cannot capture the birds in print. At the same time that the poet is marshaling his words and honing his craft, his imagination has led him out of his study and into the open, where his own subjectivity has been absorbed into the birds'. The oddly transitive use of "fly" (not normally used in conjunction with an animate object) recalls the water that sleeps the sunfish in "Beasts," and signals the literal ecstasy of the writer. This flying in turn melts into the flying of that transient moment at which language and experience intersect before pulling apart again. There is something Berkeleyan about the final line, as if the poet had momentarily crossed noetic lines with God himself, and had participated in the consciousness by which being is conferred upon the world. But there is also a cross-purpose in the negative sense, the incoherence and uncertainty of a language thwarted in its efforts to describe the indescribable. Eliot defined the Incarnation as an intersection, and it is precisely in terms of such an intersection that Wilbur's own poem takes on flesh.

Berkeley is also the hinge between "An Event" and "A Chronic Condition" (NCP, p. 275). This is yet another of Wilbur's autumnal poems, subtle and varied meditation on a summer whose richness seems inconceivable at the moment of loss. The fog that envelops him envelops his world as well, dissociating all experience in its soupy continuity, canceling color and form. Images of loss and extinction accumulate, and the very images themselves become indistinct and confused—leaves and wings both fall, and since the fall of a sparrow symbolizes the omniscience of God, God himself seems no longer to know it. And that, of course, is why Berkeley is invoked by name. He also underpins the detail of the forest tree that, unnoted by humankind, falls only in the mind of God. Wilbur conflates this with the mysterious disappearance of Hylas, the companion of Hercules whom nymphs abducted for his beauty, and then takes both images up in the precarious sense of dissolution on which the poem ends.

"The Mill" (NCP, p. 276) also has its epistemological crux, the death of memory with the death of the subject, though something can be salvaged by the telling. The poem, addressed in the second person to a man who, like every other person, took irrecoverable details of history to the grave with him, has a strong flavor of Conrad. The context of the narrative is as carefully established as those for Marlow in *Lord Jim,* and there is also a Conradian indeterminateness that reaches after meaning without being certain of its grasp. Similarly, the mill wheel that continues to turn in the undergrowth of the American South or of the Amazon jungle is also treated in the portentous manner we find in parts of *Heart of Darkness,* as though it had an inscrutable relevance to a larger theme. The subject of that discourse is never quite disclosed, but it would seem to have been *sic transit gloria* or something like it. On this occasion, as so often in Conrad, one is left holding a metaphor with a highly specific vehicle and a tenor that is maddeningly vague.

If *sic transit* is in fact the topos of "The Mill," then one might well argue that "For the New Railway Station in Rome" (NCP, p. 277) is its subversion, a sort of *sic manet.* The poem strikes me as being a brave but unsuccessful effort of affirmation. Wilbur's benign, optimistic cast of mind can, very occasionally, strike a false note. His attempts to find meaning in the mundane, to include minutiae of the region in his vision of the world, generally succeed, but something there is that doesn't like a paean to a railway booking hall. The poem courts comparison with the rather crass acclamations of the Futurists—Marinetti's hymn to the motor car, for example. If traditional ideas of the Heavenly City are a mere projection, does it follow that the railway station can function as an appropriate prototype merely because it too has originated in the mind? What Wilbur is objecting to is the life-denying kind of asceticism that glories in the downfall of the world; what he is forgetting is that the eclipse of the Forum signifies not only an aesthetic eclipse but also the eclipse of a moral order quite foreign, and even hostile, to the notion of an "eternal city." St. Augustine's *City of God* says as much.

The tone of the following extract (dug up out of an old guidebook on Rome) may sound a touch unctuous, but it balances the self-induced exaltation of Wilbur's poem:

> Pilgrims who visit the Eternal City in this Catholic *spirit of devotion* . . . will take but a secondary interest in the monuments of antiquity, the colossal works of architecture, the records of imperial greatness, the treasures of art, literature, archaeology, stored in its galleries, libraries and museums; they know that Rome has something far grander to show than these evidences of material prosperity and intellectual power; and they will long rather with St. Francis Borgia and St. Francis de Sales, to visit the venerable churches of the city, to kneel at the altars where the Saints have prayed.[22]

One imagines that even a fervent atheist would be reluctant to exchange this dim religious light for the glare of the architectural jargon in stanza 2, line 5. This has to be the least graceful pentameter that, trailing a bacchius, ever hobbled out of Wilbur's otherwise flowing pen. Its gracelessness is symptomatic of a greater unease in the poem.

Even so, the Roman railway station is undoubtedly a thing of this world and to that extent confirms the catholicity of Wilbur's spirit as it ranges through the data of his experience, recording physical forms and sensing within them the immanence of spirit. "Flumen Tenebrarum" in *Ceremony* shows that he had given some thought to the event of its extinction in the apocalypse of a reconverging universe. However, the mounting global tension of the fifties offered the possibility of a different kind of apocalypse altogether—one much less likely to issue in cosmic resignation. It was inevitable that Wilbur should in time have had to address the icy climate of the cold war, and perhaps as inevitable that he should have addressed it so tactfully and obliquely in his next collection.

four

a d v i c e
to a
p r o p h e t
and
o t h e r
p o e m s
(1 9 6 1)

Almost all the poems we have so far considered tes-
tify to Wilbur's reticence, his caution about the magniloquent gestures and
self-righteous isolation to which prophets are sometimes prone. While im-
precation and vehemence have a purpose to serve, and while the prophet
needs to dissociate himself from the world, there are less strident alternatives on hand for poets who wish to avoid them. Wilbur is a generous man,
but although he has never denounced poets who despise his particular option, he has on occasion queried the *furor propheticus* in which they indulge.
Ginsberg is a case in point, if Wilbur's observations to Joan Hutton are
anything to go by: "Allen Ginsberg recently asked an audience whether they
would consent to the proposition that the United States government, in its
foreign policy, is psychotic. Something like a third of the audience voted for
that idea. They and Mr. Ginsberg are setting themselves up as super-sane"
(Joan Hutton, "Richard Wilbur," in *Conversations*, p. 49).

By naming his 1961 collection *Advice to a Prophet*, Wilbur thus sets forth
his own way of proceeding in a world of sin. It is not by abstraction but by
regional evidence that the heart of humankind is most effectively touched;
not by frenzied iteration and angry denunciation, but by a sort of reasoning
pathos. We encounter nothing "prophetically" febrile or sensational in "Two
Voices in a Meadow" (NCP, p. 181), but rather a sense of wisdom distilled
by long meditation, something far removed from the tirades of *Howl*. While
the prophets of Judaism cultivated the virtues of urgency and insistence, the

writers of wisdom literature were altogether more deliberate in their methods. Indeed, there was sometimes tension between them, as George Anderson has pointed out: "The wise, . . . to whom we owe this literature, are mentioned in Jer. xviii 18 as a class comparable with the priests and the prophets; and in Jer. viii. 8 the wise and the scribes seem to be identified. Elsewhere . . . there are signs that the prophets were critical of the wise. There is, certainly, a marked difference between prophecy and the Wisdom books, not least in ethics, where the teaching of the wise often seems pedestrian and prudential."[1] Wilbur also has his prophetic moments, but fine though they are, they are not typical. It is in wisdom rather than in prophecy that he finds his métier—wisdom and celebration, so we had better call him a psalmist too. Anderson's account of the wisdom writer cannot be applied without reservation to Wilbur's poetry, for "pedestrian" is the last epithet it deserves. In "prudential," on the other hand, we have an adjective not wholly wide of the mark. It points to the habitual caution of the poet, the way he approaches the unknown by the known, his regionalist preference for what is there to bodiless abstraction.

Poets such as Blake have managed to combine the "Big Bow-wow strain" and the "exquisite touch" (Scott's distinction)[2] and have matched the likes of *Jerusalem* with the *Songs of Innocence and Experience*. Even so, Blake's songs are not less prophetic for having chosen a lyric route to their truths. The same might be said of Wilbur's "Two Voices in a Meadow," a poem that brings "The Clod & the Pebble" to mind. We know from "A Voice from under the Table" that Wilbur deals in "voices" (dramatic monologues) when he does not fully endorse the attitudes of his speakers, however much they might interest him. Further proof of his detachment may be found in the complementarity of the monologues, like the two aphorisms of "Epistemology," which resolve into an unstated synthesis. Indeed on one occasion, Wilbur has suggested that "from the very beginning, [he has] thought of poetry as getting one's various selves to quarrel intelligibly in public" (Irv Boughton, "An Interview with Richard Wilbur," in *Conversations*, p. 136).

The milkweed's lyric is, in a sense, the utterance of the internationalist. It derives its meaning not through attachment but through surrender to impalpable and risk-laden chance. Mention of the Nativity implies a salvific scheme in which the milkweed's desires have a part to play. Cherubs occupy a place in the great chain of being close to God and far removed from the inanimate stone's. Yet, Wilbur implies, there can be no field without rock to retain its soil. The stone, which does not aspire, has as important a role to play in the economy of creation and exemplifies the regionalist option of finding significance through an intensely lived circumscription. In a providential scheme, even chance is subsumed to purpose and the stone disposed by decision. The contingent details of prophecy likewise become significant, for according to the Jerusalem Bible, the apparently casual cow dung does in fact have a prophetic origin in the Septuagint text of Habbakuk 3:2: " 'In the middle of two living things you will make yourself known; when the years draw near you will be recognised; when the time comes, you will appear', a text which, in conjunction with Is 1:3, gave rise to the tradition of the two animals by the crib at Bethlehem."[3] So even while the utterances of milkweed and stone are antiprophetic (for prophets resist and aspire), they are finally validated by the divine purpose that it is the prophet's task to urge upon his or her audience. Wilbur seems to imply that the activity and intensity of the prophet, impressive though they are, ought not to blind us to the more passive virtue of quietism.

Quietude is a quality that prophets often lack, especially the "mad-eyed" Jeremiah who confronts us at the start of "Advice to a Prophet" (NCP, p. 182). Here too Wilbur substitutes quiet, meditative notations for oracles of nuclear war and argues for a prophecy based not on angry abstraction but on regional experience, the loss of which would seem the more poignant for being the loss of the known. If hearts are unreckoning, they are only a syllable away from being unrecking, and Wilbur should know—his use of the first person plural includes himself with the prophet's audience, for which he becomes the spokesperson. The communal "we" is thus ostensibly set in opposition to the lone prophetic "you"—ostensibly because "Advice to a Prophet" in fact deploys the old "Advice to the Painter" topos we find in poems by Waller and Marvell. Here the poet, while disowning any skill as a painter, actually paints his subject by setting it forth in visual terms, a version of the *diminutio* that enables Chaucer's Franklin to claim ignorance of rhetoric even while practicing it with great aplomb. So all through Wilbur's poem, the speaker is uttering a ventriloquial prophecy, using the terms of his own experience to make the sort of statement the conventional prophet would couch in very different language. Prophets do not generally advise; more often they favor vigor above sweet reasonableness. Wilbur, advising his prophet, in effect becomes his or her speechwriter and utters his prophecy by indirection. He is a vicarious prophet, a prophet of conference rather than denunciation. Using the figure of synchoresis, he turns to his listeners and leads them by question and answer to a position close to his own.

If "Advice to a Prophet" disavows apocalyptic visions for quieter, elegiac tableaux of loss, "Stop" (NCP, p. 184) does the reverse, moving out of the ordinary and accessible world into a dark eschatological key. The first three stanzas present a baggage truck on a platform with an annotative clarity typical of William Carlos Williams, for, as Bruce Michelson has pointed out, "Wilbur seems to rebuild Williams's red wheelbarrow into a blue baggage truck" (*Wilbur's Poetry*, p. 32). Even so, the treatment differs radically. Wilbur is not content simply to record the real with a scrupulous, hard-edged integrity, but wishes also to enlarge and spiritualize the data. He uses his diction to effect this transfiguration, much as he does in "The Death of a Toad," and, placing the joyless industrial vision *sub specie aeternitatis*, reconceives it as an image of hell. There is something very Wilburian about the simile of phosphorus on the river Lethe—it is advanced as a datum observed, as though the poet himself had seen it glittering in the wake of Charon's barge. We see something similar in "A Hole in the Floor," with its shavings unself-consciously compared to the parings of an Hesperian apple. Thus is the visionary material calmly and undemonstratively domesticated. As Donald Hill notes, "a unique event in time, once seen in the light of myth, becomes a timeless illustration of some essential human principle" (*Richard Wilbur,* p. 148).

"Junk" (NCP, p. 185) begins like "Stop" with dreary industrial images of litter and pollution and also changes key when the idea of reclamation is broached. Despite the obvious differences in texture, it brings to mind a moment in Pope's *Epistle to Burlington,* which predicts that nature will in time reclaim the vulgarity of Timon's enterprise:

> Another age shall see the golden Ear
> Imbrown the Slope, and nod on the Parterre,
> Deep Harvests bury all his pride has plann'd,
> And laughing Ceres re-assume the Land.   (*Poems,* p. 594)

Although Wilbur's epigraph from an Anglo-Saxon fragment reminds us of the typography of the alliterative line, its unfamiliarity to the modern eye results rather in our seeing the poem as a riven shape on the page, the caesuras moving like a zigzag fissure. It thus becomes a sort of technopaegnion or shape poem, embodying the very brokenness the poet deplores. At the same time it unavoidably makes a mock-heroic statement, channeling twentieth-century refuse through a verse form ordinarily reserved for heroic exploits. Because Hopkins had used similar alliterative measure for his psalmic poetry, his celebrations also resonate ironically with Wilbur's contempt for travesties of craft. In a sense these are antiregionalist; they exemplify the industrial dissociation of worker from task, a faceless, mercantile internationalism. The failure to use a native American wood for the axe shaft is symptomatic.

But once purged of their human squalor and imperfection in the Gehenna of the refuse dump, these objects gradually revert to their essential selves and are transfigured by natural craft as carbon is transformed into its diamantine allotrope. Hephaestus represents the divine principle of creativity against which even the best human craft—Wayland's in this instance—is measured and found wanting. Such a coda is altogether typical of Wilbur, a quiet exaltation of the ordinary, effected by an intimate use of mythology. Wayland figures as though he were a historical craftsperson; Hephaestus stores his tools as carefully as any of his suburban epigones. Wilbur does not, in my opinion (as Theodore Holmes claims he does), "take refuge in myth"[4] but rather brings myth out of its remote classical ambience into the living present; he *engages* with, and demystifies, the mythical.

"Loves of the Puppets" (NCP, p. 187) is an anatomy of lust, using the image of marionettes to convey its inhumanity and manipulation of the human will. Wilbur opens with a spring as tender and incipient as that at the start of *The Canterbury Tales.* The buds promise life, and their tenderness and organic contour contrast with the idol-like fixity of instinct. By referring to blood in line 2, Wilbur hints at a secular, a sexual version of redemption, like that espoused by D. H. Lawrence. In these terms coitus is conceived in itself to be a channel of grace, but all the time the apparent humanity of the urge is undercut by such images as that of the wooden face, replicated in the inexpressive, unseeing eyes (as though the beloved were not regarded, but the subject closed in by his or her self-absorption). The puppet image is also sustained in the uncoordinated, ungraceful falling of the lovers, and even in the way they are drawn together, as if by a puppeteer's string.

In traditional *reverdies* (spring songs), there is a harmony of inner and outer weather; in this, the lovers' lust proves so precipitate and heated that it bears no resemblance to the conditions of April. Indeed its desert heats point to its sterility, a sterility at odds with the "vertu" of which "engendred is the flour."[5] The lovers themselves, failing to realize the tenderness of love, become as lifeless as mechanical toys when they surrender will to instinct: the "sense" of "sensuality" cancels out "sense" of "sentience." Thus physical convergence entails spiritual separation, imaged as the jangling, uncoordinated flight of mishandled marionettes.

At this point Wilbur gives his poem a catechetic structure and parodies the sacred question and answer that we find, for example, in the opening chorus of Bach's *St. Matthew Passion:*

> Sehet
> > Wen?
> den Bräutigam,
> Seht ihn
> > Wie?
> als wie ein Lamm.–
> Sehet,
> > Was?
> Seht die Geduld,

In a similar manner, the poet hieratically poses questions and answers them, stating that the lovers sought physical sensation contemplated as an end in itself, rather as Lucretius avoided emotional engagement in his lovemaking so as to savor its sensual moments without distraction. Wilbur images the sterility of the climax by the plastic snow ejaculated in the shake of a toy—

something manipulable, a travesty of real snowstorms in all their unpredictable and humbling majesty. The lovers' tryst is presented not as a road but an impasse, and since *post coitum omne animal triste*, they weep with frustration and disappointment. Like the Red Queen in *Through the Looking Glass*, they have expended energy in getting nowhere. Far from revising their conception of love, however, they simply repeat their futile, clumsy exercise in detached sexuality.

The hollows in the final stanza are obviously declivities in the landscape, but it is hard not to read in the hollow sound of wooden limbs as they clash together, as in *Aeneid* II 11.52–53: *uteroque recusso / insonuere cavae gemitumque dedere cavernae* (Virgil, p. 296). That, together with the lovers' frenzied cries, is measured by the harmony and relaxation of nature's own rhythm (manifest in the brooks), and by the chorus of birds they disrupt with their discordance. Lust is often presented as an impulse of unregenerate nature; Wilbur here implies that such a description gives it an unwarrantable dignity. It is nature whose tenderness and quietude measures the mechanicality of lust—measures it and finds it lacking.

"A Summer Morning" (NCP, p. 188) is an estate poem *manqué*, taking the honorifics of *To Penshurst* and turning them upside down. Where Jonson separates dwelling from building, Wilbur distinguishes possessing from owning. Once again the poem is touched by his sense of regionalism, of knowing and responding intimately to a beloved landscape. In the background of the poem are the owners of the estate, giddy, socializing, drunk; in the foreground the servants, alert, responsive, dwelling—the spiritual cousins of the comadre Bruna Sandoval. The poem is simple, yet profound, and its second stanza reads like a Vermeer picture turned into words. Without wanting to claim any influence in either direction, I see a distinct parallel between this woman and the servant from White's *Riders in the Chariot*, published three years before *Advice to a Prophet and Other Poems*: "Alone in the house—for the cook would retire into livery indolence, and the gardener had a down on somebody, and the chauffeur was almost never there, for driving the mistress about the town—the maid would attempt to express her belief, not in words, nor in the attitudes of orthodox worship, but in the surrender of herself to a state of passive adoration, in which she would allow her substantial body to dissolve into a loveliness of air and light, magnolia scent, and dove psalmody."[6] Wilbur links his cook to the gardener through the montage of the sound track, and the gardener himself is related back to the cook by the *inclusio* that connects first and last stanzas. The traditional levée of the aristocracy is thus performed by more worthy surrogates, a man and woman receptive enough to receive.

Wilbur dedicated "A Hole in the Floor" (NCP, p. 189) to René Magritte, a dedication that alerts us to the subtle, unemphatic surrealism of the poem. Alan Bowness has pointed out how Magritte "isolated the object in a hallucinatory setting, but depicted it as though he were a naive painter attempting *trompe l'oeil* realism."[7] This observation applies also to the poem in hand. Not only does Wilbur depict a Magrittian hole in the floor, as alien and unsettling as the pedestal that floats at the center of *La Condition Humaine*, but he also projects a *trompe l'oeil* cityscape beneath the floor boards, like that in the background of Magritte's picture, where the infinite road matches the tangible shape of a spire.

The opening stanza is deliberately flat and prosaic. It lets us know that the hole, like the wood pile that Frost finds mouldering in a swamp, was made with a purpose in mind. But when that purpose is put in abeyance, the hole begins to unsettle the viewer. Given the quotidian style and information of the first four lines, the simile drawn from the excavation of Troy takes on an almost mock-heroic color, for how can a suburban sitting room soberly be matched with a mythic city? The answer comes in the second verse, for here, with that mythologizing enlargement we have seen in other Wilbur poems, the house itself is presented as though it were commensurate in age with the world itself, while the reference to the Hesperides imparts an additional glamor—the myth of an ultimate boundary.

A special delight of Wilbur's poetry is the way its idiom adapts itself to the task in hand. In "To an American Poet Just Dead," when describing suburban pleasure in consumer goods, he speaks the unpurified language of the tribe in a kindly way. Here he has mastered the dialect of a carpenter, using such precise, task-specific terms as lathes and joists to make their surreal adaptation seem all the more odd. For beneath the cosy sitting room, with its standard lamp and causeuse, he finds a cityscape as drear and discomfiting as any painted by de Chirico. The joists as they vanish mark the onset of an infinite darkness. We are no longer in the foundation of a sitting room but in Einsteinian space, a space whose positive curvature will bring about the convergence of parallel lines. At the same time, the convergence is also a less unsettling, painterly one, for Wilbur is painting with perspective even as he traffics in infinities. He does something similar with the radiator pipe, which he presents as a news vendor's stall in an apocalyptic *Tote Stadt*.

Parodying the reverse evolution by which, say, certain cave-dwelling fish have lost their eyes and their color, he cancels the green of life. Small wonder then that when he cuts back to the enclosure and vividness of the room, he finds them changed by that subliminal dark. It is their frailty and transience as much as the temporary manhole which invest the familiar with a sense of danger. If the known is enhanced in the process, that is because its imminent eclipse makes it all the more lovable. Once again the regional has had its thisness intensified *dans l'abime* of the infinite other.

"She" (NCP, p. 193) is named to bring the lurid adventure story of Rider Haggard to mind—a useful association, for the poem is an archive of mythic types and guises that men have applied to women. Even so, the *Ewig-weibliche* defies the constructions that men have put upon it and will wear a mysterious incognito until the end of time. Even though Wilbur eschews the more obvious stances of prophecy, his gift as a seer is apparent in "Folk Tune," which in 1946 anticipated the civil rights movement, and in "She" (1964), where he foresees an important concern of women's studies.

His survey begins in Eden, where Adam's will is whole both in the sense of being uncorrupted and also of being undivided. Division, Wilbur implies, is essential for comparison, and there can be no myth or metaphor when things are so fully themselves that they leave no room for semblance. The creation of Eve, her separation from Adam, is thus the birth of simile (similitude without perfect congruence) and allegorizes also the birth of imagination, and so of art. Before the advent of Eve, Adam had been a passive recipient, but now as he gazes into her naked face (naked also in the sense of being unmythologized), he begins forging identities for her, and so becomes a maker in the medieval sense of the word. Initially a naked figure, the icon of truth as in Botticelli's *Calumny of Appelles*, she becomes the image of motherhood, and thus of fertility. Wilbur demonstrates the continuity of her domestic and fecund guises by conflating her Ceres sheaf with a domestic implement.

Woman breaks upon the world as a nurturing sunrise, but also fragments into a multitude of semblances, bearing up under these changes like a caryatid, evolving like a *kore*. Indeed, as John Boardman has pointed out, the *korai* took many years to evolve into feminine icons—"To the Archaic sculptor, . . . women were little more than clothes-hangers. Faces are rarely prettier or more appealing than those of the men. . . . Breasts are admitted to exist, but not much admired."[8] Similarly in the list of attributes that now unrolls, the open-ended items prove that woman has long been a Rorschach blot for the obsessions of man. The captive in the tower could be Danaë or she could be St. Barbara. Taken in conjunction with the following reference to war, she could be Helen on the walls of Troy; or, if the line is read in isolation, she could be Pallas Athena. So too the reference to the woman in her garden at the evening hour—Eve, obviously, but also another avatar of the *Ewig-Weibliche*—Goethe's Margarethe, her pregnant belly the source of the oval shadow she trails. This indeterminateness reaches a climax at the start of stanza 7, where, in the absence of syntactic glue, items rock confusedly together. Such a line recalls the asyndetic virtuosity of "Puffs, Powders, Patches, Bibles, Billet-Doux" in *The Rape of the Lock* (Pope, *Poems*, p. 222). Like Arnold's Shakespeare, woman will not abide our question and waits to divulge her true self at a time untouched by desire in both its senses.

"Gemini" (NCP, p. 195) is a brace of satiric quatrains, epigrams about religious misconceptions in the manner of Martial—in the manner of Martial, and also to some extent of Pope, who does comparable things in the *Epistle to a Lady*. His Narcissa, for example, who "Gave alms at Easter, in a Christian trim / And made a Widow happy for a whim" (*Poems*, p. 562), is close enough to PUER in spirit. Both do something like the right thing for the wrong reason. The observations are immensely shrewd and, had they been written *ad hominem,* would have seemed as discomfiting as any of Pope's poisoned darts. Wilbur chooses however to keep the satire generic, though one imagines that the phonetic serendipity of "poor" and *puer* also had something to do with his decision. The standard epithet for Gemini is that of the "heavenly twins," ironical enough when we consider the unheavenly cast of the twins the poet has set before us.

We have already noted how Wilbur domesticates and naturalizes things that might otherwise seem exorbitant and strange. "The Undead" (NCP, p. 196) is a case in point, for it gives a psychological account of how vampires come about, avoiding the sensational etiologies of folklore for an explanation couched in human terms. The awkward litotic title points not only to their mythological afterlife but to their impoverished, unvital existence in the flesh. Wilbur offers a demythologized version of the horrific, rewritten in such a way as to evoke pity rather than fear. He traces the nocturnality of vampires back to a desire for dreaming above living, a displacement measured by his ambiguous use of "quick." Their horror of death is evident in the way they recoil uncompassionately from signs of decay.

But lest we imagine that horror an inverted love of life, the poet shows the undead's detachment from the richness and fertility of nature as well, setting them apart from a burgeoning plum tree. Monomania in Ovid is often the reason for metamorphosis, and here too the vampires are simply distillations of their own concern with survival, a concern that denatures life and afterlife alike. When Wilbur introduces the traditional Gothic properties associated with vampires, they have lost their terror and set about their business as methodically and unglamorously as any businessperson. They have even to induce their appetite for blood by rehearsing the omissions of their own childhoods, harping on the sort of life their lifeless prudence forbade them. Toys once avoided are now sought out, pruriently brought before the mind's eye to excite a thirst.

Against this bloodless caution Wilbur then places the selflessness and abandon of a thrush and a scholar whose deaths, marking their release from a life of commitment, are genuinely peaceful. The unnatural, unrhythmical late sleepers are set in opposition to the leaves that enwrap the bird and the eyes of the scholar, eyes which have dealt with experience, not with the phantasms of the vampiric vision. Having treated the monsters in recognizably human terms, Wilbur is able to forge a paradox that a grand guignol treatment would have had to forgo. The vampires are not out to suck blood in a spirit of demonic *Schadenfreude,* but rather to reclaim what they never have enjoyed and never can enjoy. Wilbur asks us to view them as Virgil and Dante view the denizens of the upper circles of hell. Life in all its oceanic fullness is for them a stagnant beach pool. That haunting image might well have come to Wilbur from Tennyson's *Guinevere,* where Modred's resentment of Lancelot is described "As the sharp wind that ruffles all day long / A little bitter pool about a stone / On the bare coast" (*Poems,* p. 1726).

"October Maples, Portland" (NCP, p. 198) presents itself as a Wilburian equivalent of Wordsworth's "Daffodils," the trees so vivid that they persist as an eidetic image long after being sighted. Although I prefer to read the stain of their memory in terms of the *aere perennius* motif, it is worth noting that Helen Dry has given it a strong theological color: "the stain suggests both death and eternal life. And likewise the maple leaves, from which the stain derives, neatly emblematize man's dual fate. The gold-red of the leaves indicates that the foliage is succumbing to time; but it also exalts the spirit, engendering an awe so pure it recalls the timelessness of Eden and post-redemptive eternity."[9] Certainly the poem is laced with biblical and liturgical imagery, but then so are most epiphanies in Joyce. How else can a sacramental value be imparted to otherwise prosaic events and objects? Wilbur detects a gleam of Eden's permanence in the annual fall, and so recalls the curse on Adam and its etiology of the seasons.

There is nothing in the poem that cannot bear rational inspection—the leaves are still attached to their twigs (even while the figurative meaning of "unfallen" is trying to break through), and the semblance of prelapsarian light is merely that, a semblance. But as the poet surrenders himself to the experience, so the language intensifies, and metaphor begins piling on metaphor to signify his intoxicated savoring of the moment. It is in this savoring that the poem comes to birth, and the eternity of the maples is thus assured. Even at the moment the experience is revoked its noetic *Nachleben* is guaranteed. The eye-washing, while it might also have the lustral meaning that Helen Dry gives it, is primarily the effortless application of pigment, as in a watercolor wash, and a steeping of the organ in its element, much as Hopkins rinses and wrings the ear with birdsong in "Spring."[10] Resulting in the glow of a sanguine temperament as well as redness itself, the stain is like that annealed in a church window. The coda, based on a legend of the rosemary bush, demonstrates the force of folklore, the imaginative principle that has the power to reconstitute our perception of the world. Such legends may not be true in the sense that the Virgin *did* drape her mantle on the bush, but because their prettiness gives them an aesthetic status, and so invites our willing suspension of disbelief.

Wilbur follows the vividness and elation of his maple experience with "Shame" (NCP, p. 201) a sequence which makes the grayness of the prose poem seem all the more unremittingly gray. Charles T. Scott has even suggested that its poetic status might well depend on its layout: "why do we accept Wilbur's discourse as a poem? That is, what basis do we have for categorizing 'Shame' as a poem and not a prose passage?"[11] The answer to his question is that "Shame" makes prosaism into a poetic resource, taking something gray and faceless to depict those very qualities. Wilbur's language thus becomes transparent to his theme in the best tradition of poetry. Everything is held back: the speaker relies on secondhand experience, and he fumbles with his translation of the city's inscription. This might recollect *Las-*

ciate ogni speranza voi ch'entrate, but it gives us a hell without any Dantesque grandeur. The poem is an instance of allegorical toposthesia that has its roots in Lucian, Bunyan, and Swift, but while Wilbur shares their satiric and moral purpose, he adds something further—a regional element. Like all of us, he has visited Shame, but only a poet of his peculiar genius could combine a series of moral propositions with the observed and intimate detail of the citizens' clothes and mannerisms.

In "A Grasshopper" (NCP, p. 202), the poet focuses as it were at random on an insect and, moving outwards in a series of concentric circles, makes it the contingent center of the world. Of course the procedure offers no more than a provisional truth, but it does get absolutes into focus by starting from a chance particular. As we begin reading, we are tempted to take the opening "But" as an adversative conjunction, as though the poem's discourse, like that in *Andrea del Sarto,*[12] were being taken up midstream, an effect compounded by the way in which the pronouns assume our familiarity with the object and the way the definite article attached to the chicory leaf implies that a specific leaf is under scrutiny. This gives a sense of the poem's being a frame, stopped and detached from an otherwise continuous montage. Closer inspection, however, shows that the "But" has an adverbial function, limiting the pause to a bare minimum. With an expansion of time like that in *An Occurrence at Owl Creek Bridge,* the poem dilates its moment into an eternity. Other derangements accompany this temporal arrest. Pausing is ordinarily connected with time, poising with space, and yet the two are inverted in stanza 1, and time is poised while the body pauses. Time is identified also with the tensility of the leaf, which has interiorized its momentum. As in "From the Lookout Rock," the peace that widens out from this momentary arrest is a decreating doldrums, marked once again by the withdrawal of the creative spirit. It is only when the urge to move is transitively imposed upon the creature—a Wilburian quirk that also figures in other poems—that life resumes. The resulting movement of the grasses, itself like the stridulation of a grasshopper, breaks the unison with syncopated counterpoint. Wilbur implies that peace is properly a diverse and cooperative harmony, not an absence.

"The Aspen and the Stream" (NCP, p. 205) resuscitates and modifies a genre from the Middle Ages. Donald Hill has suggested it is a flyting (*Richard Wilbur,* p. 137), but the vituperation is not mutual. I should prefer to regard the poem as a *contentio* or debate, like that *inter philomelam et bubonem*—with this difference. In most *contentiones* the contestants claim superiority to each other, whereas here the stream and aspen aspire to be the opposites of what they are. The influence of Cowper's lyric fables is evident, for such poems as "The Bee and the Pineapple" also explore the issue of discontent. Wilbur's stream desires the respite of vacancy, having been forced by nature to reflect the world; the aspen at first desires that perfect openness, assuming that the self is quenched rather than irritated by perpetual surrender. The poem unfolds as a contest between the good-natured tree, speaking in roomy pentameter couplets (a growth of rings), and the stream, which flows in quatrains of alternating rhymes. The trimetric lines insistently break the current, however, and give the utterance a short-fused, irritable quality. Resolution comes in the last stanza. Here the tree tries to reconcile the selflessness she has projected onto the stream with her own inescapable selfhood. It is a synthesis that marries the regional option of rootedness with aspiration beyond the confines of her growth. Her aspiration might fail to reach its ostensible end, but in the process it has enriched and intensified the self. For all its humility, the aspen has become an analogue of the Yggdrasill, the World Ash: "So huge was this tree that its branches stretched out over heaven and earth alike. . . . Beneath the root in giant-land was the spring of Mimir, whose waters contained wisdom and understanding. . . . Below the tree in the kingdom of the Aesir was the sacred spring of fate, the Well of Urd."[13] By combining and unifying earth and water through the principle of growth, the aspen takes on an archetypal stature.

And as if to vouch for his own aspenlike receptivity and breadth of interest, Wilbur follows the tree fable with "A Fire-Truck" (NCP, p. 207). The mandate of an object poem is very nearly met here, but as always, Wilbur shies away from mere factuality and dabs on some essence of myth—in this case the myth of the phoenix, renewing itself perpetually in the furnace of the imagination. As an instance of its virtuoso metrics one could cite the disorientation of the speaker in the first line of the third stanza, which reels in a chaos of undisciplined stress. So frequently do the caesuras cut into the line that no foot gains dominance, and we are left with a can of writhing metrical worms: a cretic, a trochee, an amphibrach and an ionic a minore!

"Someone Talking to Himself" (NCP, p. 208) is a love song of sorts, even though it seems at first glance to resemble the palinode at the end of *Troilus and Criseyde:*

> O yonge, fresshe folkes, he or she,
> In which that love up groweth with youre age,
> Repeyreth hom fro worldly vanyte,
> And of youre herte casteth the visage
> To thilke God that after his ymage
> Yow made, and thynketh al nys but a faire
> This world, that passeth soone as floures faire.
> (Chaucer, *Works,* p. 479)

These are sentiments with which Wilbur would no doubt ultimately concur, even if the title of his poem asks us to disaffiliate poet and speaker. However, the originality of "Someone Talking" lies in the way it *combines* this sober acknowledgment with the heartiness of eros. Most love poems are hermetically sealed into the present moment and into the space at hand. Donne, for example, confidently tells us in "The Good Morrow" that "love, all love of other sights controls, / And makes a little room an every where."[14] In "Someone Talking," by contrast, the speaker even in the first flush of his love, is bleakly conscious of all that love cannot reclaim. He starts with traditional lovesick similes, from the conventional (in the manner of Oscar Hammerstein's "Younger than springtime are you") to conceits as hyperbolic and exultant as any in Petrarch or Donne. Wilbur's reference to another place at once suggests "another country," the country of Sir Cecil Spring-Rice's hymn; only here the alternative is not paradise but a hell of blind, unthinking appetite of a shark—lust divested of glamor. That shark might well have swum in from Keatsian waters—the verse epistle *To J. H. Reynolds Esq.*

Again in stanza 2, where Donne would elide love and eternal life, Wilbur concedes the division of grace from sensuality. The final verse resolves the dualism by showing how the very mortality of passion gives birth to sober visions of *agape,* of a love the purer for being finally divorced from the corruptible flesh. What might at first seem a retraction of all those Wilbur poems that stress the importance of the senses as a vehicle for the soul turns out to be nothing of the kind. The exhilaration of corporal love is granted; all that the poet says is that it is not absolute. Light, for as long as there are solid objects, must cast a shadow, and yet that shadow has a unifying, binding property, like the chiaroscuro of a painting. The visions of sharks and dry marshes, negative correlates of human love, finally point to *caritas,* in which there is no evil. Wilbur offers us an image of productive failure, a failure of the individual will that issues restfully in submission.

"In the Smoking-Car" (NCP, p. 210) on the other hand, is a poignant poem about a failure altogether more passive. The title and details of the first stanza suggest that the protagonist is a businessperson commuting, perhaps, between New York and the suburbs. He has failed in some sphere of business and falls asleep on his way home. But whereas Gauguin the stockbroker went into exile in the South Pacific (a heroic, purposeful renunciation), this failed executive takes refuge in a travel-poster idyll. Women on the train cluck sympathetically as he falls asleep, and their voices are picked up in the anadiplosis that starts the next stanza. This also has a mock-heroic effect, recalling as it does the stylized echoes of Pope's *Autumn* ("Thro' Rocks and Caves the Name of *Delia* sounds, / *Delia,* each Cave and ecchoing Rock rebounds"—*Poems,* p. 134). The same figure seamlessly connects stanzas 4 and 5, suggesting the way in which the landscape, now allegorized as a valley of Failure, quietly and imperceptibly takes him to itself.

With his "Ballade for the Duke of Orléans" (NCP, p. 211) Wilbur recurs to the issues of "Someone Talking," that sense of incompleteness indivorcible from even the most spectacular triumph, which registers, say, in the sorrow of Alexander the Great. Wilbur's form is well chosen, for the statutory refrain has a nagging effect: it arrests and reproaches irremissively. There is also a sense of stalling and neutralization, produced by self-canceling antithesis. As is usual with Wilbur, the subject matter ranges unself-consciously from the mundane and the regional (trout fishing) to the mythological (Ulysses) before the strands are wound together in the figures of Conquistador and Argonaut.

The first leap of the trout recalls a rainbow as much as it does a weapon and that promise is violated in the fading iris, which recalls the Greek word for "rainbow" at the same time that it describes the eye of a dying fish. Having killed the creature, the angler feels self-disgust. So too Ulysses, having spent the night with Calypso as a break from all the heroics of his odyssey, wakes to a yearning for Penelope, the end of all his journeying. Even in the midst of his pleasure, guilt supervenes, turning, in Keats's words "to Poison as the bee-mouth sips" (*Poetical Works*, p. 220). The *envoi* reads like a version of Herbert's "Pulley." The restlessness of human beings is a condition of their birth, a measure of their original sin. Satisfaction, "enough-making," is not to be found in the sublunary world.

"To Ishtar" (NCP, p. 214) is an ode to a goddess that demythologizes its subject all the while it is hymning her. While conventional odes to deities deal with persons, Wilbur's melts Ishtar into her attributes as they are manifest in seasonal change. Even though Ishtar belongs to the Babylonian pantheon, the thaw he describes is a New England thaw, not remotely connected with the Middle East. However, the distinctiveness of the poem lies in its *concordia discors*. Keats is a possible inspiration here, for in his ode to autumn he also assimilates his personification to plausible figures in the landscape, figures to be observed by any comer: "Who hath not seen thee oft amid thy store?" (*Poetical Works*, p. 219)

If autumn is manifest in gleaners and harvesters, it is easy enough for Wilbur to take the assimilation one step further and equate his goddess with impersonal aspects of the landscape. He keeps braiding details of the myth into his regionalist pictures. In the Gilgamesh Epic, tablet 7, for example, we read that "Ishtar, the daughter of Sin, turned her ear to the abode of darkness, the dwelling of Irkalla to the house whose enterer goes not forth, to the road whence the wayfarer never returns."[15] By means of a simple "low" Wilbur fleshes out this vague description, conveying the meanness and ultimacy of the final gate in Irkalla, and the submissive posture of the goddess as she enters the underworld.

"Pangloss's Song: A Comic-Opera Lyric" (NCP, p. 215) is the fruit of Wilbur's collaboration with Lillian Hellman and Leonard Bernstein on *Candide*. Given the speaker's conviction that this is the best of all possible worlds, it is not surprising that it should unfold as a tissue of sophistries justifying venereal disease. The bright paradoxical manner (not unlike the start of "Lamarck Elaborated") plays against the dark subject, and so does the easy, balladic roll from tetrameter to trimeter. Wilbur has kept things simple to make space for the music. And although "Two Quatrains for First

Frost" (NCP, p. 217) does not owe its provenance to a musical comedy, it too constitutes a song lyric, plain and immediate enough to carry a musical burden as something enriching rather than supernumerary. Like the seasonal lyrics of *Love's Labour's Lost,* the quatrains resemble leaves in the Duc de Berry's *Book of Hours* and document the pause between summer and autumn with two plausible conceits. The roundsong of summer's end is not only a rondelet but a round delay, the tiresome interruption of the cycle; and the zero the gambler bets on is also the zero of the first frost.

Turning to "Another Voice" (NCP, p. 218), we might be forgiven for expecting a monologic poem like "A Voice from under the Table." We soon discover, though, that Wilbur is speaking not *in* but *about* another voice, one that persists as a ground bass against his own. It is the voice of faith in the goodness of God, the voice of theodicy that has somehow to reconcile that goodness with the suffering of the world. The assent can be made only in faith, and there are times when even a "fairly orthodox Christian" (Wilbur's own description of himself)[16] will rebel at the effort it demands. "Another Voice" therefore presents itself as a sort of colloquy between the doubting, urgent voice of the poet and the silent, persisting voice of faith—another instance of "intelligible quarreling" between the poet's selves. Attempts to justify misery must always seem devious and sophistical, a mere play with words.

That is why the crows cry *Corcyra* in stanza 1, for in the counsel before the war of Corinth against Corcyra, Thucydides has the Corinthians accuse their enemies of double-talk:

> "Wisdom" and "Moderation" are the words used by Corcyra in describing her old policy of avoiding alliances. In fact the motives were entirely evil, and there was nothing good about them at all. She wanted no allies because her actions were wrong, and she was ashamed of calling in others to witness her own misdoings. . . . So this neutrality of theirs, which sounds so innocent, was in fact a disguise adopted not to preserve them from having to share in the wrong-doing of others, but to give them a perfectly free hand to do wrong themselves.[17]

Lives are lost in the ensuing battle, but how is one to console the dead with justifications for the war? The suffering is real, the deaths irreversible. Cutting from myth to the present in his customary way, Wilbur hints his distress over the Vietnam war by pointing to Corcyrean crows in the skies of America. The poem thus adduces examples of human grief that are difficult to defend or rationalize: theodicies—even secular ones like Keats's "vale of Soul-making"[18]—often sound glib in the face of suffering.

Donald Hill has noted that "something of the manner of Yeats is recognizable in these spare three-stress lines" (*Richard Wilbur,* p. 143)—something of the manner of Yeats and, I would add, something of the manner of Housman. One is reminded of such terse, bitter claims as that which privileges beer above Milton in justifying "the ways of God to man" in *The Shropshire Lad.*[19] Perhaps throughout the poem Wilbur means us to think of Christ's refusal to speak during his arraignment by Pilate. It is that mute voice of which he entreats forgiveness in the last stanza, where he explains that his horror of misery is based, after all, on sheer compassion.

Because "Fall in Corrales" (NCP, p. 222) is set in New Mexico rather than in New England, autumn seems not so much a season of fulfillment as of depletion, the dry riverbed and tumbleweed anticipating the sterility of winter. Wilbur opposes winter and summer (which he conceives as times of stasis) with the intermediate seasons. Spring and autumn are dynamic, phases of transition that more fully engage the human soul than the seasons of arrest. So while the summer and winter idylls separate humankind from its setting (shut doors resonating with shut heads), in spring the soul is transfused through the landscape and participates in its fertility. This energetic participation is evident also in the autumn, for as life dwindles, so it functions as a *memento mori* and rehearses the soul for the onset of death. The sentences of straws and stones are *sententiae*, pithy statements of mortality, for straw was once grass, flesh is like the grass, and stones (like the bones revealed by the corruption of the flesh) are disclosed by its dying. Wilbur envisages his skeleton's whitening in the desert landscape (*candor* in the Latin sense), a vision more truthful than those the shut minds of summer and winter entertain. The result is also candor in its modern acceptation.

There is also an opposition of life and mortality in "Next Door" (NCP, p. 223), a lyric in which Wilbur reverts to the Eastern seaboard of America. The title suggests intimacy and contiguity, and yet the worlds it documents are worlds apart. Gone is the happy communal integration of ace and youth that Goldsmith hymns in *The Deserted Village:* "The hawthorn bush, with seats beneath the shade, / For talking age and whispering lovers made."[20] Now the old are segregated from the young, who, like the birds, drown out their voices. The poet can only speculate on the thoughts and feelings of the old, projecting possible conversations, possible thoughts. The girls and boys are obviously living for the future, but the old are facing backwards, reaching even to myth by euhemerism, and yearning for such conquests of death as that recorded by Euripides in *Alcestis.* A dissonance between the bird cries and the grief of age recalls the dissonance of birdsong with grief itself in another eighteenth-century poem—Gray's "Sonnet on the Death of Mr. Richard West": "The birds in vain their amorous descant join, / Or cheerful fields resume their green attire" (*The Poems of Gray, Collins, and Goldsmith,* p. 67). The difference is that in "Next Door" the birds do not even make the effort of consolation, they simply occlude.

The collection ends with "A Christmas Hymn" (NCP, p. 225), which like "Pangloss's Song" shows how well Wilbur has understood the symbiosis of word and music. The poem moves so resolutely and clearly across the page that it seems to call for a big tune, as all fine hymns do. Nothing is obscure, and yet nothing is banal. A congregation would not be baffled, for the graph of the poem is plotted purposefully from Nativity to Judgment, and with this graph in the background, Wilbur can afford to include a few suggestive moments. One example is his play with synecdoche and paradox, as in the genre detail of the lantern, the light of which merges with the star's, and ultimately with the radiance of the angels singing the *Gloria*. The doublet about the vocal stones recurs from verse to verse, giving the hymn its prophetic vigor and acting also as an incremental refrain that steadies the pattern and develops the thought. The cries of acclamation, for example, are at one point displaced by the cries of sorrow, and at another the heart of humankind takes on its own paradoxical stoniness. Not only can Wilbur advise contemporary prophets, but he can also catch the urgent tone of the biblical kind as well.

five

w a l k i n g
to
s l e e p

n e w   p o e m s
and
t r a n s l a t i o n s
(1 9 6 9)

having advised a prophet in his previous collection, Wilbur devotes a long poem to advising a sleeper in his 1969 volume. It might therefore be as well to begin with the eponym, since this collection, unlike the others, is divided into four sections, three of them named after dominant poems: *In the Field*, *Thyme*, and *Walking to Sleep*. Although I shall follow the internal arrangement of each of these, I shall read "Walking to Sleep" (NCP, p. 158) out of sequence, for being assigned a section all of its own and conferring its name on the whole, it virtually demands to be taken first.

There is much in the content of the poem that is atypical, although it is as suavely crafted as anything that has gone before. Usually Wilbur has enlarged his scope and shifted his concerns circumspectly and cautiously, so much so that some commentators have accused him of marking time. James Dickey, for example, writing about *Advice to a Prophet* says that "Up to now, . . . there has been no *development*, or even change, in Wilbur's work, and there is something vaguely disturbing in this, even though you hear people on all sides saying that if someone is already the most charming and amiable man in the world there's no need for him to try to be something or somebody else."[1] While poems like "Another Voice" call such judgments into question, one can at least see how they came to be made. But in the earlier parts of "Walking to Steep," Wilbur's departure from cherished tenets is marked enough to seem baffling. For a start, he often counsels evasion, the kind of evasion deplored in "The Undead." Again and again we find " 'Thou shalt not' writ over the door." Such decalogues of denial are not unknown to poetry, but when they are issued, it is often to intensify the experience that the negatives cut out in silhouette. Think, for example, of the proem of cancellations in Keats's "Ode on Melancholy": "No, no, go not to Lethe, neither twist / Wolf's-bane, tight-rooted, for its poisonous wine" (*Poetical Works,* p. 219).

In "Walking to Sleep" on the other hand, the negatives are the negatives of the undead, recoiling from the beautiful because it courts the danger of commitment. So, like the vampires, dreamers are urged to skirt any compacts with the dying. Their paranoia is such that they defoliate landscapes to expose would-be aggressors—sure sign that there is something rotten in the State of Denmark (or Vietnam). The dun, unvital landscape they create helps underline the sterile nature of the enterprise. Bruce Michelson has described the poem as "an extensive guide to survival in the hypnagogic state"[2] and related it to Wilbur's quarrel with Poe. Even so, no matter what Wilbur's misgivings about the state might be, it is uncharacteristic for him to be so concerned with survival by surrender, so eager to neutralize and nullify where his regionalist impulses would ordinarily lead him to inventory the streaks of the tulip and dwell on objects in all their mortal richness. Only the undead should feel alarm at the possibility of wolves or skull-naked cats, especially if it involves deleting all regional evidences of life, the barns that figure so poignantly in " 'A World Without Objects,' " and "A Black November Turkey." How then are we to reconcile the pinched maxims of "Walking to Sleep" with Wilbur's usual generosity and commitment? One way, obviously, is to detach the speaker from the poet and read it as a dramatic monologue. We are in bed, and at our bedside a father turned psychopomp is mediating our passage from waking to dream. There, at any rate, is the concrete situation of a dramatic monologue, though it is not a very developed one.

There are other ways of viewing the poem, however. Urged on by that negative capability that is the hallmark of all good poets, Wilbur could be sampling the world from a radically different vantage. He has already done so in his "voice" poems, but one feels here that the assumptions and attitudes are much farther removed from those of the poet's accepted position. Then again, what one dreams is not always what one believes, and *Walking to Sleep* could simply be a compilation of nightmares that have haunted the poet, the dark side of a moon otherwise polished and radiant. Viewed this way, the poem must be taken *sui generis* and ought not to be aligned with Wilbur's characteristic poems of waking. Indeed, one of its chief interests is its oneiric transitions, its dream logic. These are especially manifest in the section beginning ten lines up from the bottom of p. 159. Robert Boyers, in his intelligent but hostile appraisal of the poem, has this to say:

There is something fundamentally dishonest about such a passage, for it suggests so much that might be relevant to Wilbur's vision without ever confirming anything at all. Though we are almost inclined to accept the still obscure significance of "the fuse-box" and "vacant barracks," we must be hard put to make much of Wilbur's "sheeted lawn-chairs" and "vast stone tent where Cheops lay secure." What are all these things doing here, we want to ask, only we suspect that Wilbur would look askance at such questions, confident that we ought to accept what has been set so deliciously before us.[3]

"What are all these things doing here?" The answer is that they are being dreamed, and the implausible continuities of dreaming thus anatomized. Well might one ask the same question of a lyric in Gilbert's *Iolanthe*:

> For you dream you are crossing the Channel,
>   and tossing about in a steamer from Harwich—
> Which is something between a large bathing machine
>   and a very small second-class carriage—
> And you're giving a treat (penny ice and cold meat)
>   to a party of friends and relations—
> They're a ravenous horde—and they all came on
>   board at Sloane Square and South Kensington Stations.
> And bound on that journey you find your attorney
>   (who started that morning from Devon);
> He's a bit undersized, and you don't feel surprised
>   when he tells you he's only eleven.[4]

The right question to ask of such poems is not "What are all these things doing here?" but rather "How do they come to be here?" In the case of Gilbert's poem, an item introduced for the sake of comparison ("a very small second-class carriage") suddenly edges out the original object and becomes the center of the next phase of nonsense. Surprising displacements are the very stuff of comedy, and they are also the very stuff of dreams.

It is easy to see the same principle at work in the passage that Boyers deplores. Its transitions are not smooth, but neither are they wanton. It would be better to describe them as being preparedly arbitrary, rather in the manner of enharmonic modulations, which allow the composer to shift key by giving a dual construction to one note, say G sharp = A flat. The fuse-box that we pass on the cellar steps is comfortingly familiar, and yet it also seems to function as an emblem for the meltings and short circuits out of which the poem is formed. So too the gritty steps, whose grittiness gives them the texture of a stope and so anticipates the mining images that the poet is about to marshal. We have come into the basement in order to repair a fuse (for why, otherwise, should we be groping?), but before long our torch becomes a carbide mining lamp. And the deck chairs, likely enough features in a suburban cellar, take form as shrouded catafalques in vault, triggering associations with a cathedral crypt. It would seem to be the sanctity of such a space that then causes our foreheads to glow as if with aureoles, mining lamps in a religious key. The crypt pillars modulate enharmonically into mine props, and the rock face pocks and scars take on the appearance of Egyptian inscriptions, a cue for the allusion to the pyramid at Giza. This itself is an allotrope of the cathedral crypt, while the tent that Wilbur has invoked to image the shape of the pyramid is also a likely enough home for a pioneer miner, and this in turn prompts the allusion to the "shed of corrugated iron," suggesting another structure, this one typical of a turn-of-the-century boom town.

Wilbur is writing a fantasia with startling yet justifiable modulations, and the interest in the poem centers less on the motifs than on the way in which they are assembled and blended. These associative chains are familiar enough from surrealism—think of that notorious dissection of moon by cloud, of eyeball by blade in the Buñuel/Dali *Un Chien Andalou*—and they have led Henry Taylor to call "Walking to Sleep" "the most surrealistic poem the poet has published to date."[5] A Freudian would no doubt have a field day with the vaginal mines and phallic pillars, and there is nothing in the poem to forbid such an approach to its meaning. However, the image in which it finds its resolution suggests that Wilbur has deliberately conceived it as a series of wrong turns and cul-de-sacs, releasing dreams from the control of emotional and mental censors. In fact he has adapted the poem of journeying (that rare form, the hodoiporikon), and blended it with the more familiar lullaby. As a result of this cross-generic pollination, the journey now serves to induce sleep through the fatigue of traveling.

In order to resolve its hypnotic insistence, registered above all in the way the syntax often escapes the line in a wakeful enjambment, Wilbur absorbs the will to movement into static contemplation—quietude in the mind of Vishnu (NCP, p. 161, four lines from the bottom), the creative and sustaining principle in the Hindu *trimurti*. If we are to reach that state of divine passivity, we must accommodate the world in its entirety, welcoming its images as they come. While Robert Boyers has noted "that Wilbur is at last here confessing his conviction that the proper project of imagination is to set itself at rest" ("On Richard Wilbur," p. 80), it is just as important to realize that the poet is also projecting creative indolence á la Keats—that undistracted, uncensored exposure of the soul to experience from which the imagination will forge its art.

After the alien landscapes of "Walking to Sleep," let us turn to the Wilburian attentiveness of "The Lilacs" (NCP, p. 118). We are back on familiar regionalist ground, for both Whitman and (dare one say it?) Louisa May Alcott have associated lilacs with New England. However, the blooms that Wilbur brings before our eyes are cousined also with the international hyacinths of *The Wasteland*, for like them they suffer the cruelties of April. The Anglo-Saxon measure of "Junk" has been reemployed with excellent results, since the breakage and staggering of the lines dramatizes the lilacs' reluctant coming to birth, while the same pattern, associated later with established blooms of summer, has a top-heavy fall not unlike that of the flowers themselves. In the manner of Herbert's "Flower," Wilbur's poem records a discontinuity of sorrow and joy, somehow reconciled in the flower itself. Herbert, for instance, exclaims that "Grief melts away / Like snow in May, / As if there were no such cold thing" (*Works*, p. 165) and describes the flower as having retracted to its "mother-root," "Where they together / All the hard weather, / Dead to the world, keep house unknown." At comparable points of "The Lilacs" Wilbur records the silence of the flowers with regard to their own sufferings, so removed from their present generosity and abundance. The fruition of the spring, like that in Herbert's poem, could not occur without the sterility of winter, and the lilacs' beauty is interinvolved with their hardship. They transfigure and at the same time contain the suffering from which the poet recoiled, and which he refused to justify, in "Another Voice."

"On the Marginal Way" (NCP, p. 120) also moves from anguish and despair to affirmation. Somewhere on the Eastern Seaboard—Maine, according to Michelson (*Wilbur's Poetry*, p. 93)—the poet has discovered volcanic intrusions in a system of shale. Differences between the igneous and sedimentary rock prompt a series of metaphors, each darker than its predecessor. They begin innocently enough with an allusion to George Borrow. Wilbur is a bowerbird and often finds a snug place somewhere in his poetry for odds and ends from his encyclopedic reading. Fabre figures casually in "Cicadas," Borrow here. How odd to find a hundred naked women at the start of a meditative poem, and yet there they are, straight, as Wilbur himself tells us, from *The Bible in Spain*. The spectacle is not however treated with the composed sensuality we find, say, in "Five Women Bathing in Moonlight," but rather as a Rubensian torrent of bodies, too insistently fleshy to amount to an affirmation of the flesh.

The negative color is supplied by idea of a catch (which gives the women the sprawled inanimacy of still-life fishes), by the fragmenting synecdoche, and by the prim, anatomical diction that will have no commerce with such terms as "breast" and "sex." Having tumbled down bodies as if from a fishnet, Wilbur moves enharmonically to other images of brutal disorder and presents the same scene as a Géricault in the next stanza, and then again as a horrendous outpouring from the ovens at Auschwitz. Bruce Michelson has raised half an eyebrow at Wilbur's apparent conflation of Géricault with Delacroix at this point (*Wilbur's Poetry*, pp. 94–95), but it seems to me that the reference is better read as a kind of antonomasia. The indefinite article seems to make *The Wreck of the Medusa* stand for any pyramidal composition of needlessly dead and dying persons, whether they figure in *Sardanapalus* or *The Massacre at Chios* or in concentration-camp footage.

The poet's compulsion to turn experience into disconsolate metaphor is attributed to the *Zeitgeist*. His fright has something to do with the cold war, threatening to recapitulate the horrors of World War II on a scale vastly magnified and its local outcroppings in such conflicts as that in Vietnam, hinted by the shabby, mean war in the penultimate stanza. Just as Keats assuaged his fears of mortality by standing on the "shore of the wide world" and thinking "Till love and fame to nothingness do think" (*Poetical Works*, p. 366), so Wilbur spends the hours of darkness contemplating time itself, not as it issues in an apocalyptic climax (the resolution of "Flumen Tenebrarum") but as it stretches back to the Paleozoic period. The effect of this is to subsume human terror to a sense of evolutionary purpose, well caught in a synthesis that has Darwin lie down with Genesis as lion with lamb. Having thus regained his sense of a shaping purpose beyond chaos and evil, Wilbur is able, as dawn breaks, to reconceive the carnal rocks in terms of prelapsarian innocence, hinting at a text from Deuteronomy 33:27—"The eternal God is thy refuge, and underneath are the everlasting arms"—as well as the apparition of the risen Christ (returned Son/sun) on the shores of Galilee. Time has been abolished in eternity or, if not abolished, then made into a vehicle for our fulfillment rather than our extermination. Once again Wilbur threads in scriptural references—this time from Ephesians— to point and shape his climax. Time, as St. Paul projects it in that epistle, is simply the revelation of purpose: "That in the dispensation of the fulness of times he might gather together in one all things in Christ" (Eph. 1:10) and "Till we all come in the unity of the faith, and of the knowledge of the Son of God, unto a perfect man, unto the measure of the stature of the fulness of Christ" (Eph. 4:13). These texts are conflated in the coda of "On the Marginal Way."

"Complaint" (NCP, p. 123) is a pastiche poem, recollecting the form of the *planctus*, venerable forerunner of the torch song. Wilbur seems at first to be writing a Browningesque monologue, one set at the time of the High Renaissance and haunted by the figures of Ficino and Castiglione. The interest of the poem is not, however, restricted to its psychology, for the poet also uses the occasion to offer a critique of Neo-Platonism. His epigraph from Ficino reads "In reality, each love is that of the divine image, and each is pure." That is the theory, but experience fails to match. The speaker feels an unrequited love for a duchess who cannot see beyond his gracelessness and unattractive habits. But in no way does his passion open up an avenue to divine *caritas*, for he is too obsessed with the duchess as she is to care what she might symbolize.

Heaven itself is imaged as an extension of the speaker's servitude on earth, not a return to primal unity, where the bumbling of the servant approximates the more usual formula of *cortesia*, "your humble servant." This sort of wan Petrarchism cannot be blamed on Ficino, however, for he insisted that *Amanti convenit ut re amata fruatur et gaudeat, is enim est finis amoris.*[6] The *res amata* in this instance remains unobtainable, a fact hinted also by such Petrarchan images as the castle of her pride. Even so, the love is potentially complete, for it embraces the faculties of body, mind, and soul, each addressed by the speaker in the guise of buccaneer, poet, and priestly confessor. One is reminded also of a later Platonist for whom "Life, like a dome of many-coloured glass, / Stains the white radiance of eternity,"[7] since the courtier projects each of these guises as refractions of a prism, breaking up the white light of the beloved who contains and resolves its prismatic division in herself. Hyperbole is symptomatic of an imbalance in the speaker's vision, for he has lost sight of the woman in the vaporous abstraction of his creed. The halting, unrhymed stanzas, sapphics manqué, serve to project an unbalanced, fumbling persona.

"Fern-Beds in Hampshire County" (NCP, p. 125) is vintage Wilbur—a poem rooted in the minutiae of the region and yet ready to amplify these with meditations on primordial time. As in "The Death of a Toad," the poet places his topic *sub specie aeternitatis,* though it is an *aeternitas* viewed through the wrong end of the telescope, recessive rather than proleptic. We need to remember that the plants are filicinids, a primitive form of life more advanced than the mosses, but less evolved than flowering and fruiting plants. Like crocodiles and sharks, they reached their evolutionary apogee comparatively soon and persisted in that final form while other plants continued to develop more complex features.

Such primitive persistence is rendered in the syntax at the start of "Fern-Beds," where an elaborate concessive structure is resolved in a blunt main clause. By repeating the verb "to be," Wilbur further conveys the idea of unchanging sameness. The ramifying, hypotactic tangle of subordinate clauses within a subordinate clause dramatizes the wild growth of the thicket and hints also at a complex evolution, arraigned and even judged by the unchanging tenacity of the ferns. Working in tandem with the syntax is the metrical form, in which couplets marry unequal lengths of line. Albert Hayes has explored this phenomenon in the poetry of George Herbert and called it "counterpoint"[8]—not an ideal term, but useful enough in the absence of any other.

The effect of such "counterpoint" in Wilbur's poem is to convey an energy repeatedly curbed and reined in, as though the fern were resisting the urge to evolve and reaffirming its chosen form. This is most vividly demonstrated by the way a three-foot line at one point pushes out into a pentameter only to flare and die. The couplet, moreover, provides an image of pairing, like the pinnules of a fern. With these resources at his disposal, Wilbur first of all evokes the plants in repose and then records their response to the wind. Having initially likened them to the passive vegetation of rock pools, he subsequently transmutes that image into an oceanic deluge in order to convey their wavelike motion in a gale.

However, what starts out as a transpositional metaphor is gradually turned to fact, since the ferns come to signify the movement of life from the sea to land, a function further confirmed by the vertebrate imagery of spines. Reconciling religious myth with zoology, Wilbur gives the ferns the proleptic faculty of loving and at the same time demythologizes the *appareat arida* of God's command into an oceanic roar. An aqueous, refracted green thus solidifies before our eyes into the vital green of life itself.

"In a Churchyard" (NCP, p. 127) also finds comfort in the idea of evolutionary purpose, though its "solemn stillness" is far removed from the windy exhilaration of "Fern-Beds." Indeed Wilbur starts his poem in homage to Gray's great night piece, richly paraphrasing the line on the ocean gem. He is typically alert to its Berkeleyan quality, fascinated as always by the fact that being can be conferred by consciousness. Just as Gray's visual imagination is able to function in a void of sense experience, so (Wilbur points out) can the aural imagination. The conceits locate this sensory void in the vacant skulls and in the clefs of dead ears (combining cochlear form of the ear with the cochlear symbol of tonality); and yet of course the percipient is the poet himself, who implants these puzzles in the "minds" of the dead. Not content with having offered advice to prophets and sleepers, Wilbur here addresses the contents of the grave!

His atemporal, asonic music is in physical terms as inconceivable as Keats's "ditties of no tone" (*Poetical Works,* p. 209), and yet as an extrapolation it does make paradoxical sense. Music construed as purposive pattern can exist in the inner ear, as it must have done for Beethoven, and can thus be realized in the mind. The spiritual semblance has an existence involved with, and yet separate from, the physical experience from which it derives, just as Gray's rose and gem exist for the mind that imagines them in the absence of sense data. Wilbur is thus leading us outward by a series of concentric circles—from the mock-aurality of the silent grave to the notional aurality of a silent bell, which itself is made into an anagogic symbol. As the first of the four last things, it quiets and cancels all that comes within its compass.

Wilbur drives this home with a typically domesticated treatment of myth, presenting Charon's ferry as a motor launch. The tolling of mortality in each of our souls subordinates everything to our obsession with death, even to the detriment of savoring present beauty. The *contre rejet* of the phrase "set free" makes this clear. At first we read it as means to liberation ("setting free" in the abstract), and then, as it gathers its object, we realize that it is disencumbering us of our concrete surroundings. This might do quite well in Marvell's garden, where the soul casts "the Bodies Vest aside" (*Poems and Letters,* p. 52), but it does not accord with Wilbur's bedded, "regionalist" sense of the spirit.

Recalling the treatment of God's *appareat arida* in "Fern-Beds," we realize that the boom in the penultimate stanza functions as the indicator of a divine purpose. It does not cancel the accidents of birds and vestry windows, but rather contains such details and invests them with meaning. Human words are caught up into the creating and sustaining Logos. For Wilbur the sublime, traditionally vast and inexpressible, can be apprehended only through what we *are* able to grasp. That New England churchyard is reestablished after the poet's metaphysical flights, and he finds his anchorage there.

A similar kind of statement is made by "Seed Leaves" (NCP, p. 129) which can be read as a regionalist emblem. Being entails definition; there can be no life without a body. Wilbur's first stanza reads like a kenning, his reference to "something" left deliberately vague and the identity of the plant uncertain. He has admitted that the poem "seemed to have enough Frost in it so that [he] could honestly dedicate it to him and call it a memorial poem" (Robert Frank and Stephen Mitchell, "Richard Wilbur: An Interview," in *Conversations,* p. 24), and yet to my mind it is a good deal less like Frost than many poems in *The Beautiful Changes.* The abrupt trimeter couplets have more the flavor of Lear's poem on the Akond of Swat, which is full of jumpy, additive rhymes: "Does he sit on a stool or a sofa or chair, or SQUAT / The Akond of Swat."[9] Additional notes of quirkiness are supplied by feminine rhymes that wriggle in the clamp of the three-foot measure and syncopated statements that defy the couplets to catch them. The one-line rider at the end of the stanza has an effect of laconic doggerel.

The seedling's staple has to straighten in time, and the crown of the plant to be distinguished from its root. Implicit in this spatial end is a teleological one, the end of growth, ideas neatly dovetailed by the poet in the first line of stanza two. But even at this stage the cotyledons give no evidence of their adult destiny, their unserrated margins and fleshy texture like the gums and flesh of a baby. If life were simply infancy magnified, there would be no differentiation, none of the specificity and uniqueness that are the stuff of being. Just as the "undead" pursue existence for its own sake but fail to live in the fullest sense, so the seedling might wish to escape the pain of life and take refuge in the bodiless sublimity of myth, a fate exemplified by the Nordic world ash, phrased with discomfiting bombast. This is not Wilbur's option, however, for even at his most ideal and mythic, he always makes contact with the real. Indeed, it is only with the security of roots, the security of knowing and being known, that regionalists can essay the ideal realm. The teleology of life is finally death, but death that releases the individuated being into a universe that, unborn, it never would have known. In my end is my beginning, and in my beginning is my end. Even at the moment of definition, the plant diversifies and begins to encompass the skies.

Like the seedling, the following poem ("In the Field"—NCP, p. 131) also takes aim at the sky. The definite article of its title refers to a particular New England meadow, but also carries its idiomatic charge of "experiencing at first hand." The field ultimately earns its definite article because it becomes a specific, measurable field—a field of *Lebenslust,* a yearning for life both temporal and eternal that centers on the heart of humankind. At the start of the poem, the meadow is only incidentally present, and the poet and his wife only half-conscious of the grass. This brushes their legs with a hint of mortality (1 Peter 1:25 comes to mind) and is further devalued as the dregs of a cup otherwise filled with heady starlight. Even here, however, there is a hint of imperfection when a sublunary object, a pine tree, blots part of a constellation. The appointments to which the poet refers in stanza two are deliberately ambiguous, suggesting the magisterial furniture of a public hall and also the appointments of diary. Whether taken as appointments of space or of time, they supply only passing comfort.

At first the Wilburs delightedly trace out stellar patterns, seeing in their fixture a permanence not only more lasting than bronze but even *poese perennius*. However, delight gives way to despondency when they remember that those patterns are projected, untrue in the logical sense and untrue in the geometric sense as well. Old measurements no longer apply, for the stars, once conceived as immobile, are in fact rushing outward from the cosmological big bang (though Wilbur, some decades before the "proof" supplied by the Hubble telescope, hedges his bets with the pulsating theory). The void left by the dismantled Ptolemaic scheme is rendered as a version of chaos, the stars dashed as from a fallen printer's form, although Wilbur no doubt also uses "type" and "form" for their aesthetic implications of shape and control. (One is faintly reminded of the change from ecstasy to disillusionment in another nocturne—Howard Nemerov's "The Goose Fish."[10]) A universe reconceived as an aleatoric cast from the hand of a gambler is altogether more discomfiting—Einstein himself recoiled from the idea— than one inhabited by anecdotal shapes and figures, and the stargazers have accordingly to reorient themselves. This entails adjustment, a truing in both senses, although the verb "chat" in stanza ten trivializes and "tea-tables" the inconceivable, as though the spectators were bravely whistling in the dark. It is one thing to reel off facts, however, and another to absorb them imaginatively. The talk of Antares' red gianthood is at first as anecdotal as the vision of Andromeda and Arion: Wilbur turns the disparate size of planetary orbit and stellar diameter into a boxing match between cosmic bully boys. Then the imagination goes cold trying to picture a spent universe, and a sense of mortality supervenes. The couple returns to a bedroom, where, like the blessing of an epithalamion, a lamp shines more brightly than the stars.

This is the turning point of the poem and prepares us for the daylight affirmations that come with the dawn. Here it is not chill abstraction but regional immediacy which fills the poet's mind. As he watches his wife gather flowers in the same field that witnessed their terror, he sows it with terrestrial constellations, connecting the colors of the meadow blooms with the spectral classes of stars. White daisies become a milky way, hawkweed yellow and red giants, while the heal-all could signify the "extremely youthful pleiades cluster, displaying its typical hot blue colour"[11]—for why otherwise would its blue be a "minor" one? The infinity of the universe and its apocalyptic destiny cannot be known, but the infinity of human yearning can, the yearning for a mode of life more permanent than that of the universe. But even as he adopts this posture of faith, Wilbur—ever bifocal, even at moments of affirmation—concedes that science will find his solution irrational. Even so, he casts his *credo* in the teeth of skepticism.

"A Wood" (NCP, p. 134) also acknowledges skeptical alternatives to the vision it affirms. The poem bears comparison with Wilbur's "Still, Citizen Sparrow" and also owes something, perhaps, to Cowper's *Yardley Oak*, in which the poet also shifts from description to fable. But whereas Cowper focuses on the oak as an emblem of mutability, Wilbur has a different moral to draw—pluralism in preference to a dominant mode, coexistence above hierarchy. For sensibilities impressed only by sublimity, by epic rather than lyric, by cathedrals rather than chapels, the wood is conceived in terms of its dominant trees. Converting the allegory, we are able to see that while Wilbur is generous enough to concede the traditional standards for "major" poethood—voluminousness, the assay of lengthy forms—he is conscious that grandeur has its costs. William Heyen has pointed out that " 'Distinguish' works in two ways: in the sense of seeing (reading) at all, and in the sense of honoring."[12] "Adumbrator" also has a dual implication: it casts shade, but it also renders sketchy. Big strokes are sometimes blunt strokes. If the sun stands for poetic inspiration, then the very existence of flora in the understory shows that it sustains and creates a variety of forms.

The next stanza is a regionalist record of plants that might otherwise be overlooked, but which achieve a humble beatitude and exemplify a courage that the quiescent trees above them lack. Wilbur draws a fabular conclusion in the final verse, using a pararhyme for "spirit" to show how even the most ambitious literature falls short of its platonic ideal. A failure to recognize decorum as the Augustans conceived it (propriety in the sense of suiting style to purpose) also serves to make the critic "properly" foolish in a quite different sense.

As if to prove his point, Wilbur places an intimate, undemonstrative elegy alongside "A Wood." "For Dudley" (NCP, p. 135) approaches its ostensible subject, death, by tacking from concrete object to concrete object. It is only once Wilbur has apprehended real sunlight on a real table that he is able to clear his throat and amplify his discourse. As always, myth is summoned without effort into a familiar setting, and we shift from a Vermeer-like tableau to the gloom of Hades. The Homeric notion of immortality is a sunless, sapless one, and it is not surprising that Achilles should say "Put me on earth again, and I would rather be a serf in the house of some landless man, with little enough for himself to live on, than a king of all these dead men that have done with life."[13]

As a poet deeply attached to the things of the world, Wilbur gives his partial assent to this. Partial only, for the infinite other borders on and colors our daily lives. However, the "quick" (or life-giving) sunlight modulates in the last line to a more radiant vision of eternal life, the *lux perpetua* of the Requiem Mass. It is correlated with the physical sun's withdrawal, in contrast with the Homeric myth that has been aligned with its first streaming in.

"Running" (NCP, p. 137) is a suite rather like "Looking into History"— three discrete pieces in the same key (or its relative minor). The gerund-title is perfectly embodied in the first poem, an experience of speed so intense that it has remained even when memory of its context has vanished. The route of the twelve-year-old boy across the farm is recalled with regionalist precision, but other details of the occasion have already begun to blur. Here the race has issued in raciness—an energetic dishabille of speech that sanctions the vivid whacking and the spanking and the slight syntactic solecism of an adjective-cum-adverb ("right"). It is the voice of the twelve-year-old Wilbur, caught, like his movements, in a near-mystic "spot of time."

The second section takes up the story many years later, and the poet, now a father, is watching a marathon with his son. The purposeful running of the first has yielded to sedentary spectatorship, the restless mobility of the athlete to the restlessness of dissatisfaction and boredom, while "appease-ment" hints at an unhealthy, narcotic "appeacement" in the men who are shamed by the energy and dedication of the runners who pass them. In a strange way, the perspective on the runners serves to recapitulate the transition from heady youth to age. They seem at first to be small, but soon, with something like a visual Doppler effect, they burst upon the scene as men, a fact which the phrasing detaches and throws into prominence, just as the winner's resting in his will rebukes the will-less, restless spectators. Kelley stamps on the sun with a momentary sense of omnipotence, of conquering time. This recalls comparable moments in Donne's "A Lecture upon the Shadow" and even W. J. Cory's famous paraphrase of Callimachus—"how often you and I / Had tired the sun with talking and sent him down the sky."[14]

Callimachus's epitaph might in turn (and at a pinch) have suggested the Heraclitean flux in the final poem, where the whole universe is likewise seen to run, subsuming the speaker in its movement. He has been jogging and is forced now to walk. In his vigilance he notices farmland like that he sped through as a child, land that is no longer fruitful. Yet its very exhaustion allows aspen and pine to repossess the deforested tract, just as the depletion of his own strength is countervailed by the vitality of two boys—Henry Taylor says they are Wilbur's sons ("Two Worlds Taken as They Come," p. 97). These run along with an abandon very like his own at the age of twelve, and he watches them without envy, passing on the experience as if it were a sort of baton in a relay race. It is only people who have failed to give them-selves wholly to experience (the undead) who allow their lives to be deflected into circuits of meaningless habit, turned in by morbid introspection. The speaker then bluffly hails his readers and invites them on a walk—a strategy that recalls Frost's invitation in "The Pasture." It is in moving forward to meet death, not in deflection or stagnation, that our human destiny is realized—a New England credo reaching as far back at least as Longfellow's "Excelsior." Wilbur is not foolhardy or undignified, however. Having known the exhilaration of the run, he surrenders it in a dignified, unconditional ceremony of transmission to the hungry generations that are about to tread him down.

The same stoic dignity informs "Under Cygnus" (NCP, p. 140). We are familiar with poetic contemplations of death, those unwavering proleptic epitaphs composed by those who have no fear of the end. One thinks of *Hamlet*, Gray's *Elegy*, Christina Rossetti's sonnet "Remember me when I am gone away," and Yeats's Irish airman. "Under Cygnus" belongs to this tradition, but in other respects it is unique. There is surely no other poem that has the solar system as its speaker. Wilbur has cast it in the form of a kenning, tossing off paradoxes in the opening stanza in the manner of Symphosius' *griphi*, which he has twice felt a compulsion to translate. Samson is a type of Christ, and so is hell-defying Hercules. It is through heroic submission that purpose is achieved, the kind of brisk walk that the older Wilbur adopts at the end of "Running."

By synergism the aspiring soul helps Providence forge its destiny, shaped not only by the active flight of the galaxy away from the big bang, but also by the positive curvature of space, and by the thrust of its rotation. This is conveyed in the emblematic ritual of the second stanza, where sword and cross, Pauline and soterial symbols, collapse into each other, and each in turn is subsumed to the brave death-song of the swan. Here the poet seems to allude to the heroic, active passivity in Keats's "Ode to Melancholy," which also has a decor of pendant trophies. He also uses the swan myth to carry the ordering assertions of art to the very threshold of its own extinction. Far from being a passive predestinate of forces beyond its control, the solar system claims to have been their resolute author, stepping behind the *ananke* of the stars.

"Thyme Flowering among Rocks" (NCP, p. 142) reads like a watercolor title, but the poem itself is much more like a versified botanical plate. Metaphor, imaged through the emblematic formality of a Japanese sand garden, is put in abeyance, and the plant is described systematically and rigorously, as by a field botanist. It seems straightforward enough, even if the tercets, haiku-like (as Henry Taylor points out—"Two Worlds as They Come," p. 91), do create a picture of leaves paired rhymingly on either side of a rachis. However, in this poem, as in so many others, Wilbur is trying to show that even in simplification there is complexity, and infinity even in limitation. As much as Matsuo Basho, whom he quotes at the end of the poem, Wilbur is a poet of *sabi*, defined by the *Encyclopaedia Britannica* as "love of the old, the faded and the unobtrusive."

To describe even a simple herb is finally to arrive at at its indescribable

haecceity, and the spindly little plant suddenly becomes as complex and in-
decipherable as a rainforest. The sublime is present at the end of a micro-
scope as much as at the end of a telescope. At this moment of imaginative largesse, figurative language is readmitted, although it has been
skulking in the ricketty implications of "rachitic" (for "rachial") and half-
alive in the "trumpets" of the thyme. The swimming head that tries to understand what it has so scrupulously described is compared to a bathysphere
that cannot comprehend the ocean into which it is dunked, its spherical
shape half picked up in the craning of the head. It is craned because it has
been peering into rocks, but it is also craned by its enclosure in the cranium.
Even the most uncompromising regionalists will have transcendence thrust
upon them.

"A Miltonic Sonnet for Mr. Johnson on His Refusal of Peter Hurd's
Official Portrait" (NCP, p. 144) does what other sonnets have done
(Wordsworth's "England, 1802," for example)—it measures present corruption against past glory. Milton himself is Wordsworth's yardstick for a lack-
luster and venal society; Jefferson (a Renaissance "man") supplies Wilbur's
with a touchstone when he confronts the crudity and philistinism of L. B.
Johnson. The sonnet is presumably "Miltonic" because, like many of Milton's, it is an occasional piece, conceived in the warmth of indignation (e.g.,
"On the Late Massacre in Piemont"). Wilbur might also have had the sonnet "On the Lord General Fairfax at the Siege of Colchester" in mind, since
it speaks of Public Faith's being "clear'd from the shameful brand / Of
Public Fraud" (*Complete Poems and Major Prose*, p. 160), the germ of the
conceit by which Wilbur converts the free world into a vast Texan ranch.

The sestet has something of the ventriloquial mockery we find in Browning's "Soliloquy of a Spanish Cloister," where the poet assents to Johnson's
feeble grounds for rejecting the picture, not at the literal level at which the
president intended them, but as metaphors for the stature and *claritas* of the
picture itself. In the *sententia* of the last line, Wilbur reverses the pattern of
literal and figurative reference, suggesting that abstract political vision will
find no purchase in a world improperly *seen*. This might at first seem to elide
moral and aesthetic issues, and so to sacrifice truth to the heady panache of
epigram. Close inspection shows, however, that the aphorism is consistent
with everything that Wilbur has stated in the poems that precede the sonnet, and in those that come in its wake. Love calls us to the things of this
world, not least to the pictures of Peter Hurd.

The poem that follows the sonnet in this somewhat miscellaneous patch
of the collection is "A Riddle" (NCP, p. 145) a riddle to which, before I
stumbled on Wilbur's endnote, I had supplied the wild answer "Brünnhilde." Perhaps my thoughts were directed away from campfires to Romantic opera by the sinister desolation of the glade, much more suggestive, in
its gaslike underlighting, of the Wolf's Glen in *Der Freischütz* than of a boy
scout excursion. That vivid inversion of darkness and radiant snow has a

metaphoric charge not often found in riddles and confers unwonted distinction on a form that has fallen on evil days. Nonetheless, Wilbur points out that riddles, like other kinds of figurative language, provide a means to getting "everything connected" (John Graham, "Richard Wilbur," in *Conversations*, p. 104). One might add, in the case of campfires—which, to be anecdotal, do not ordinarily attract me—that riddles can also reclaim alien experience by opening up the predispositions of their decryptors. Even as they supply such wrong answers as "Brünnhilde," some readers are being catholicized out of their otherwise narrow tastes.

In "Playboy" (NCP, p. 146) Wilbur reverts to the satiric mode of the L. B. Johnson sonnet, though here it is altogether less heated and altogether more affectionate in tone. His ridicule targets not only the prurient youth but also the notion of playboyhood exemplified by the magazine he is reading, for the immaturity present in the "boy" of the title is highlighted by its application to an actual adolescent, and so is the factitiousness of "play" (as it is used in the childish adjective "play-play"). Wilbur sets the lyric in a stockroom with dusty shelves to intensify the contrast between ordinary life and the tawdry wish-fulfillment of pornography. The similes of dunce and sage neutralize each other, and the subject vanishes into his reverie. While Archimedes is there to point the geometric abstractness of the body that has been airbrushed to perfection, his name also brings with it the idea of displacement, and the humdrum sandwich in the boy's left hand, balances the glamor of the goblet in the farther hand of the woman, which contingently puns on "father" and balances the mother bird image.

The poet provides an anatomy of the decor in the photograph, posed in something akin to a Wild West bordello, and stringing together tired erotic images and archetypes—the Romantic rose, the phallic vase, the sour clash of pink and vermilion, the contradiction of spontaneity and calculatedness. Indeed the inventorial stock list has been taken into the fantasy, which engrosses the boy as he has earlier engrossed the contents of the storeroom. The items here are so inconsequential that they trench on surrealism—a pose dictated purely by pornographic considerations contingently takes on the festivity of a toast; a color so shrill as to earn the figurative adjective "poisonous" becomes literally fatal to moths. Part of Wilbur's joke is to name things only for the sake of deleting them—for when, with feigned innocence, he asks if the boy's attention has focused on the background or the flesh it offsets, the self-evident answer gives his question a comico-rhetorical status, as in the cry "Is the Pope Catholic?"

But beneath the satire there also sounds a note of pathos, a pathos akin to that we find in *Madame Bovary*. After all the absurd, swashbuckling Romance, with its Jacobean word for desire ("will") and its masculinist fantasy of strength, the boy will find himself once more in his dusty storeroom. The language suggests a mystic "spot of time"; the content subverts that mysticism as mere self-abuse. We think of Bernini's St. Teresa on the one hand,

and recall on the other the roué's notorious response to the statue—"If that is divine love, I know it well." By invoking the formulae of transcendence, the poet means us to feel compassion for a being pitifully trapped in the closed circuit of his lust.

"The Mechanist" (NCP, p. 148) is an especially deft triad of couplets, taking up some of the misconceptions satirized in "Playboy." In folklore, if daisies are stripped of their petals to the chant of "(S)he loves me—(s)he loves me not," they are said to reveal whether or not a lover is faithful. But to put faith in a mechanical count is to forfeit human judgment and, in the process, to deny human selfhood. No longer animal, the prospective lover turns vegetable in the process of consulting one. The daisy observes this violation of the great chain of being and, likewise resigning her proper vegetable role for a mineral one, acquires a set of gears. What at first seems to be perfecting the humanity of the lover—self-denial—proves at second glance to be its cancellation. Hence a mechanical being infects nature itself with its own mechanicality.

"The Agent" (NCP, p. 149) is a blank verse narrative a little in the manner of "Shame," but much more colorful and varied in its expression. It centers on a spy who has been sent to pave the way for an imperial invasion. The exact locality and time is left open to give the poem the status of parable, but Wilbur does hint, all the same, that the poem plays out in Eastern Europe (in a land rather like the Syldavia of the Tintin books) and that the invaders come either from Nazi Germany or from the Soviet Union. The point is that the imperial culture is faceless, deregionalized. It could be the sterile, book-burnt, "purged" culture that Hitler foisted on Germany, or the equally impoverished program that Zhdanov imposed on Stalinist Russia. In any event, the agent is able to absorb the customs of the country he has been sent to undermine because his native inheritance is so gray and unmemorable. Set against the regionalist intimacy of the "adopted" country is the nakedness and exposure of a "drafty" land, suggesting the plains of East Germany or the Asian steppes.

This carries its own nemesis, however, for in his eagerness to attach himself to what is colorful and charactered, the agent has irrecoverably lost his native identity and runs the risk of being killed as an inhabitant of the Transylvanian town by the imperial army. At the end of the poem, Wilbur passes judgment in the contrast between the rooted permanence of the trunk and the miserable, *deraciné* being that shrinks against it, shrinking not only in an effort at self-concealment, but also by the measure of its dignified stature.

When we turn to "The Proof" (NCP, p. 152) we are inevitably led to think of St. Thomas Aquinas and his proofs of theism. The poem in question is not a proof in that logical sense, but it does amount to a sort of apologia. Wilbur has Adam speak the poem, presenting creation as manuscript proof that waits revision—a conceit apt enough for the God of the

Logos. Adam/Wilbur, drawing on his own experience as a wielder of words, asks whether a creature is compelled to love its maker. The argument is false, of course, an argument by analogy that compares animate with inanimate object. But it is necessary for the next step of the poem, which reconceives God not as a demiurge bringing the best of all possible worlds into existence at a stroke but rather as a patient artist who labors on a work.

Such thoughts inevitably take us back to the writings of Cardinal Newman, who as early as 1843 had taken the Virgin Mary as a type of the Church, pondering things in her heart and letting them evolve in all their slow complexity. Ian Ker's summary of that sermon runs as follows: "In the course of the history of Christianity, 'a large fabric of divinity' has been 'reared, irregular in its structure, and diverse in its style as beseemed the growth of centuries.[']"[15] Wilbur takes up a similar stance vis á vis the rambling inclusivity of God's plan (as opposed to a scheme of cold efficiency). He brings the whole economy of Christian salvation and apocatastasis into focus in the last line, which activates the Latin sense of *patior* ("suffer") in "patient." The *stet* clearly carries with it the standing-in of the Atonement.

Although Robert Boyers has claimed that "A Late Aubade" (NCP, p. 153) is addressed to the speaker's mistress ("On Richard Wilbur," p. 81), it makes more sense to assume that Charlotte Wilbur is its true addressee. To begin with, aubades were quite often associated with illicit love and regretfully marked the end of a night of pleasure—the anguished lover (Chaucer's Troilus, Shakespeare's Romeo) is forced to leave because there is a social ban on the love. But if we assume that Donne's "The Good Morrow" is addressed to Ann, then that poem breaks with the tradition and presents itself as a *marital* aubade, restful, contented, unanxious. So too does Wilbur's. The aubade is late in the sense that it written after a morning in bed, but it is also late in the sense that it derives not from heady courtship, but from the middle years of a marriage, which remains as vital and passionate as before.

In old-style marriages that have lost their glow, a wife might have had recourse to the standard pastimes of a suburban matron, which Wilbur flashes on to the page in a succession of vignettes—scholarship, shopping, uncreative gardening, counseling, and "self-improvement." Noon is about to strike, just as in the Dutch aubade (the *wagterlied*) the watch would call the hour of parting. And indeed the lovers do separate, but only for as long as it takes the wife to go downstairs to the kitchen and return with a love feast as beautifully painted as Porphyro's in *The Eve of St. Agnes*. While the meal items might have the glow of Keatsian luxury, they also have the outlined clarity we find in William Carlos Williams. Those pears are cousined with the plums from the icebox.

"Matthew VIII, 28 ff." (NCP, p. 154) owes something to T. S. Eliot's *Journey of the Magi*, for, like that poem, it mediates a biblical narrative from a point of view ignored by the original and modernizes the subject matter in the retelling. Eliot's Wise Men, for example, use the jargon of twentieth-century tourists, while Wilbur's Gadarenes speak the dialect of suburban stockbrokers. These are rich young men who do not even have the grace to weep at the sacrificial demands made by the kingdom of heaven, men who have faith in materialism. Where Eliot's Magi are transfigured by what they find, the Gadarenes prefer insanity to material loss and urge Christ to leave in harsh, peremptory slang.

Although Wilbur has hailed the organizational skill of William Smith (the compiler of *Walking to Sleep*), I find that "Matthew VIII, 28 ff." makes an odd neighbor for the birthday poem that flanks it—"For K. R. on Her Sixtieth Birthday" (NCP, p. 155). This is a miniature genethliacon addressed, it would seem, to Kathleen Raine, or so the references to Blake and Plato would suggest. (Raine, furthermore, turned sixty the year before the collection was published.) It is a cheerful, well-turned occasional poem in the form of a rondeau, but not otherwise remarkable. Indeed, the recurring line does not have enough weight to bear continued repetition, and it even has the unfortunate effect of making the subject seem a little short of breath.

Incidental lyrics such as the K. R. poem (and a later marriage toast to one of Wilbur's sons) are nonetheless to be welcomed as humble satellites of the magisterial, "planetary" poems around which, in each collection, they seem to orbit. They project an air of intimacy and casualness that further humanizes the humane sensibility of those greater pieces, and in this respect they bring to mind the later poems of W. H. Auden. Wilbur himself has described *About the House* as being "the book of a man [who] . . . just wants to print some puttering poems" (Peter Stitt, Elessa Clay High, and Helen McCloy Ellison, "The Art of Poetry: Richard Wilbur," in *Conversations,* p. 191).

six

the

m i n d –
r e a d e r

n e w   p o e m s

(1 9 7 6)

Wilbur's 1976 volume is, like its predecessor, di-
vided into sections, one of which is occupied solely by the eponymous poem.
As before, I shall start with this, the dominant piece. Because it also deals
with the control and shaping of consciousness, "The Mind-Reader" (NCP,
p. 106) bears some resemblance to "Walking to Sleep," except that here it is
not the poet who guides the reader half-hypnotically into ways of seeing, but
a clairvoyant who tries to articulate the nature of his gift. Mary Kinzie has
distinguished Wilbur's poem from Browning's *Mr. Sludge, "The Medium"*
by pointing out that while Mr. Sludge is "peccant, garrulous, and small,"
the mind-reader is a "true *poeta vates*, the witness / maker of magic."[1] But
there is another important difference: while Browning is above all interested
in the personality of his fraud, Wilbur is more concerned with a mode of
consciousness than with character. The poems converge only when the seer
confesses that his seizures are staged and that he lies whenever his gift of
insight deserts him. We are reminded of Mr. Sludge's ability to "turn,
shove, tilt a table, crack [his] joints . . . Work wires that twitch the cur-
tains."[2] The heart of the matter is not to be found in that outward stagi-
ness, but rather in the way the *veggente* has a near-deific omniscience thrust
upon him.

Wilbur dramatizes the dilemma in his opening description. Here, as in
the earlier churchyard meditation of *Walking to Sleep*, the mind provides an
existential warranty. Even as the seer describes the falling hat and the dis-

appearance of the wrench, he is, like Berkeley's God, locating them in consciousness. Nothing is "truly" lost once it has been conceptualized. A poet is a version of a prophet, and the prophet in turn the mouthpiece of Deity, *ergo* the prophet in speaking participates in the omniscience of God and becomes the Berkeleyan repository even of things that he claims have vanished from consciousness. Wilbur tries to fight his regionalist, rooting instincts in the opening paragraph of the poem. As if to desubstantiate the event he records, he tosses in "what you will" expressions to suggest that the record has no real integrity and can be adjusted to suit the client/reader. The effect, however, is of a cadenza written out, an improvisation that has received a mental fixative. One is reminded of similar moments in Keats's "I stood tip-toe," where the descriptive procedure combines the observed with the imagined, cunningly spiced with contingencies and subjunctives, but nonetheless vivid and real for such sleights of hand:

> Then off at once, as in a wanton freak:
> Or perhaps, to show their black, and golden wings,
> Pausing upon their yellow flutterings.
> Were I in such a place, I sure would pray
> That naught less sweet, might call my thoughts away.
> (*Poetical Works,* p. 5)

Whether they imagine or document their materials, concrete poets like Wilbur and Keats cannot but give it a local habitation and a name.

But it would be wrong to say that Wilbur is attempting an effect and failing. Its "failure" is strategic, designed to clarify the nature of poetic and prophetic consciousness. The poet's impulse to concretize provides a metaphor for the compulsion on the *veggente* to reveal to others what they have forgotten. It is as much a donnée of *his* consciousness as it is of the corporealizing poet's. Anthony Hecht has written eloquently about this paradoxical side to the poem:

And he manages with infinitely graceful tact to remind us how merciful is that Greek myth which tells us that the dead drink of the waters of Lethe, and are immediately blessed with forgetfulness. For, indeed, who could bear, even in life, to be afflicted with total and perfect recall of all his own failures, his acts of clumsiness and unkindness, his foolish errors and stupidities? Yet it appears that this old man has been singled out for this especial torment. Given the exquisite, interminable anguish of his life it is not surprising that he should seek oblivion in drink ("The Motions of the Mind," p. 602).

It seems to me, though, that Wilbur is making a statement even more radical than that. It is not only his own past which weighs on the seer, but also the collective past of the race. What the world might on a superficial glance consider a gift—the Midas touch, say, or perfect pitch—can prove in fact to be a species of torture. Midas forfeited his contact with organic nature;

people with perfect pitch suffer agonies over the intonation of even the greatest performers. And prophets too are discomfited by their "omniscience." Wilbur underlines this by glossing "gift" with the near-antonym of "burden" (NCP, p. 109, four lines from the top). This has been the lot of prophets since time immemorial. Elijah, measuring the corruption of Israel against his consciousness of the Law can only cry "It is enough; now, o LORD, take away my life; for I *am* not better than my fathers" (1 Kings 20:4), while in Thomas Gray's translation of an old Norse poem, a prophetess utters her oracles with a fatigue not unlike the mind-reader's: "Now my weary lips I close: / Leave me, leave me to repose" (*The Poems of Gray, Collins, and Goldsmith*, p. 226).

Such fatigue is only partly the exhaustion of a man whose individual mind has become a *tabula rasa* for the inscription and erasure of other people's obsessions. It is also the fatigue of a spirit that has had persistently to view the human underside. To be apprised of inner being is more often than not to encounter squalor and meanness. One might imagine that glory would be the reward of inward vision, but the consequences, like those for Midas and the perfectly pitched ear, are actually catastrophic. It is one thing to have God's ability to see "not as man seeth; for man looketh on the outward appearance, but the LORD looketh on the heart" (1 Samuel 16:7); it is another to have this vision and yet to lack his beneficence and ready forgiveness. God conceives human sin in terms of the atonement, but the *veggente* cannot do so. He is agnostic, for even though he is able to view the inward person, he stops short of extrapolating any divine consciousness from his own. For him the sparrow's fall is a matter of physics rather than a measure of divinely compassionate notation, even though the poet's unusual use of "weighty" (NCP, p. 110) tilts the line toward the latter reading. Similarly, almost in spite of himself, his large capacity for attention gestures at Berkeley's theistic solution to a crux of epistemology.

It is not, however, enough that God should be passively omniscient. His correlative omnipotence carries in it the possibility of action, the redemption and shaping of the contingent squalor the *veggente* can witness but cannot change. Suffering in this context is therefore no mere tolerance, but rather the heroic enterprise of the Passion. The capacity to forgive and purify is also hinted by a resonance of the Anglican Collect at Communion: "Almighty God, unto whom all hearts be open, all desires known, and from whom no secrets are hid: Cleanse the thoughts of our hearts." The clairvoyant can offer no such purgation, since he deals with the form, not the sacrament of confession (NCP, p. 108, ten lines from the top). Lacking God's teleological vision, he is unable to perceive how the sordid can be transfigured, or how providence can pattern random events. It is not surprising, therefore, that the *veggente* should wish to abdicate his consciousness, to become the insentient items that have fallen from sight—the hat, the wrench, and the book mentioned at the start. Of course in Berkeleyan terms there is no escape from that existential omniscience, and even those random items have been imagined by a poet, projected by a seer, and caught up in the consciousness of God.

An interesting feature in the construction of the poem is the split and hanging line. It first occurs on page 106 and then at regular intervals, the projecting lower half like a tongue that, with a little pressure, will fit against the groove of the upper. This creates an image of potential unity needing only a key to lock it into place. It would be wrong to talk of this sober, unexalted blank verse in terms of the Italian *canzone,* but the short half-lines do have a faint resemblance to the *chiavi* of that form, especially since a hanging key is one of the symbols the speaker himself comes to apply to the recovery of lost experience (NCP, p. 107, ten lines from the bottom).

In "The Mind-Reader" experience is retained in minds both human and divine as an existential key, as a source of potential meaning. A different kind of retention, much less portentously treated, gives birth to the conceits of "A Storm in April" (NCP, p. 52). In "Walking to Sleep" Wilbur showed himself adept at enharmonic modulation, shifting key by contingent similarities between things to embark on a new tonality. The same effect, though it is altogether less sinister here, enables him to find spring analogues for winter snow and so smooth the transition between contrary states. We generally regard snow as something hostile and infertile, an outlook embodied in the simile taken from the scorched-earth policy of the Punic Wars. This particular storm, on the other hand, is more like an anticipatory spring, the snow having the organic softness of petal and leaf and seed. In terms of this shift, spring will simply be an imperceptible changing of the guard, not unlike that moment in D. H. Lawrence's "Bat" when, unnoticed, bats take over from the birds.

This is not the first time that Wilbur has scrambled seasons. "In the Elegy Season" took eidetic images of autumn and screened them on a winter landscape. That simple act of enrichment is reversed when, as here, he turns a storm into a burgeoning. With his customary stanzaic expertise, Wilbur sets the milkweed floating in a final pentameter altogether more airy and unbounded than the brisk trimeters that have gone before.

"The Writer" (NCP, p. 53) also demonstrates the poet's gift for novel verse forms. It feels at first as if Wilbur had attempted, like many poets before him, to render a quantitative pattern in accentual syllabic terms. But, so far as I can tell, there is no classical measure that asks for tercets of anapestic trimeter and tetrameter. Why then the rattle of trisyllabic feet? The reason becomes evident if we recall that the subject of the poem, the poet's daughter, is busy at her typewriter, for the characteristic rhythm of that machine is better caught in flurries of three syllables than in a more regular disyllabic measure. Ellen Wilbur is writing a story, and her father pauses to wish her creative Godspeed, a sort of propemptikon before a voyage. As so often in Wilbur, attention makes infinity, and the whole house seems to organize itself around the story that is coming to birth, as earlier it had organized itself around the release of a trapped starling. The final departure of that brave, resilient bird after several failed efforts becomes a parable for the writer's flight in the same room, and this in turn causes the poet to redouble his Godspeed wishes, recovering that sense of urgency and commitment that has faded with adulthood. Wilbur confesses to being proud of the colloquial tercet at the end of the poem, and there is indeed an interesting shuffle in the tense pattern. Orthodox syntax would not ordinarily allow the juxtaposition of gnomic present and pluperfect, and the solecism from someone whose grammar is otherwise immaculate enacts the jolt of being thrown back, as an established poet, to his first raw struggles with form.

According to M. Pallottino, doubts "may arise on whether a true literature ever existed among the Etruscans," but he goes on to argue that "Its total loss . . . is no valid argument against its existence."[3] In this context of doubt and speculation, Wilbur writes his simple elegiac address "To the Etruscan Poets" (NCP, p. 55). Poetry, he implies, is only partly a matter of words and much more a thing of vision. The poets whose utterances have vanished with their language are nonetheless a part of the confraternity— "still" in the sense of having been silenced by the passage of history and "still" also in persisting as notional poets through time. The couplets melt poignantly into each other as fluency of thought blends with the fluency of milk, the actual womb with a metaphorical matrix, the milk in turn with liquefying snow. Wilbur hints that his lines are a case of *de se fabula*. Poets have traditionally boasted about the lastingness of what they write; here the writer contrasts the *aere perennius* motif against the engulfments of time. The programmatic stanza break between subject and simile helps confirm that image of tenuousness and fragility.

"The Eye" (NCP, p. 56), giving its name to the first section of the volume, invites comparison with "The Mind-Reader," if only because it is concerned with privileged perceptions, perceptions otherwise unavailable to human sight. Here the enhancement is supplied by binoculars rather than by clairvoyance, but the effect is the same, viz., the bestowal of illusory godhead. The speaker finds himself on a Caribbean island and, like another island denizen, becomes the monarch of all he surveys. The greater part of the poem comprises a catalog of the items onto which his binoculars latch— the crowns of palm and banana, a holiday couple on a terrace, the presence of what might be the *Queen Elizabeth* in the bay. Wilbur has chosen couplets to fragment and tessellate the perception, an effect further enhanced by the faceless metonymy that reduces a man and a woman to the shoes they wear. His absorption in these minutiae is so great that he keeps on for an hour without any mention of wrist fatigue—a feat which, to this ornithologist at least, suggests an astonishing strength of arm!

When the speaker is done, he too is astonished by his fascination. It could be accounted for in regionalist terms—that desire, even in a cosmopolitan resort, to encompass a setting in all its fullness. But the reasons Wilbur himself adduces are many and form the kernel of the poem. Trivialities of the passing scene can be very entertaining, as the chorus of dragoons informs us at the start of *Carmen,* and even Wilbur's agent confesses to pleasure in the *passeggiata* (NCP, p. 149). Then there might be motives of gastronomic voyeurism, the desire to analyze the contents of that tall tropical drink to the last detail of flavor; as well as voyeurism of a less savory kind. More important still is the aesthetic issue of framing, of detaching objects from their context in order to canalize the attention. The entire scene is encompassed by the poet's analytic view as it were from alpha to omega, except that the English alphabet supplies the abecedarian imagery here. (It is the presence of that *Z,* incidentally, that leads me to assume that the legend on the ship is *Queen Elizabeth.*) The hint at the Revelation of St. John prepares us for the sense of godhead to which the eye, thrown forward by the focal point of the binoculars ("promoted" as in *pro movere*), feels itself "promoted" in the hierarchical sense. But, like the mind-reader's, that delusive state is predicated on a loss of individual identity, as the startling swing from godhead to nonexistence makes plain.

Part 2 of "The Eye" does penance for this rather fruitless and indulgent survey. It shakes off the lax, self-promoting milieu of internationalist *dolce vita* and urges the eye not to luxuriate in glamor, but rather to view all things with an inclusive, agapic love. St. Lucy is invoked because, according to Dante, she is "the foe to every cruelty,"[4] and Wilbur implies that the eye is cruel to all that is not superficially attractive. It blinds itself to whatever it cannot apprehend as beautiful, so turning sensuous percept into non-sense. The other meaning of nonsense is relevant as well, the nonsense of which spoiled and self-indulgent people are guilty—groundless whims and ridiculous fancies. Wilbur uses a rough, unrhymed stanza to contrast with the smooth, compacting couplets of part 1. Dante's Lucy is moved to compassion by the plight of a mortal, and Wilbur begs her intercession for the identical gift. Gone are the trappings of cosmopolitan leisure—its tropic settings, its luxury liners—and in their stead a drooling commuter, a crippled man, and a blind woman. The prayer is twofold: a prayer for self-knowledge and a prayer for a moral rather than merely superficial vision. What in part 1 had been an illusory inclusiveness gathering its selected data into alphabetical order becomes in part 2 a genuine encompassment, an enriched, spiritualized vision.

"Sleepless at Crown Point" (NCP, p. 58) is a haiku that probably dates from the same Caribbean holiday as "The Eye." Like most of its kind, it is so spare and resolved and balanced that it leaves the critic with little to say, unless it were to admire the pun on cape-work, which takes the geographical cape up into the garment and the transference of motion which has the land move energetically into a yielding sea. Bruce Michelson, on the other hand, gives it an allegorical interpretation—not strictly admissable in the orthodox haiku, but interesting nonetheless: "For three decades Wilbur's head-land, that wakeful, witty sensibility of his, has been lunging into dark, vaporous, disheveled places. Everything takes place on the border between light and shadow; it is no good if you go to sleep at your crown point and never go sleepless into the dark; it is no good if you go out there and never come back again."[5]

"Piccola Commedia" (NCP, p. 59) also proves to be a touch inscrutable. In it Wilbur has incorporated a part of his travels in early manhood, some of which earlier figured in "Water Walker." It brings the dialogue of *The Wasteland* to mind insofar as it marshals dialectal speech into formal verse, and also at the same time it recalls the pregnant, inconsequential drift of a Robert Altman film—*Thieves like Us*, say. Alongside a Kansas highway a Rabelaisian woman directs the speaker into the tourist cabin. Here he encounters her daughter (or worse?), a girl like that in the centerfold of "Playboy." The poem, we discover, is meant to exorcise a moment of lust, its manipulative coldness counterpointed by the heat of a Kansas summer. The disjunctive "But" in the final stanza has the suddenness and sharpness of the cry at the end of "She dwelt among the untrodden ways," where it also takes a past event into the experiential present. Wordsworth's is a cry of pain, Wilbur's a cry of relief at somehow having escaped this latter-day "Bower of Bliss."

If the little comedy of "Piccola Commedia" turns on the littleness of lust, "A Wedding Toast" (NCP, p. 61) is a hymn to the generous abundance of love. In reading the miracle of Cana as a symbolic statement, Wilbur follows the trend of most recent exegetes of the Gospel of St. John (a trend deplored by C. S. Lewis, incidentally, in *Christian Reflections*).[6] Here, for example, is the exegesis of John Marsh:

> The wedding feast lacked wine, not water; yet it is precisely to the water, concerned with the admission to the feast by purification, that Jesus turns to supply the deficiency of wine. And this is the significant part of the miracle. That which had, as water, never been able, and never would be able, in any quantity, large or small, to prepare men by an adequate purification to enter worthily even into an earthly marriage or union of persons, was to turn, in the presence of the true bridegroom, and by his grace and power, into the very substance of the joy of the divine marriage between God and his people.[7]

Since he is a poet and not a biblical scholar, Wilbur gives the miracle his own symbolic slant. St. John regards water, even lustral water, as something far inferior to wine; Wilbur knows its quotidian importance. It is humble water not wine that he wishes on his son and daughter-in-law, water regarded with that reverence for ordinary things for which he prays in "The Eye." Only when the soul is properly disposed will the sacramental value of unremarkable things become clear—an obvious corollary of a regionalist vision.

"March" (NCP, p. 62) is one of those seasonal vignettes that crop up in all Wilbur's collections—crisp, narrowly observed, quasi-imagist poems. The musical analogue for such morceaux would be Tchaikovsky's *Seasons*, Op. 37b, a suite encapsulating each month in a clear (and clarifying) musical statement. For Wilbur, the piquancy of March lies in the miniature autumn it inlays at the start of spring. Beech foliage often clings brownly to the branch long after other deciduous leaves have fallen. It takes a March wind to dislodge it before the advent of the new growth. Wilbur images the leaf movement as that of migratory birds, miniaturized to fit a New England meadow, which, because of its remnant snow, he accordingly presents as tundra. The crux of the poem lies in the last stanza, however, where the birds themselves are treated anagogically (rather as Marvell treats his bird in *The Garden*)—transfigured souls awaiting the resurrection of spring. There is nothing in the landscape of snow and heatless sunshine to warrant any belief in the imminence of life; it takes a prophetic leap of faith to bridge sensory evidence and future events.

Whereas "Walking to Sleep" explores the hypnagogic state, "In Limbo" (NCP, p. 63) examines the hypnopompic. It presents the disconnectedness that most of us have felt at the point of waking, and which a Freudian would no doubt describe as the superego's gradual ascendancy over the id. Since so much of the collection has been given over to meditations on sight, one is at once arrested by the formless dark in which the poem begins. Milton's account of Limbo in *Paradise Lost* might lie in the background of the poem, for it too has vanities that rattle in the dark:

> A violent cross wind from either Coast
> Blows them transverse ten thousand Leagues awry
> Into the devious Air: then might ye see
> Cowls, Hoods and Habits with their wearers tost
> And flutter'd into Rags, then Reliques, Beads,
> Indulgences, Dispenses, Pardons, Bulls,
> The sport of winds
> (*Complete Poems and Major Prose*, p. 270)

The fragments in Wilbur's consciousness, on the other hand, are not the trappings of Catholicism, but bits and pieces of his past life, from a boyhood holiday on the coast of Massachusetts, through his ramblings across America (the South, perhaps?), to his early manhood during World War II.

Some of this disparate material figured in "Water Walker," but there it was ordered and steadied by a Whitmanesque "I." "In Limbo" differs in showing no continuity or existential completeness; there is only the clamor of semblances to self. Pretenders are invariably the cause of wars, wars fought to secure a dubious succession to a throne. Here that "throne" is the true, the actual, identity of the speaker. Not only does he desire the warring selves and personae to make peace with each other, but also to fuse and integrate, for the etymon of "atonement" is "at one."

But even as he prays for unity, he finds his petition counterpointed by a babel of voices as various as the reified versions of his past self. The monism he is seeking is impossible this side of paradise. Two Latinisms enhance the meaning in the last three lines of the third stanza (NCP, pp. 63–64)—the invention of discovery (as in *invenire*) and the infancy of speechlessness (*infans*). Only in death can the flux of being solidify, and only in purgatory can the soul be mended. Human language is inadequate to the task, "breathless" in the asthmatic and the mortal senses of the word. The howl that demands the world is of course the cry of the redeeming Word, made dumb by his nativity, for in that howl the reclamation of humanity begins.

The poem has hitherto focused on unidentifiable objective sounds and on the incoherence of the speaker's past objective selves. Stanza 4 repeats these disorientations in subjective terms, presenting the combined breaths of the poet and of his wife as a twisted susurrus, and recapitulating the history of their marriage as that of life itself. The sounds resemble the male sperm in its frantic efforts to beat toward the ovum. As in other poems, a veiled reference to Berkeleyan thought in the final stanza helps the poet regain his sense of being, aware at last that the effort of recollection and restitution is not his to make. He thus gathers and focuses the alarmed and fragmentary perceptions of the preceding four. By switching on the light Wilbur reaffirms his objective form and at the same time reassembles the scattered elements of his dreaming in a subjective coherence. Flux and continuity are in the last resort compatible terms. Even as the poet reestablishes his context, he is conscious, as he was in "Marginalia," that transition cannot be hypostatized; it can be glimpsed only as it passes. Plato remarks that while Er is granted an eschatological vision, "in what manner or by what means he returned to the body he could not say; only, in the morning, awaking suddenly, he found himself lying on the pyre."[8] The nightmarish fluidity of limbo has congealed, but its passing has tainted the stability and reassurance of home.

In "A Sketch" (NCP, p. 65) Wilbur falls back on the impressionism that serves him so well in the earlier collections. Sketches were once regarded as subordinate, preparatory exercises, as Richard Cocke has pointed out: "The study of Raphael's drawings is of particular value, since we can trace in them the transformation of the old tradition in which drawings were used simply as a means to an end, without artistic value in themselves."[9] Once that value has been allowed, however, the sketch becomes a potent means to expressive ends. The *disegni* of Leonardo, to take a random example, prove that fleeting impressions—formations in water, say—are better caught in rapid notations than in carefully worked surfaces. In Wilbur's sketch, a goldfinch darts about in a garden outside a window, the mullions and transoms of which give it aesthetic context. Of course, like all apparent improvisation, the poem is nothing of the kind and depends on a stanza so difficult that Wilbur himself cannot meet its specifications in the second verse, where the failure of "shining" to pick up "pine" functions rather like the error for Allah by which the weavers of Oriental carpets steer clear of hubris. The hanging last line gives an impression of poetic dishabille, and also perhaps of the projecting perches onto which the bird springs throughout the poem. Above all it has a kinesthetic quality, evoking a skitter, a rapid movement as much of an artist's pencil as of golden wings. Just as the golden feathers gleam their common denominator through all these dashed-off portraits, so does the rhyme, especially the virtuoso internal rhyme of each third line that the stanzaic topography lays bare.

"Peter" (NCP, p. 67) resembles "Matthew VIII, 28 ff." in offering an imaginative supplement to a Gospel story—an impulse as old as the apocrypha, as the *Protevangelium of James* and other such documents testify. Wilbur presents St. Peter as a somnambulist, walking through the days of Christ's passion in a dream of disappointment. The wine of the Eucharist, new in being fresh from the vintner's and new also in terms of the covenant it seals, has drugged and slowed his reflexes, and he perceives reality through a veil of sleep. St. Peter, according to Matthew 16:18, is the foundation stone of the Church—*Petrus/petra*. Wilbur takes this image of apparent strength and unassailability as an image of weakness, of entrapment in self, showing how human disability is involved in the very origin of the Church. Shut in by the clichéd grandeur of his messianic notions, St. Peter can exist only in a state of stony insentience as, one by one, the events of Holy Week give them the lie. A frigid conceit á la Crashaw dramatizes his emotional detachment with images of grilles and moats and gives a sardonic rather than impassioned sense to the Gospel claim that he "wept bitterly" (Matthew 26:75).

If there is a poetic genre peculiar to the twentieth century, it is the memoir poem, a poem in which the speaker describes an encounter with a well-known personality in terms that would fit it for an autobiography—terms quite different from the recollection usual in elegies, say, which presents the subject as a public figure and subordinates intimate detail to that end. Examples of the type I have in mind are David Day's "On 'Meeting' Dr. Leavis and His Wife in a Northern Second-Hand Bookshop,"[10] Robert Pinsky's "Peroration, Concerning Genius" (a recollection of Yvor Winters),[11] and Wilbur's "Cottage Street, 1953" (NCP, p. 68). No two persons could be more different than Sylvia Plath and Richard Wilbur, the poets who face each other in this poem. He is a poet of affirmation, she the poet of Thanatos. To compound the irony, this elemental conflict of values occurs at a tea party, the restful, trivial exchanges of which hint at the deadlock they cannot resolve. The poet finds himself unable to bless his antitype, whom he sees in terms of a *Tempest* sea-change, already lost to life—but that is only part of the point. Much more important is the figure of his hostess, framed in her phoenix fire-screen, the emblem of self-destruction conceived as self-renewal. Even if the tea party has failed in its pleasant normality to address Plath's despair, even if its tame pleasantries (as of brewing tea) are engulfed by the sinister brewing of the dusk outside, Edna Ward has at least reached out to her, as later, with unconscious symbolism, she will reach out *in articulo mortis*. She embodies not suicidal self-destruction but the denial of self that love enjoins, and the failed tea party testifies to her noble spirit. Hers is that quiet, unobsessed heroism that the poet has already hymned in "Lightness."

In "The Fourth of July" (NCP, p. 69) is a breathtaking fugue of a poem, its different voices all raveled up in a satisfying design. It features a technique more common to novels than to poems—the technique of simultaneous layering illustrated in this excerpt from Ken Kesey's *Sometimes a Great Notion:*

> . . . While Indian Jenny, . . . looked out through the spider web that laced her lone window and finished her spell: "Oh clouds . . . oh rain. I call down all sorts bad weather an' bad luck on Hank Stamper, u-huh!" Then turned her black little eyes back into the empty shack to see if the shadows were impressed.
>
> . . . And Jonathan Draeger, in a motel in Eugene, wrote: "Man will do away with anything that threatens him with loneliness—even himself."
>
> . . . And Lee, riding with his brother across the river toward the old house, wondered, Home again all right, but now what?[12]

This is not the simultaneity secured by a "Meanwhile back at the ranch" formula, but a different, more poignant kind. Simply by recording them, Kesey imparts coherence in his random data, a coherence centered partly in chronology and partly in the consciousness that knits them into simultaneity.

Wilbur achieves a comparable effect in "The Fourth of July." Stanza 1 is given over to an English picnic on 4 July 1862, the day on which Lewis Carroll began narrating *Alice in Wonderland.* Stanza 2 describes General Grant as, on the same day, he plans the siege of Vicksburg (a touch of Yeats's "Long-Legged Fly" here). What seems, however, to be a random conjunction is all the time being shaped by the ordonnance of the poem. The otherwise pointless allusion to Liddell's lexicon prepares us for a later meditation on words and on taxonomy; the Thames and the Mississippi are both in motion as images of irrecoverable time, and the metaphor that presents Vicksburg as a house of cards seems to have been prompted by the cards of Carroll's story. The faint parallels also set off the difference between the events: an English idyll and a tense martial atmosphere, the improvised fantasy of *Alice in Wonderland* and careful strategic plotting. The poet does not value the one at the expense of the other, for he presents both as necessary manifestations of the human spirit (the imaginative and the rational), and both contain elements of each other. Carroll, after all, was a fine mathematician, conversant with the "grammars" he overthrew in *Alice*, and Grant's scientific management of space and topography was in its turn predicated on imaginative principles.

In stanza 3 Wilbur starts on a new tack. Having linked two unrelated events by the happenstance of chronology, he is forced to admit that while pattern gives shape, it cannot preserve its data. As the rivers are endlessly spending themselves in waves, as light loses its identity at the point of absorption, so all the pageantry of life cannot be arrested by the word (though, as always in Wilbur, there is a hint that it is preserved in the consciousness of the Word). Picking up the reference to Carroll, he implies that Alice's aphasia allows her to befriend a fawn because it too cannot articulate (and therefore perceive) any difference between itself and the girl. Wilbur gives this a messianic color, as though lion and lamb lie down only with the abolition of history and of the word that is its vector. The wood is "termless" in having neither temporal nor linguistic term. As he plays with the Carroll text, Wilbur also subtly works in an allusion to Grant. In *Through the Looking Glass*, Alice does not thank the shade as the poet claims she does: " 'Well, at any rate it's a great comfort,' she said as she stepped under the trees, 'after being so hot, to get into the—into the—into *what?*' she went on, rather surprised at not being able to think of the word. 'I mean to get under the—under the—under *this,* you know!' putting her hand on the trunk of the tree."[13] Ostensive gesture displaces word (an event that Wilbur associates with paradise in "Games Two"), but there are no thanks. However, in Handel's *Serse*, a warrior does indeed apostrophize a tree in "Ombra mai fu." Thus very lightly the two threads are twined together and spun over into the next stanza, which distinguishes memory loss from a paradisal conflation of language and experience.

Alice was convinced that the tree beneath which she stood began with an L (*Alice in Wonderland*, p. 187), and it takes no effort of imagination to realize that it must have been a lime or linden tree (*Tilia cordata*). It is from the lime that Linnaeus took his name—the Linnaeus, who having sorted and named in the best tradition of Adam, ultimately forgets all that he has patterned; he forgets even his own identity. Wilbur presents this as though the botanist himself were a tree branching out like his taxonomical diagrams but preyed on by a fungus that issues in leaflessness. This emblem of *sic transit gloria* does not, however, deter the poet from hymning the fruits of art and science and history itself in his coda. The ordering of Linnaeus is cognate with the ordering of Copernicus and represents a patient, responsible empiricism; and yet the quirky hunches and gaiety of Carroll's invention resemble the imaginative leap that the astronomer took in departing from the Ptolemaic model. Everything finally connects and harmonizes. Even the surrender of Vicksburg, so remote from the present, is finally perceived as the first step in a chain of circumstances that led up to the civil rights movement, and so to the universal application of Jefferson's ideals. The poem thus ends where it began, on the Fourth of July.

After the giddying range and deft interconnections of the Independence Day poem, "A Shallot" (NCP, p. 71) seems a little flat, though smoothly written. Systematically presenting an onion in terms of fertility and generation, the poet traces the contour of the object, first by having the rhyme slip off "convex" (which takes the stress on the first syllable) and then by repeating the word "curve." Like many imagist poems, it is content with a simple apposition of object and associative image—but, unlike its many congeners, it fails to establish any priority of one above the other. Given the tender personal pronouns, we cannot be certain whether the speaker is depicting his wife in a vegetable image or a vegetable as an uxorial icon.

From the sensuality of the onion we move to the weazen textures of "A Black Birch in Winter" (NCP, p. 72). Although at first the poet plays with conceits, envisaging the bark as mosaic and shriveled human face, he is too much of a regionalist to let these distract him from the tree itself and revokes them as he did the Clevelandisms of "Praise in Summer." A mosaic is finite and mechanical, appliquéd rather than integral. And while human skin is undeniably organic, humans are mortal and have no need to accommodate a cycle of growth—hence the ironic "finish" of the wisdom, picking up the gloss of the mosaic but actually implying desuetude and depletion. The tree has both the longevity of art and the flexibility of human tissue and has to reconcile their difference. Wilbur's last verse demonstrates the tree's response to perfection, for he unleashes unruly, asyndetic phrases in a stanza that has to stretch to make them fit. But although it gives, it never breaks.

"For the Student Strikers" (NCP, p. 73) is one of Wilbur's rare occasional poems, written in response to an antiwar protest on a New England campus. Although it is hardly vintage Wilbur, it at least shows how even in the midst of a crisis, he is faithful to his tenet that prophets should persuade and reason rather than denounce. "C Minor" (NCP, p. 74), which follows the strike poem, also fights shy of prophetic grandeur—in this case for reasons of decorum in its technical generic sense. Breakfast in a suburban kitchen is not a fitting context for the scherzo of Beethoven's Fifth Symphony. It is a critical commonplace that Beethoven reserved the key of C minor (as Mozart the key of D minor) for his most intensely felt music. E. M. Forster is one of many commentators to have pointed this out: "He has invested in it deeply. If we lost everything he wrote except for what is in this key, we should still have the essential Beethoven, the Beethoven tragic, the Beethoven so excited at the approach of something enormous that he can only just interpret and subdue it."[14] Indeed Forster has one of his characters fix an apocalyptic program to the same C minor scherzo: "It was as if the splendour of life might boil over and waste to steam and froth. In its dissolution one heard the terrible, ominous note, and a goblin, with increased malignity, walked quietly over the universe from end to end. Panic and emptiness! Panic and emptiness!"[15]

Small wonder that the poet's wife should switch off the wireless and let the day begin less strenuously. The heroism is grand and thrilling, but it does not bear on the everyday life, which Wilbur proceeds to document, and which takes us back to "A Summer Morning." Like the cook and the gardener, Wilbur and his wife practice the sacrament of the present moment, as it was announced by George Herbert in "The Elixir" and reformulated a century later by Jean-Pierre de Caussade: the "senses despise mean trappings but the heart worships this royal majesty in whatever form it appears, and the more humble its disguise, the more the heart is pierced through with love."[16] It is not only Wilbur's heart but *also* his senses which revel in this framing and sanctifying of quotidian experience, offered not as an alternative to the visionary splendor of Beethoven, but as its complement. The regionalist's astute attentiveness makes possible such humble yet radiant visions as this of the Wilbur vegetable patch. How adeptly the inflections of everyday talk about the weather preface these visionary vegetables, vegetables that bring to mind the orient and immortal wheat of Thomas Traherne. Because they have been cut out of time—the poem refuses foreknowledge of any kind—they resemble the unprospective flowers of the Sermon on the Mount. That sermon's vision of temporality, its acquiescent submission to the moment, lies at the heart of Wilbur's poem. "C Minor" is faintly reminiscent of Longfellow's "The Day is Done," which relates similar sentiments not to morning but to evening quietude:

> Come read to me some poem,
>   Some simple and heartfelt lay,
> That shall soothe that restless feeling,
>   And banish the thoughts of day.
>
> Not from the grand old masters,
>   Not from the bards sublime,
> Whose distant footsteps echo
>   Through the corridors of Time.
>
> For, like strains of martial music,
>   Their mighty thoughts suggest
> Life's endless toil and endeavour;
>   And tonight I long for rest.[17]

In "A Wood," Wilbur was careful not to privilege one style above another. And even the most strenuous epic longs for rest, intercalating what E. M. W. Tillyard has called "passages . . . forced into harmony with more spontaneously composed ones."[18]

There is a touch of Donne in "To His Skeleton" (NCP, p. 76)—the choleric tone of the first line recalls that of "The Sun Rising," some of the diction is Metaphysical pastiche ("Informous"), and there is also the brusque, hectoring slang of "The Canonization." Afflicted by various mineral deposits in his body, the poet takes these for colonial outposts of a skeleton bent on usurpation. All this makes for a charming coup d'esprit, but the poem remains a slight one.

"John Chapman" (NCP, p. 77) on the other hand, combines charm with substance, being a meditation on the famous speech of Polixenes in *The Winter's Tale:*

> You see, sweet maid, we marry
> A gentler scion to the wildest stock,
> And make conceive a bark of baser kind
> By bud of nobler race.[19]

John Chapman, like Perdita, is on the side of nature, forgetting, amid his colonial projection of paradise, that nature is fallen. It is paradoxical that he should plant the apple in Eden, for the poet presents him as a figure of faith. Thomas D. Clark has written in the *Encyclopedia Americana* that it "was . . . his life of an altruistic orchardist in a day when men were seeking to claim large blocks of western land that has assured him a warm and affectionate place in American history."[20] This is also Wilbur's vision of the man, differentiated from the violators, whose waggons ambiguously rut the virginal frontier. Against the swing of the destructive phallic axe Wilbur sets the tenderness of fostering gardener, and, picking up *Kubla Khan,* makes a garden in the wilderness with the epithet "girdled." Chapman, however, like many children of nature—Rousseau among them—is affected by Pelagian error and, throwing himself on nature's mercy, reaps the bitter fruit of the fall. This mocks the sanguine hope of perfectibility, for "sanguine" also describes the rich complexion of hybrids far excelling those apples that revert to type. The play extends into "double-dyed," an adjective often associated with villainy, which here flaunts the brilliant colors Chapman's weazen apples lack and at the same time gathers up the doublet of the Linnaean name—*Malus malus. Malus* means both "apple" and "evil."

Wilbur ends by doing honor to the holy fool, whose resurrection he images as an apple tree in blossom. At the same time, entertaining an altogether more cautious view of nature, he acknowledges the need to hybridize with scions of grace the unregeneracy of the stock. "Spotted" in stanza six means maculate with sin, but also teasingly refers to the freckles on certain hybrids—Golden Delicious, for example. I am tempted also to read the parable on another level. John Chapman could stand for regionalists who impoverish their art by refusing the artifice of graft and scion. Only those artists who, acknowledging the stubborn, entrenched, resilient root and yet ready to use resources richer and more varied than those the native culture by itself can offer, can produce a hybrid both beguiling and strong.

Wilbur begins "April 5, 1974" (NCP, p. 78) with an up-and-down reference like that at the start of Gautier's "Noel," except that where Gautier
stresses the decorative brilliance of white earth against black sky, the American poet is doing something more—explaining the source of the steam that
destabilizes his sense of the landscape. A momentary disorientation engenders wonder at the ordinary, so that a natural law, the evaporation of fluids
under heat, suddenly seems aberrant. In the same way, fact is elided with
fantasy. The ground is "giving" in a textural sense (as when mud gives to
the foot that presses it), but its giving also entails the figurative idea of surrender and compromise. In much the same way, the coming out of the freeze
is the "coming out" of a debutante as well as an ejection. At the end the poet
returns us to the dissolution with which he began, seeing in his stable categories a fixity of mind. Once loosened, they allow the poem to flower.

Wilbur has an especial fascination for the saints, a fascination greater,
perhaps, than an orthodox Episcopalian ought to entertain. He seems above
all to be arrested by their commitment and self-denial, whether these qualities are manifest in an uncanonized comadre, or in St. Francis prostrate in
the snow, or in St. John Chrysostom burning in the desert. As a poet in love
with the refractory, undismissable concreteness of the world, he no doubt
feels a fascination with wholly different vantage points and keeps circling
back to the lives of these uncompromising espousers of *contemptus mundi*.
St. Teresa of Avila is the saint portrayed in "Teresa" (NCP, p. 79), which
begins lushly and erotically in the style of Bernini's statue.

Saints are very often visionary and almost as often distrustful of the same
visionary insights. Donald Attwater has said of St. Paul of the Cross that he
"was to experience such mystical communications all his life, and came to
distrust them,"[21] while of St. Gemma Galgani he writes "she occasionally
behaved in a way that she attributed to diabolical possession" (*Penguin Dictionary of Saints,* p. 146). Likewise St. Teresa, whose vision comes so close
to mingling Eros and Agape, a mingling attested by the anecdote about the
roué and the Bernini sculpture. Her vision nevertheless receives its validation
in the fruits of her life: her reformation of the Carmelites, discalced and
therefore bent on barefoot tasks. St. Teresa is said to have locked herself in
a chastity belt and thrown away the key, a (rather horrifying) austerity that
haunts the final couplet, bringing the poem full circle. Wilbur has pondered
the exclusivity of sainthood in his discussion with Aidan Matthews: "It
seems to me that it would be impossible to accomplish today what George
Herbert achieved in his day: to house the entirety of one's being within the
diction and doctrine of one's faith, to accommodate everything inside one's
experience of faith. But perhaps that's why Herbert is the only saint my
church ever made" (in Snodgrass et al., "Writers and Wrongs," p. 125).

"Children of Darkness" (NCP, p. 80) exemplifies the more familiar
Wilbur, the poet of both/and rather than either/or. If "John Chapman" is
in part a cautionary parable about Pelagianism, then "Children of Dark-

ness" is leveled at the would-be Manichee seeking to segregate nature into categories of good and evil and shore them up with myth and folklore. The phrase "children of light" occurs four times in the New Testament, but it has no antonym. Wilbur's title therefore affirms the universal fatherhood of God and the integral nature of his creation. What a false vision has orphaned and disaffiliated from the Creator is now restored. The regional bias of Wilbur's art equips him perfectly for the task, since regionalists, unconstrained by any glamorizing selectiveness, record all aspects of their region.

The poet begins with the standard topos of the forest-cathedral, reminiscent, say, of this from *Bleak House:* "Seated among these, we looked through a green vista supported by thousands of natural columns, the whitened stems of trees, upon a distant prospect made so radiant by its contrast with the shade in which we sat, and made so precious by the arched perspective through which we saw it, that it was like a glimpse of the better land" (Dickens, *Bleak House,* p. 253). Then, describing all the fungi he encounters there, the poet asks how their gothic qualities can be reconciled with that topos. His answer, after he has compiled a balancing catalogue of richly colored mushrooms, is that they are the gargoyles of the cathedral, apotropaic images of evil, not the evil itself. And even if they were, evil is a *felix culpa,* that *sine qua non* of God's salvific ends. Notice how in the final line the volition of "would" is taken up into the unchanging nature of the "wood" itself.

The remaining poems of the collection are squibs and hardly invite the reader to ponder their meanings. All their graceful succintness requires is a passing smile of acknowledgment—the application of astronomical data to the cult of personalities, so that an *eminence grise* becomes by virtue of red gianthood an *eminence rose* ("Flippancies 1: *The Star System,*" NCP, p. 90) and the kindly but sharp epigram on confessional poets whose despair supplies the only unifying thread in their ragbag utterances ("Flippancies 2: *What's Good for the Soul is Good for Sales*"). "Rillons, Rillettes" turns mashed pork into a metaphysical poser, and "The Prisoner of Zenda" summarizes a film in terms that the Kansas girl might have used ("Piccola Commedia"),[22] mixing up the characters and the actors who play them as naive film-goers often do. The lightheartedness is enhanced by coercive rhyme (rhyme designed to make language mechanically laughable): "end a"/ "Zenda" and "behavia"/ "Flavia." This little scatter of poems is no doubt meant to set up an antimasque for the "The Mind-Reader," which follows on their heels and with which this chapter began.

seven

n e w
p o e m s
(1 9 8 7)

New Poems is the most neutrally named of all Wilbur's collections. The reason is perhaps to be found in the fact that while "Lying" would seem to be the banner poem of the collection, it would make an ungraceful (not to say rebarbative) title for the whole. Even more than the others, then, this collection invites us to treat it as an assembly of units. There is no dominant poem to set the tone or to furnish an aphorism that cuts to the center of the poet's vision.

"The Ride" (NCP, p. 4) stands in line of succession to other dream poems by Wilbur, and also of those that cross the margin of sleep into waking. Like Fuseli in his picture of a nightmare, Wilbur to some extent relies on a folk etymology connecting nightmares with horses (though "mare" is not of course the real etymon of the word). But whereas in Fuseli's picture the horse *is* the dream, storming with all its potent terror into a bedroom, in Wilbur it traverses a nightmare identified not with itself but with the landscape. Indeed, the horse has a solidity and reassurance distinct from the horror of the dream that encases it, and instills a peace like Wordsworth's in "A Slumber Did My Spirit Seal." Both poets know the quiescence of acquiescence. But even though there is a Wordsworthian resonance here, it is not Wordsworth but Emily Dickinson who haunts the lines. Wilbur has caught something of her stoic isolation and her deadpan, uninflected narration of harrowing states. She too undertakes journeys into nothingness that have the semblance of a normal outing, and we sense her presence most especially in the slippage from a trot (a specific, recognizable datum) to the faceless, ontological absolutes of vacancy and nonexistence. There is a faint suggestion that the horse is a psychopomp leading the poet toward death, the pillar of the mane evoking the Israelites' fiery pillar in the wilderness. But the lyric ends before any destination is revealed, and the speaker, liminally conscious that it was a dream but still inhabiting its space, wishes to reward the unreal animal. It is a cryptic poem (dream poems often are), but it says something about imaginative engagement and levels of truth that "Lying" will pick up and elaborate a few pages later.

Gnomons are, among other things, rods that measure the altitude of the sun. In Wilbur's "Gnomons" (NCP, p. 6) they also measure equivalences of spirit and humanity. Thirteen centuries separate the American poet from the English historian, thirteen centuries and a vast cultural divide. A universal "man" of the Dark Ages—his head the repository for much learning—Bede had a mind commodious enough to find place for gnomonics. That interest supplies Wilbur with a point of contact, even though his findings at first seem little more than inert and useless facts. But, just as in the case of Rossetti's woodspurge, it is not the fact ("The woodspurge has a cup of three")[1] that is significant, but the circumstance and consequence of discovery. Testing his tables on a different continent in the twentieth century, Wilbur finds a satisfaction both human and aesthetic when they are ratified. He relives the experiment, putting both time and space in abeyance and entering that eternal present in which the laws of physics subsist, and which Bede himself inhabited when he drew up his list. There is a faithfulness in physics that offsets the transience of things whose passing it measures; and there is a similar fidelity in the human quest for knowledge, whether prospective or retrospective. The shadows fall on the specified mark and create a rhyme, a symmetry of fact and aspiration that somberly elides a post-Enlightenment world with the Dark Ages—the darkness persists—and associates the head of the poet with that of the cleric, backed by the sun as if by the aureole of his beatification.

If "The Ride" presents itself as successor to the line of Wilbur's dream poems, then "Alatus" (NCP, p. 7) belongs to that of his seasonal lyrics, or, more specifically, lyrics of seasonal transition. He reuses the haiku-esque stanza of "Thyme Flowering among the Rocks" to frame aspects of a New England autumn for contemplation. At the same time, however, he runs the stanzas into each other to convey the urgency and drive of "Time's winged chariot." The wingedness of time is implicit in the title, and so too is the wingedness of leaves. We are familiar with *contre rejets* that invite us to revise a preliminary reading of a line by giving the syntax an unexpected turn; less familiar is the *contre rejet* we find at the end of the first stanza, which cancels our metaphoric reading of the data and reinstates the literal. Having begun with a conceit drawn from warfare, Wilbur seems to extend and elaborate the parallel line after line. But leaves really do have supply lines, vascular bundles that channel the nutrients up and down. Withdrawing these before hibernation, trees literally cut the lines, leaves literally "go down" to the tug of gravity, literally turn (turn color, that is, not tergiversate), and literally fly (alatedly, not ingloriously). It is the epithet "bravely" that subverts the metaphor, since it blocks the constructions of cowardice and defeat that Wilbur has prompted us to make. That bravery also proves two-pronged, for it suggests both the valor and the *vivid* bravery of an earlier usage, as in Herbert's account of a rose "angrie and brave."

Having revoked the war metaphor, Wilbur reinstates it in images of pennons and blood, only to concede that the metaphor is beside the point. Fall cannot be imaged as war because its circumstances are incontestible—the passage of time cannot be resisted and the outcome of any attempt to do so is simply foredoomed. Human misprision might construe the leaves as soldiers battling their destiny, but their bravery is more properly to be found in their surrender. In stanza 7, Wilbur recalls Bunyan's hymn of constancy ("Who would True valour see, / Let him come hither; / One here will constant be, / Come Wind, come Weather")[2] only to revoke it, as before he let his lambent metaphor flare and fade in the uncertainties of our interpretation. While the individual leaves entertain no hope of resurrection, having been heaped on the bonfire and reduced to their mineral constituents, the tree can hope for new life in the spring. By the same token, human efforts at resisting mortality are futile, but the hope of spiritual transfiguration is not. That is why the poet ends with a fire-bush, emblem of godhead's pure being (it was from the burning bush that Yahweh told Moses that he is who he is). Its leaves have fallen but it resiliently yearns for the continuity of life that is not biological—it passes the sun, and so transcends Blake's sunflower, aspiring to an effaced source of order. We can gather from the use of the Jacobean participle "hid" that Wilbur wishes us to think of Colossians 3:2–3: "Set your affection on things above, not on things on the earth. / For your life is hid with Christ in God."

"Lying" (NCP, p. 9), which is not about ethics but about the imagination, is a subtle and often cryptic meditation on a topic at least as old as Plato's *Republic*. There a distinction is made between levels of lying: "deception, or being deceived or uninformed about the highest realities in the highest part of themselves, which is the soul, and in that part of them to have and to hold the lie, is what mankind least like. . . . And . . . this ignorance in the soul of him who is deceived may be called the true lie; for the lie in words is only a kind of imitation and shadowy image of a previous affection of the soul, not pure unadulterated falsehood" (*Republic*, pp. 79–80). As we all know, Plato has little time even for the "lie in words"—the pseudo-statements of poetry—but it is these that Wilbur is concerned to rehabilitate in "Lying."

Beginning with suave, worldly advice á la Chesterfield, the speaker condones and even counsels lying if it gives life to a dull party, for a lie in words is an imaginative construct by another name. In conversation that centers on taxes and golf (its vigor the mere ebullience of alcohol), the lie about the grackle offers a momentary glimpse of a world beyond that of getting and spending. Grackles are perfectly ordinary corvids, and yet to ears attuned only to birdies and rebates, they must have a mythological ring, portmanteaued by a latter-day Lewis Carroll from "gryphon" and "cackle." The claim to have seen one would seem extravagant only to the ignorant, as extravagant as a claim to have seen a dodo, and therefore amusing party nonsense. The speaker, however, secure in the knowledge of having indeed seen grackles—the lie relates only to recency—finds himself colluding with the unseen bird at the expense of the golfers and taxpeople, conscious that it is shrugging its dismissal of the sorry men and women who know nothing either of its real or its fictive existence. The "severance" is primarily a dissociation, but the noun is also colored by the French sense of weaning.

Bored by the party, the speaker hastens to add that boredom is an indefensible state of mind and must never be blamed on the objective world. The lie has been born of the boredom that Wilbur defines as frustrated action, an impulse to do without the passion to do properly. The poet couples making and doing in line 16 so as to pick up the gimcrack tolerance of the phrase "make do," and points out that mendacious invention (and even scientific invention) is nothing more than rearrangement of preexisting matter. The mind accesses the world to take or leave what it finds; unlike God, it cannot create *ex nihilo*. Ergo some lying is closer to omission and negation than it is to creativity.

Wilbur describes all the multifariousness of the day as if consciousness were a train slowing down as it passes through a town at dawn and then gathering speed as it reaches the outskirts. The list of data is a regionalist's list, full of miraculous ordinariness (as when the sun on windowpanes becomes an astonishment) and domesticated miracle (as when the word "usual" is inserted into Job 39:19—"hast thou clothed his neck with thunder?").[3] We know from Wilbur's Berkeleyan convictions that while a train might enter a town, it does not create that town by its entry. There is thus a double charge, both temporal and physical in what is there before us. These objects preexist us, and they are there for the seeing. The ordinary is as miraculous as the aberrant and deserves as much attention as unseasonal snow. So too does "nothing," for to perceive nothing is to confess to a failure of attention. The water imperceptible in a dry well has not been disembodied but rather transposed into the magisterial waves of the Atlantic. And of course the patron of nothingness is what Wilbur terms the "arch-negator," Goethe's Mephistopheles. He overturns the devil's boast ("Ich bin der Geist, der stets verneint! / Und das mich Recht; den alles, was entsteht, / ist wert, das es zugrunde geht")[4] by pointing out that while matter might change from state to state, it cannot be destroyed. The negativity of Satan is purely subjective—Milton had him turn into black mist for his reconaissance of Eden, and Wilbur gives this a nice optic twist by pointing out that while black might seem to be an absence of color, it is merely its absorption. Withdraw the self-obsession of the negator and the earth once again seethes with vaulting colors—"vaulting" by containment and "vaulting" also like the heart that leaps when it beholds a rainbow in the sky.

Simply to perceive, then, is to relive the pleasure the *Deus Artifex* in the completion of his task. There is poetry ("making" has its medieval charge) in the act viewing. To communicate that vision, language must become comparative and so engage with the deft fraudulence of metaphor. Wilbur prepares us in a New England idyll of catbird and mock-orange for the displacement and approximation of likening. There can be no oranges in a temperate climate, but onlookers can create their own equivalences and find the delicacy of orange blossom in philadelphus flowers. The catbird too will recur later in the poem as a type of the poet. As Anthony Hecht points out, "the catbird . . . like a mockingbird, or a poet, is distinguished as a mimic, gifted in the art of imitation."[5] That is so, but mimics who simply mimic would forfeit selfhood and in a different but comparable way become as unreal as Satan. The catbird's mimicry is an *additional* resource; it uses it to spice its *own* call, which Bruce Campbell has described as "Short song phrases of 5 or 6 notes interspersed with mewing and mimicry."[6] A lie, to be defensible, must be framed and separated from the self and so become the basis for a work of art. And it must always serve truth, whether that truth be conceived as fidelity to experience (good metaphors are apt metaphors) or fidelity to spiritual truths inexpressible in any terms but those of myth.

It is with a conspectus of these myths that the poem ends. Wilbur views the education of Achilles as integrating and resolving discordant elements in the psyche. He represents the Creation myth as the fall not only from innocence but from wonder, that ability to comprehend the everything (in contrast to Satan's nothing) proceeding from the hand of God. And in the euhemerism of the death of Roland he finds an instance of the ennobling properties of art, the mythic transfiguration of ordinariness. The last seven lines about the integrated world are themselves a masterful example of dovetailing, intergrooving items in an ordonnance like that the spirit of God drew from the waters of chaos. There is something immensely satisfying in the way the mechanical triangle of a dovetailed joint is suddenly vivified as a metaphor by the bird, which is itself a metaphor for inexpressible divinity. So too the hint of the old proverb ("Tell the truth and shame the devil") at the end of a poem about lying and the father of lies.

"On Having Mis-identified a Wild Flower" (NCP, p. 12) makes an attractive lyric pendant to the grave blank verse of "Lying." Here the poet is chastened not so much by the fact that he has made a mistake in naming something, but by the fact that taxonomy in no way refashions the world it classifies. The world, as he remarked in "Lying," is there before us, Whorf's hypothesis notwithstanding. While the speaker might be wrong, the thrush is right, uttering what it knows by instinct. It is right also in the sense of fitting (as in eighteenth-century decorum), fitting the design that *does* govern a world fixed and clarified in the mind of God.

Some of that clarity comes with distance, with the Olympian point of vantage that, as its name suggests, gives the viewer a godlike sense of pattern—pattern that from close-up might otherwise seem random and unfocused. This Wilbur explores in "Leaving" (NCP, p. 15). As he departs from a party in the late afternoon, he becomes aware of a formality and purpose that hitherto he has failed to observe. Syntaktika are often melancholy affairs, and "Leaving" has a touch of that generic sadness. One senses a connection between the ebbing of the daylight and the ebbing of life itself, and in the telescoped, reduced scale of vision, a hint of frailty and transience. More important, though, distance enables the poet to perceive gesture and stance in iconic, archetypal terms. Icons are never portraits of personalities, but images whose divinity is assured by the artist's abstraction of the human element. Their forms are frontal and simplified, designed to create religious states by avoiding accidents of flesh and circumstance, which the iconographer accordingly reduces to the level of ancillary emblem. It is enough, for example, that an icon of St. George depicts a young man on horseback; nothing more is needed for the devotional purpose it serves. In much the same way, Wilbur now perceives his friends as though they were Theophrastan characters rather than living personalities.

Distance lends clarity rather than enchantment to the scene. The dynamics of the marriage between an ineffectual scholar and his determined, birdlike wife suddenly become apparent; so too the habitual insolence of the wit and the self-satisfied poise of the belle whose cheek is enameled by gaze (not glaze). This is reminiscent of the moment in *Aeneid* 2 when the Trojans flock to the camp that the Greeks appear to have abandoned and visit various landmarks in a spirit of excited discovery. Even the children, whose play might otherwise seem random, now execute figures as stately and as formal as the choreography of a masque. From which recreational sense of "play," Wilbur moves to "play" as it pertains to drama. Human instinct, so long as it remains unself-conscious, helps us to perform functions and to serve purposes that only a consciousness much greater than ours can encompass. Gray says much the same thing about the children whom, in the "Eton College Ode," he sees playing from a distance: "Alas, regardless of their doom, / The little victims play!" (*The Poems of Gray, Collins and Goldsmith*, p. 59).

"The Catch" (NCP, p. 17) is a spirited trifle, connected with its predecessor by the notion of filling, only here it is a dress, not some ordained identity, that is filled by the person of the poet's wife. Wilbur would appear on the whole to be a shy man and, like Cowper (another shy poet before him), good-naturedly records the moments in his life when his diffidence has prevented him from rising to an occasion. The effect can be as endearing as this portrait by Cowper of his own gaucherie:

At length, improv'd from head to heel,
    'Twere scarce too much to say,
No dancing bear was so genteel,
    Nor half so dégagé.[7]

Comparable poems by Wilbur would be "Cottage Street" and "The Catch," with its confession of male obtuseness. Its comedy also centers on the exorbitance of its conceits (Charlotte Wilbur becomes an angler, the coathanger a gaff), on the allusion to the wicked queen in *Snow White* and in the decorously deadpan way in which a slang expression ("It's you" = "It suits you") is taken up into the meter.

In "Icarium Mare" (NCP, p. 20) we leave the Herrick-like world of "The Catch" for an altogether more earnest manifesto poem, which like others in previous collections sets out the poet's regionalist program. *Icarium Mare* is that part of the Aegean (named after Icarus) where the islands of Samos and Patmos ride. Each of these is associated with an important figure—Samos with Aristarchus the Mathematician and Patmos with St. John. This juxtaposition of the scientific and the spiritual, of painstaking empiricism and brilliant imaginative flight has already been made in "The Fourth of July," and there, as here, they were not regarded as opposing but as complementary visions, visions that are even interfused. Both men resemble Icarus in aspiring to a world beyond this, a world that is given the nonce name "True Earth"[8] in relation to which the sublunary world, as the real Jerusalem to the Heavenly City, is only a murky approximation. Enclosed in our atmosphere as by a sea ("All These Birds" called it a claire), most of us lack the heroism or foolhardiness that prompted Icarus to flight. Aristarchus and St. John, on the other hand, have imaginative and mental strength to equip them for such a voyage, though neither leaves the planet. Aristarchus rounds the sun conceptually, and St. John has a "bejeweled" vision, bejeweled by its effort to lay the foundation stones of the New Jerusalem.

We must also bear in mind that Aristarchus was led to formulate his theory of a heliocentric universe by trends in religious thought as much as by his measurements. As John Burnet has observed:

> The central fire received a number of mythological names, such as the "hearth of the world," the "house," or "watch-tower" of Zeus, and "the mother of the gods." That was in the manner of the school, but it must not blind us to the fact that we are dealing with a scientific hypothesis. It was a great thing to see that the phenomena could best be "saved" by a central luminary, and that the earth must therefore be a revolving sphere like the other planets. Indeed, we are tempted to say that the identification of the central fire with the sun was a detail in comparison. It is probable, at any rate, that this theory started the train of thought which made it possible for Aristarchos of Samos to reach the heliocentric hypothesis, and it was certainly Aristotle's suc-

cessful reassertion of the geocentric theory which made it necessary for Copernicus to discover the truth afresh.[9]

It is also noteworthy that Wilbur should use an astronomical term to describe the mystic transports of a visionary. The mathematician and the saint thus to some extent synthesize the values attached to the other as well as to himself. But there is also a vertical synthesis to match this "lateral" one— each experiences *from the earth* what Icarus assayed in heaven and was consumed by.

With the most delicate of touches, Wilbur reminds us of the important vertical synthesis to which these lesser instances approximate. The shed in stanza five is the allotrope of the barn in " 'A World without Objects' " and therefore signifies the Incarnation of the Word. It contrasts with St. John's celestial city in its humility, and the chinks of light admitted by its slats are the refractions of *Lumen de lumine.* Our task is somehow to appreciate the heavenly without depreciating the earth, to learn the habits of attention that all good regionalists have cultivated, and so to arrive at an understanding that is not the less real for being partial. Wilbur recalls Herbert's definition of prayer as "something understood" (*Works,* p. 51) in the third line of the penultimate stanza.

Like Marvell before him in "The Garden," Wilbur toys with the myths of metamorphosis in "Under a Tree" (NCP, p. 24). Daphne and Syrinx might have escaped defilement by changing, but were at once laid open to an intercourse more consenting and intimate—that of the wind as it takes the leaves, the leaves as they take the wind. The poet conveys this restful mutuality in the lilting repetitions of "caress." "Wyeth's Milk Cans" (NCP, p. 25), which flanks "Under a Tree," is also a mood poem, though it substitutes the chill of winter for summer ease. Wilbur is a past master of the ecphrasis, and he manages in these tercets to catch Wyeth's undemonstrative, spare mode of composition. He also plays with the silence of painting by creating a potentiality of noise, turning cans into bells whose pealing would be the sound of the season itself. This apparent whimsy is not as foreign to the painter as it might at first seem. Wyeth himself has pointed out that his regionalism is not simply transcriptive. He strives also for a symbolic absolute:

> If what I'm trying to do has any value at all, it's because I've managed to express the quality of the country which I live in. . . . I wandered over these fields, knowing the neighbors here and the farmers, and being part of them. So what is important about my pictures, I feel, is a sort of organic thing of country . . . being able to find something which expresses it symbolically, not just a scene of a beautiful countryside with a rainbow effect or a storm coming up. That doesn't particularly interest me. It's the symbolism I want to realize.[10]

For Wilbur, the Wyeth cans symbolize the spirit of winter.

In earlier chapters we have noted the way in which Wilbur often has all sorts of random and contingent details concenter on a theme rather as iron filings are patterned by the field of a magnet. "For W. H. Auden" (NCP, p. 26) exemplifies this feature in a particularly vivid way. The poet's retentive memory has accumulated an image-hoard of sensations waiting the occasion of a poem in order to be brought into relationship with each other. In this elegiac poem mortality supplies the common denominator. Items form up behind the dead poet in a marche funèbre like the cortège of death in Kurt Jooss's ballet *The Green Table* or like the figures on the hill in Bergman's *The Seventh Seal*. Wilbur adjusts the topos of Death the Leveller and offers us Death the Unifier in its stead. The images of movement from which the poem is fashioned are finally resolved in the closure of a door. The question that, according to legend, St. Peter asked of Christ—*Quo vadis*—is answered, as before, with a statement of death, but it is death couched in the reassuring language of a creed. In their tentative, twentieth-century way, the expressions of knowledge and certainty recall Job's great *Scio enim*.

"Orchard Trees, January" (NCP, p. 27) recalls the situation of "Boy at the Window"—snug spectators inside a house and forlorn objects outside. But whereas the snow effigy of the earlier poem owed its existence to the iciness, the fruit trees experience an anthropomorphic discomfort, their bark failing to exclude the cold by which—in another sense than that supplied by "fur"—they are pelted. In the life-cycle of deciduous trees, the inactivity of winter is a pause before the effort of fructification. Without it there would be no fruit, and so, in a half fabular way and in the manner of most theodicies, Wilbur hints that suffering will make for a noble character. The cold purges of the life sap, which in turn converts to vegetable gems in spring, gems held in place by green sepals of their setting. Those hidden jewels, because they are unseen before the spring, recall the unfathomed gems of Gray's *Elegy* and thus hint at the huge attention that seems to haunt a good many Wilbur poems.

In "The Death of a Toad" and in "Fern-Beds in Hampshire County" Wilbur switches suddenly to primordial time to give a new and often giddying slant on his topic. True to these established precedents, "Trolling for Blues" (NCP, p. 29) also darkens a fishing expedition with an overcast of evolutionary time. The poem begins innocently enough as the mind seeks out semblances for itself in bird and cloud and fish in the confident, uncomplicated spirit of the emblematist. Most emblematic art is concerned to pare away any detail that impedes the perception of equivalence. So it is that Wilbur, having presented the fish as a reflector, proceeds as cavalierly as any of his seventeenth-century antecedents to block out the features that get in the way of the moral, not least the instinctuality of an animal that he has presented only a line before as a passive mirror. The fish, with the arbitrary application of emblematic codes (blue = the color of truth), is offered as an image of thought in stanza 3. And as in the expression "blue-eyed boy," blue comes eventually to signify the poet's own blind exclusions, endorsing his similes by the partiality of his vision. The fish as it seizes the bait does not follow the clew to its own human evolution, but rather escapes and takes its would-be captor's imagination back to the late Devonian period when cheirolepis began the evolutionary path from chondrostei through holostei to teleostei, the family to which both the blue and the chiasmodon belong.

Wilbur's decorative harping on blue gives way to a chill darkness, and in that darkness, mere existence and the evolutionary struggle to survive. The mêlée has nonetheless furnished a prototype for the human consciousness that, eons later, so patly and confidently finds itself reflected in the blue. "Unthinkably" has, as Michelson points out (*Wilbur's Poetry*, p. 59), a hint of "unthinkingly"; and "rose" implies two inter-involved movements—from deep sea to continental shelf and up the hierarchical rungs of evolution.

This disturbing poem is followed by "Advice from the Muse" (NCP, p. 30), an altogether more reassuring lyric. It adapts the "advice from" formula that Wilbur has more than once had occasion to use, and purports to be the counsel of the "Muse" (viz., the poet himself) to a novelist (conceivably the T. W. W. of the dedication).[11] The first stanza presents a domestic scene á la Vermeer or Chardin that the speaker attributes to the novelist but that clearly proceeds from the same pen that wrote "For Dudley." Its function in the "novel" is textural and circumstantial, designed to impart a necessary lifelikeness, but even here the chiaroscuro prevents any exhaustive catalog of furniture that a naturalist might have been tempted to supply. The plot of the story proceeds but is soon subordinated to Wilbur's discourse on the form. This owes something to Henry James on the one hand and to Virginia Woolf on the other. Wilbur's advice to withhold final clarification recalls James's desideratum that fiction resemble life in its open-endedness and impalpability: "Experience is never limited, and it is never complete; it is immense sensibility, a kind of huge spider-web of the finest silken threads suspended in the chamber of consciousness, and catching every air-borne particle in its tissue. It is the very atmosphere of the mind; and when the mind is imaginative—much more when it happens to be that of a man of genius—it takes to itself the faintest hints of life, it converts the very pulses of the air into revelations."[12] Wilbur, like James before him, is careful to distinguish subtle kinds of incompleteness from the loose ends of rough, undisciplined craft. But because experience "is never complete," it is finally too complex to be expressed in finite terms: "Reduction to exploitable knowledge is apt to mean for many a case of the human complexity reduction to comparative thinness . . . "(*Selected Literary Criticism*, p. 365). Virginia Woolf, in her notorious contemplation of "The Mark on the Wall," likewise refuses any resolute and definite treatment of a subject: "No, no, nothing is proved, nothing is known. And if I were to get up at this very moment and ascertain that the mark on the wall is really—what shall we say?—the head of a gigantic old nail, . . . what should I gain?—Knowledge? Matter for further speculation? I can think sitting still as well as standing up. And what is knowledge?"[13] This reads like a parody of Pontius Pilate and rather deserves its send-up by E. M. Forster: "life is such a muddle, oh dear, the will is so weak, the sensations fidgety . . . philosophy . . . God . . . oh dear, look at the mark . . . listen to the door—existence . . . is really too . . . what were we saying?"[14] I quote this more extreme instance of closure refused in order to offset the tact and plausibility of Wilbur's version. The "credible" circumstantiality of the interior with its cherry wood table and its vase of roses cannot of itself secure the verisimilitude to which a great deal of fiction aspires—the author must confess a limitation of consciousness to avoid the drunken "godhead" to which the sight fell prey in "The Eye."

We sense that ever-present Berkeleyan Deity in the penultimate stanza of the poem, retaining and fixing all that is lost to human consciousness. Omniscient narration is all very well, but it remains at odds with reality, hence the desirability of blurring the mirror or window in the penultimate line. As we know from the end of *King Lear* ("Lend me a looking-glass; / If that her breath will mist or stain the stone, / Why, then she lives"),[15] there can be no life without breath, and the breath that inspires the fiction is also the breath that blurs a pattern too insistent or definitive.

"The Rule" (NCP, p. 32) is an odd little poem in defense of apparently capricious conventions. It sets out the rubric for chrism as baldly and as flatly as it can. Wilbur uses a deliberately circular argument in line two to create the sense of unreasoned imposition, exactly as it might strike the eye of an unbeliever. To the eye of faith, however, there *is* a symbolic purpose. The oil of the viaticum is fittingly linked to the eve of the Crucifixion, with Christ's own death. The bishop, furthermore, can claim his relevance to the events of Maundy Thursday by the fact of apostolic succession. What seems an arbitrary imposition is therefore nothing of the kind, and much more defensible than efforts to seek out the "unruled" abundance of the forest, where, thinking themselves exempt from the formality of ritual, skeptics will find (with John Chapman) that nature is unmerciful. The manchineel to which Wilbur refers is a euphorbia with a deadly latex, and although it is fabled to rain death on people who lie beneath it, I have not been able to find any confirmation of the legend outside Meyerbeer's *L'Africaine*. However, it suits Wilbur's satiric purpose to have the tree parody various rites of the Roman and Anglo-Catholic practice and exude a venomous equivalent to chrism and a poisonous rain that inverts the aspersion of holy water. "Caustic" and "fierce" also pick up the scorn and contempt of persons seeking to escape formality in the bosom of nature, only to find that formality transposed into another key. All the stages of life have to be undergone, and convention simply helps to make them meaningful.

"The Rule" is a parable, and "A Fable" (NCP, p. 33) its generic first cousin. Fables fell from grace toward the end of the eighteenth century and have never really returned to favor. Most modern attempts at the form smack of pastiche, a problem that Wilbur addresses by enhancing rather than disguising the Augustan flavor of his poem. The rattlesnake might seem *echt Amerikanisch,* but his egotism and self-applause is very much in the style of an English cat called Selima:

> Her conscious tail her joy declared;
> The fair round face, the snowy beard,
>   The velvet of her paws,
> Her coat that with the tortoise vies,
> Her ears of jet and emerald eyes,
>   She saw; and purred applause.
> (*The Poems of Gray, Collins and Goldsmith,* p. 82)

The lightness of Wilbur's tone ought in no way to blind us to the shrewdness of his message. He has already advised prophets not to rant about the arms race and, taking a leaf from his own book, writes a prophetic poem in the form of a joke. The face is designedly pat, but Wilbur creates a sinister undertow by having the stanza pattern come and go out of focus. Stanza 1 is patterned 5a3b5a2b; stanza 2 3a5b5a2b, and so on—a wavering that undermines the security and complacency the snake is meant to feel. In the *Moral,* tetrameters enter the design to steady the flux of three- and five-foot lines, and the jargon of Defense Secretaries is brought into pert conformity with the meter.

Even though "Transit" (NCP, p. 34) might bring to mind a pretty Caroline trifle, it lacks the pastiche elements of "A Fable." The title can mean "She goes" (as Herrick's Julia had gone before her):

> When as in silks my *Julia* goes,
> Then, then (me thinks) how sweetly flowes
> That liquefaction of her clothes.[16]

However, *transit* also recalls the topos of earthly transience (*sic transit gloria mundi*). Although Wilbur has had an epiphany of loveliness, he cannot, like Petrarchan poets before him, freeze it into a decorative tableau. But even if the times prove inauspicious for pastoral hyperbole, he uses it all the same in a gesture of defiant nostalgia, invoking attendant cupids and a stupefied sun as readily as any Metaphysical, but taking care at the same time to limit their application. Because the subject leaves a train of images in her wake, Wilbur invokes a conceit to turn this progress into the stages of a pilgrimage. Even as he disavows the extravagances of courtly love, however, the poet smuggles in little touches of *religio amoris*—the displaced religiosity of crux, and stations, and even beautiful feet (cf. Isaiah 52:7).

"Shad-Time" (NCP, p. 35) is another variation on the seasonal lyric to which Wilbur keeps recurring, always with some fresh nuance to document.

Here he records the signs of spring as they impinge on the blankness of winter. The first stanza is a *tabula rasa,* as flat and featureless as he can make it. By withholding all color adjectives, Wilbur secures an effect of mono-chrome, which the insistent, canalizing doublet of "bank" and the elision of river and sky compounds. The flat "intervals" suggest musical intervals that have not the energy to make their proper stretch and fall a semitone short of their destination, in much the same way that "Flat" levels out "vales."

In this undifferentiated continuum amelanchiers burst into bloom and color enters the poem for the first time. So too does harmony, for the poet is reminded of Orpheus in the featureless realm of Hades, able to compose the leitmotiv of substantial "things" even in the face of absence and dele-tion. The perception of the Juneberry flowers sets off a train of further sightings—three birds, green moss, red maple pollen—minimal, but like the olive leaves at the subsidence of Noah's flood, evidences nonetheless of life and color. Wilbur's sensuous, annotating habit of mind is uncomfortable with vacancy; he always needs a focus to help center and direct his imagi-native response. Once his frozen sensibility has been warmed by sight of the shadblow, he is able to affirm with Hopkins "That Nature is a Heraclitean fire, and of the comfort of the Resurrection." Harmony and coherence are enhanced by the way in which the poet gathers up the similes (dreams com-ing into focus; Orpheus in the underworld) that he had earlier used to reg-ister the advent of spring. The shadows are dream shadows, and the numbers in the abyss are not simply the prodigality of nature, but also the numbers of Orpheus' song, as in the Latin adjective *numerosus.*

"Worlds" (NCP, p. 37) is an epigram about ambition and humility, a dip-tych that sets Alexander the Great against Sir Isaac Newton and shows them to be "worlds" apart. Alexander strung countries together to form an em-pire, a portion of a speck in the cosmos. Failing to encompass even that, he feels a petulant disappointment. Newton, on the other hand, having pos-sessed the universe by the imaginative brilliance of his physics, is humbled by the scale of what he has discovered, knowing that (as in "Lying") it was there before him.

In "All That Is" (NCP, p. 38), falsely imposed patterns and solutions trivialize a universe that will always defy our efforts to contain and define it. Alexander tried to encompass everything, but his knowledge of the countries he annexed was the superficial knowledge of the imperialist, and it had no effect on his soul, as witness Pope's epigram—"The *Youth* that all things but himself subdu'd" (*Poems,* p. 178). Crossword puzzles are also Alexan-drine to the extent that they take the whole range of human experience as their province and reduce it to arbitrary patterns. Instead of liberating the imagination, they force it to jump through lexical hoops—the mental exten-sion of the order that prevails in suburban gardens.

These Wilbur describes in the opening lines of "All That Is," the forced patterns of the topiarist no longer innocent emblems, but rather the hellish *carceri d'invenzione* of Piranesi. Arbor vitae seems at first sight to refer to the trimmable conifers that flourish in the suburbs, but Wilbur probably means us to think also of the transverse section of the cerebellum, and so to regard this falsified pattern as being something mentally ingrained. Be that as it may, the cypress hedges supply the dark background upon which the windows light up and transform suburbia itself into the arbitrary crisscross pattern of a puzzle, light on dark. And, to a person, the denizens begin their nightly crosswords, looking at the larger world as through the fugitive and cloistered security of a convent screen. Wilbur now heaps up a jumbled pile of crossword clues, as startling as the data thrown up by surrealists but without the surrealists' purpose to give it form. Indeed he contrasts the otiose materials of the puzzle with the revelations of three visionaries—the proto-surrealist Lautréamont; Blake, who finds a world in a grain of sand, and the writer of the *Markanadeya Purana*. This records the Hindu vision of all exists, in the genesis of the great mother from the combined breath of the other gods. As Henrich Zimmer has noted, the "particularized and limited powers of the various divinities, their severally specialized and one-sided attitudes, thus became integrated in an apparition of the divine mother of the universe. They formed a single overwhelming totality, which was identical with the primeval, cosmic life-force and so connoted omnipotence."[17]

It is the visionaries' role to find experience unified at a divine center; it is the crossworders' to force experience into meaningless pattern. Infinity does, however, enter the coda of the poem, where Wilbur spots a mushroom beneath the sterile hedges. Its intricate weave of fibers signifies the true interconnections of experience: an organic multiplicity, a webwork far removed from the geometric crudity of blocks and numbers. It connects two infinities at opposite ends of the scale of being—and the connection holds. Where puzzles decompose, the universe persists in its Heraclitian exchange of energies.

It is more usual than not for positions of faith to be treated with wistful optatives. Yet Wilbur does precisely the opposite in "A Finished Man" (NCP, p. 40), which is unusual also in being a dramatic monologue conducted through *style indirect libre* rather than in the first person. The thinker/speaker feels that all the demeaning and faithless incidents of his life will be expunged from existence as one by one the witnesses die—but expunged only in the absence of divine consciousness like that suggested by the mind-reader, in the absence of a *liber scriptus*. He yearns for finite oblivion as others yearn for immortality. The perfection in the last line naturally takes up the finish in the title. This connection has already been activated by the sculpting presence of the sun, as though the man were becoming the simulacrum of himself that will eventually grace the building. But of course the "finish" that Wilbur has in mind in "Finished Man" is the finish of life-in-death—extinction and inertia.

"Hamlen Brook" (NCP, p. 41) reverses the self-centered deletions and erasures upon which the finished man has based his peace of mind and celebrates instead a zest for experience so intense as never to be satisfied. The poet, tired from the sort of jogging excursion he records in "Running," is about to slake his thirst in a stream. Even as he stoops to drink, however, his delight in the illimitable variety of the world supervenes, and he pauses to swallow the beauties around him. Keats's minnows in "I stood tip-toe" have long been famous for their minnowiness:

> Where swarms of minnows show their little heads,
> Staying their wavy bodies 'gainst the streams,
> To taste the luxury of sunny beams
> Temper'd with coolness. How they ever wrestle
> With their own sweet delight, and ever nestle
> Their silver bellies on the pebbly sand.
> (*Poetical Works*, pp. 4–5)

Wilbur's account of the inchling trout in "Hamlen Brook" worthily takes its place alongside such lines. If I had to choose the poet of the century who is most nearly Keats's avatar, my choice would fall on Wilbur. He has something of the same disinterestedness, that faculty of projection (the more remarkable for being exercised here in the face of a fierce physical thirst!). Even the ache that ends the poem is the Keatsian ache of being too happy in others' happiness and springs from a yearning to record and hymn all creation. The ache also recalls the prophet's postvisionary sense of unworthiness. Having momentarily glimpsed the hidden web-work in the brook, Wilbur knows that its complexity cannot be relayed. Isaiah's vision of Yahweh had a similar effect: "Then said I, Woe *is* me! for I am undone; because I *am* a man of unclean lips, . . . for mine eyes have seen the King, the LORD of hosts" (6:6).

The last section of *New Poems* is reserved for the text of a cantata. This Wilbur wrote for the composer William Schuman, an occasional poem to celebrate the Statue of Liberty's hundredth year. As he remarks in the introduction to *New and Collected Poems*, it is set apart because "it asks to be read as words for music, and as an effort to say something clear and acceptable, yet not wholly predictable, on a national occasion" (NCP, p. xv). Not all poets who write musically have a proper grasp of music and of the demands it places upon the word. Wilbur (like Gray and Auden before him) is blessed with both faculties, with mellifluity and with musical understanding. He knows how important it is to thin and simplify poetic textures, for as Shenstone once observed, "a certain flimsiness of poetry . . . seems expedient in song."[18]

The five sections of "On Freedom's Ground" (NCP, p. 44) alternate between a fairly loose rhapsodic poetry (we might want to call this "recitative") and tighter, strophic sequences—the "arias." "Back Then" gives us New York as it was before the advent of the colonists and presents a version of nature so blindly driven by instinct and compulsion as to know no freedom. This is good so far as it goes, but it is marred by its omission of the native Americans, who were already on shore, fully aware of freedom and almost certainly in possession of a name for Bedloe's Island. The Eurocentric claims that the island somehow comes into its own in English and that the thought of liberty came ashore (instead of being there aboriginally) are the only false notes struck by a poem otherwise remarkable for its justice and humanity. If Wilbur had left out the reference to disembarkation, the emphasis would have centered more firmly on the desolation of an *unpeopled* landscape before the crossing through Alaska, rather as Virginia Woolf in one of her novels projects London (as it was not) in its primordial past.

"Our Risen States" records the War of Independence in fine martial quatrains, a roll call of battles and leaders. But it is not all martial music. Wilbur presents the colonists as inheritors of a tradition that began at Runnymede and as mediators of that tradition to France, a moment that catches some of the prophetic energy of Blake—it is as if the hapless soldier of "London" had galvanized into action by a sense of injustice.

"Like a Great Statue" is also a roll call, but it is much less telescopic and brisk than its strophic predecessor. Here Wilbur seems to regain that inclusive, Whitmanesque vision he managed in the early "Water Walker," fusing the ritual and dignity of Binyon's "For the Fallen" with many intimate "regionalist" details. It is followed by a confession of national sins: the displacement of native Americans, slavery and exploitation in various guises. Like most confessional prayers, it ends with a resolution to amend. Wilbur here seems to have made his texture slightly more complex than in the strophic interludes, as if to invite the sort of declamatory setting that gives us ready, undistracted access to the words—something like "Pari siamo" in *Rigoletto*, where Piave's increased verbal density inspires Verdi to greater melodic spareness.

Having dispensed with sin and shame, Wilbur takes up the traditional comic symbol of the dance, symbol of social harmony and integration. "Come Dance" is another roll call, but this time of dance forms—a golden opportunity for the composer to write an illustrative medley. The title summons up that lovely little lyric of the fourteenth century, "Ich am of Irlaunde," and seems to invest America with a comparable holiness:

> Ich am of Irlaunde
> And of the holy londe
> Of Irlande.
> Good sire, pray ich thee,
> For of sainte charite,
> Come and dance wit me
> In Irlaunde.[19]

The medieval atmosphere is enhanced by Liberty's turning avatar of the Blessed Virgin Mary, invested with the traditional Catholic title of "Our Lady" rather as Hunt playfully catholicizes her in *The Descent of Liberty:* "To nip the sides and shrug the shoulders / Of our Lady's fair beholders."[20] Wilbur chooses the John Paul Jones as the final dance for his catalog, the concentric circles help to signify matrimony, that dignified and commodious sacrament. The linkage also has the effect of gathering up all the other dances and, with that, the nationalities associated with each. A linked circle seems an altogether more attractive metaphor for America than the proverbial "melting pot."

"Immigrants Still" takes us back to the Hudson, but the Hudson of 1986. The Marian image is reaffirmed, and the Statue of Liberty becomes an image of redemption, redeeming the blind, instinctual nature that Wilbur presented in the opening movement. The cantata ends with a syntaktikon designed to offset the complacency threatened by Wilbur's circular design. There is no finality, no perfected arrival for any but "finished" men. Perfection might be impossible on earth, but the will to perfect must never be paralyzed by that fatalistic assumption.

The evidence of the "New Poems" suggests that, painstaking and slow though his compositional method might sometimes seem, Wilbur too is holding course. The poetic surface remains as lovingly crafted as ever, the content as wise and inwardly consistent. Unlike Eliot and Auden, say, whose poetry documents profound shifts of ideological commitment, Wilbur repeatedly consolidates a position taken up quite early in his career. He confesses to some waverings, some wrinkles in the steady projection of the graph, but the various alternatives are embraced and tried out in the poetry without any dramatic shift of position. There is something reassuringly stable about this, something that makes the poetry as sound and as dependable as the seasons to which it so often recurs. Whereas each successive volume of Lowell seems to present a wholly new poetic self, Wilbur's own persona is always recognizably continuous with its past utterances, even though the mask might be adjusted here and there and the angles of vision adjusted. Far from constituting a limitation, it seems rather to offer a radiant testimony to the poet's mental health.

conclusion

Bruce Michelson's fine book on Wilbur came out after I had completed the first draft of this study, but even though I have learned a great deal from it, I have not felt compelled to alter my more conventional reading of the poet. Michelson's avowed program is to find "darker" sides to Wilbur than have hitherto been acknowledged. Given a Zeitgeist of infidelity and despair, such tactics make good apologetic sense. It seems that whereas pills were once sugared to make them palatable, now they need a statutory coating of gall—not that such pharmacological clichés do honor to Wilbur's fine poetry. But even if it is not medicinal, there can be no doubting that it has distinctly restorative properties, properties which should be stressed rather than underplayed.

John Stuart Mill recovered from his breakdown by studying the verse of Wordsworth, verse that is rooted and transcendent and feelingly impersonal. A diet of Byron would have had nothing like the same effect. Even with their differences of scope and tone and intention, Wilbur, like Wordsworth, seems to offer his disaffected contemporaries a similar kind of healthfulness, the more cherishable for being so rare. Michelson, with an eye nervously cocked on Wilbur's detractors, tries to preempt the charges of confinement and reduction that might be leveled against a poetry so firmly and purposefully shored up by a system of beliefs beyond itself, beliefs both epistemologically and dogmatically secure. Doing so, he runs the risk of recreating the poet in the image of a Giacometti he treats with such ambivalence:

> One could write a long book which did nothing but catalogue this side of Wilbur's discourse, this stream of language and symbol which expresses important values in his imagination, his heritage, his dread, and his hope. But because this is only part of his eloquence, sensibility and range, to read too much into the religious vocabulary of his poems is, I think, to reduce and confine his achievement unfairly, and portray his vision as more bounded and safe than it is. We should hear and attend to the religious voices of Richard Wilbur, yet not at the expense of everything else (*Wilbur's Poetry*, p. 99).

A bounded vision, however, is also a *vue racinée*. We will not find Wilbur *dans l'abime*, and it is not wise to try to win converts by locating him there. He can instead be found, like Keats's Autumn, in concrete, familiar settings—the New Jersey of his boyhood, the Italy of the war years, the Rome and France of his adult excursions, and the Massachusetts of his maturity.

Tertullian, were he canonized, would be the patron saint of people whose belief begins from abstract principles—*Credo quia impossibile est*—and figures like Cardinal Newman might be seen to have gathered beneath his pall. St. Thomas, on the other hand, exemplifies a different capacity for faith, one that works in terms of sense experience—*Nisi videro . . . non credam*. The findings of Peter Stitt and several other critics before him make it clear that Wilbur belongs to this tradition of empirical spirituality—"he much prefers that this spirituality not be abstract and disembodied, but indissolubly linked with quotidian reality" (*The World's Hieroglyphic Beauty*, p. 17).

That of course is the hinge that connects the regional impulses in Wilbur to his sacramental penetration of things. In *De Incarnatione Verbi Dei*, St. Athanasius speaks of the Incarnation as the means whereby "the incorporeal and incorruptible and immaterial Word of God entered our world. In one sense, indeed, He was not far from it before, for no part of creation had ever been without Him Who, while ever abiding in union with the Father, yet fills all things that are. But now He entered the world in a new way, stooping to our level in His love and Self-revealing to us."[1] He is careful to distinguish omnipresence (God "fills all things that are") from Incarnation, in which the incorporeal and incorruptible spirit locates itself ("now He entered the world in a new way"). What had been a generalized "filling" is now canalized and specified, and so made comprehensible. This doctrine proves an important resource for Wilbur, concerned as he is with fusions of spirit and matter. Almost all his poems, like those of Hopkins before him, are incarnations, shadowed recurrences of the Word made flesh. Confident that all matter is sanctified by the indwelling spirit, Wilbur presents himself as the celebrant of things, and thus to some extent redresses the failure of many Christians to get the balance right.

Christian thought, even despite the foundations laid for it by St. Athanasius and other Fathers, has sometimes lost sight of the synthesis upon which the Incarnation is predicated, so that versions of Manicheeism can sometimes haunt even its most orthodox adherents. Here, for example, is the pronouncement of a nun otherwise good and pious: "You know all that I ask the good God for you. May He alone, He alone possess your heart without reserve, without division and for ever. Everything else is unworthy of us: we are destined for an end too noble, too glorious, to think of resting in created things. A far grander object ought to fill these hearts of ours."[2] While St. Athanasius sees God as filling all things, Blessed Julie Billiart implies that created things are ignoble and inglorious, even though she does not quite put this (heterodox) sentiment into words. Wilbur is poles apart from her facile separation of spirit and matter, where things detract from godhead instead of representing it. The spirit for him is to be discerned in *all* its incarnate forms, discerned and glorified. Universal and impalpable Being is commensurate with a specified, regional form.

The balance is as likely to elude materialists as much crypto-Manichees, though here it is the spiritual dimension that goes out of focus. Robert Boyers has complained that "Wilbur does not really care for things. What his verse celebrates is not the hard things of this world, but the imagination that makes possible delight, its own and others' in appropriating things for a variety of spiritual and psychological purposes" ("On Richard Wilbur," p. 77). We have seen, on the other hand, that Wilbur very deeply cares for things, cares for them so deeply that he rescues them from the inertia of mere existence. Things are there in all their palpability, but he clothes them with a nimbus of spirit. This is not appropriation; it is revelation. Again and again Wilbur's poems fall back on the Berkeleyan idea of a deific consciousness that reifies the world *in spirit:* the world is there before us and survives in the mind of God after we have gone.

Conscious as he is of the inexhaustible variety of creation and aware that no single mind can encompass it, Wilbur is led to document what he knows. It is from this narrowing of attention that his regionalism derives, though, as we have seen, it is not a regionalism that closes itself to the resources of cosmopolitan culture. Anyone who has read the *New and Collected Poems* will have made the acquaintance of New England's birds and trees and flowers, will have experienced every nuance of its seasonal change, and yet will also have encountered Baroque fountains, French painters, and troubadour verse forms. Wilbur's secret lies in his attentiveness. He counts the streaks of the tulip as painstakingly as Hopkins, and having counted them (knowing they will never again be replicated) is led to contemplate the infinite imagination that gave them form. Attention, to paraphrase one of his lines, is the genetrix of infinity.

notes

INTRODUCTION

1. Gregory Fitz Gerald and William Heyen, "The Window of Art: A Conversation with Richard Wilbur," in *Conversations with Richard Wilbur*, ed. Butts, p. 57; hereafter cited parenthetically in the text as *Conversations*.

2. Wilbur, *On My Own Work*, unpaginated; hereafter cited parenthetically in the text by the title.

3. All page references are to Wilbur, *New and Collected Poems*.

4. Stitt, *The World's Hieroglyphic Beauty*, p. 18; hereafter cited parenthetically in the text.

5. Wilbur, "Commentary: WALKING TO SLEEP," p. 106.

6. Ferry, "The Diction of American Poetry," p. 143.

7. Williams, *Selected Essays*, p. 148.

8. Wilbur, "The Writer's Role: Responses to Hortense Calisher," p. 38; hereafter cited parenthetically in the text an "The Writer's Role."

9. Rubin, *The Faraway Country*, p. 157.

10. Wilbur, *Responses: Prose Pieces 1953–1976*, pp. 152–53; hereafter cited parenthetically in the text as *Responses*.

11. Wells, *The American Way of Poetry*, p. 87.

12. Wilbur, "The Genie in the Bottle," p. 7; hereafter cited parenthetically in the text as "Genie."

13. Stepanchev, *American Poetry Since 1945*, pp. 105–6.

14. Whitehead, *Science and the Modern World*, p. 219.

I. *THE BEAUTIFUL CHANGES AND OTHER POEMS* 1947

1. Rochefoucauld, *Reflections, or Sentences and Moral Maxims*, p. 41.

2. Reibetanz, "What Love Sees: Poetry and the Vision of Richard Wilbur," p. 67; hereafter cited parenthetically in the text as "What Love Sees."

3. Auden, *The Dyer's Hand and Other Essays*, p. 305.

4. Jobes, *A Dictionary of Mythology, Folklore and Symbols*, p. 338.

5. Graves, *The Greek Myths*, 1:150.

6. Jarrell, *Poetry and the Age*, p. 229; hereafter cited parethentically in the text by the title.

7. Quoted in Chapman, *Faith in Revolt*, p. 201.

8. Cambon, *Recent American Poetry*, p. 12.

9. Whitman, *Leaves of Grass and Selected Prose*, p. 66.

10. Michelson, *Wilbur's Poetry*, p. 107; hereafter cited parenthetically in the text by the title.

11. Hill, *Richard Wilbur*, p. 27; hereafter cited parenthetically in the text by the title.

12. Clark, *Civilisation: A Personal View*, pp. 14-17; hereafter cited parenthetically in the text as *Civilisation*.

13. Quoted in Fermigier, *Bonnard*, p. 84.

14. Prideaux, *The World of Delacroix: 1798-1863*, p. 191.

15. Quoted in Prideaux, *The World of Delacroix*, p. 176.

16. Quoted in Phipson, *The Animal-Lore of Shakespeare's Time*, p. 219; hereafter cited parenthetically in the text by page number.

17. Hecht, "The Motions of the Mind," p. 602; hereafter cited parenthetically in the text by the title.

18. Donoghue, *Connoisseurs of Chaos*, p. 120.

19. Duffy, " 'Intricate Neural Grace': The Esthetic of Richard Wilbur," p. 177.

20. Bloom, *Figures of Capable Imagination*, p. 48.

21. Warlow, "Richard Wilbur," p. 224.

22. Rourke, *American Humor*, p. 184.

20. Beddoes, *Works*, p. 118.

24. Flavius Vopiscus, *Dives Aurelianus*, p. 250.

25. *The Greek Anthology*, 2: 337.

26. Mann, *Death in Venice*, p. 83.

27. Kenneth Clark has noted "the scientific care with which these appalling catastrophes [floods and cataclysms] are studied," in *Leonardo da Vinci*, p. 151.

28. Pater, *The Renaissance*, p. 123.

29. Deneke, *Gestalten deutscher Dichtung*, p. 65.

30. Hölderlin, *Sämtliche Werke*, p. 240.

31. Snodgrass et al., "Writers and Wrongs," p. 125.

32. Williams, *In the American Grain*, pp. 55-60.

33. Bixler, "Richard Wilbur: 'Hard as Nails,' " p. 2.

34. Michelson, "Wilbur's Words," p. 271.

35. Ciardi, "Our Most Melodic Poet," p. 54.

36. Karsavina, *Theatre Street*, p. 177.

37. Golffing, "A Remarkable New Talent," p. 33.

38. Abbott, "Wilbur's PRAISE IN SUMMER," p. 13.

2. CEREMONY AND OTHER POEMS (1950)

1. Wilbur, "The Poetry of Witter Bynner," p. 3.

2. Welland, "The Dark Voice of the Sea," p. 199.

3. E. V. Gordon, "Introduction," in *Pearl*, p. xxviii.

4. Levey, "The World of Objects in Richard Wilbur's Poetry," p. 50; hereafter cited parenthetically in the text as "The World of Objects."

5. Altieri, *Enlarging the Temple*, p. 59.

6. Stevenson, *A Child's Garden of Verses*, p. 17.

7. Yeats, *Collected Poems*, p. 44.

8. Wilbur, "Eight Perspectives and a Poem," p. 31.

9. In *Out of Africa*, Karen Blixen (Isak Dinesen) writes "still here the shot was a declaration of love, should the rifle not then be of the biggest caliber?" (p. 230)

10. Wilde, *The Complete Works*, p. 860.

11. McMullen, *Degas*, p. 456.

12. Milton, *The Complete Poems and Major Prose*, p. 219; hereafter cited parenthetically in the text by the title.

13. Quoted in Martz, *The Poetry of Meditation*, p. 30.

14. Keats, *Poetical Works*, p. 5; hereafter cited parenthetically in the text by the title.

15. Wilbur, "Poetry and Happiness," p. 458.

16. Whittemore, "Verse," p. 44.

17. Quoted in Scott, "Typography, Poems and the Poetic Line," p. 158.

18. Benoit, "From 'The New American Poetry,'" p. 167.

19. Michelson, "Richard Wilbur: The Quarrel with Poe," p. 258.

20. *The Poems of Gray, Collins and Goldsmith*, p. 176.

21. *Hymns Ancient and Modern Revised*, p. 217.

22. Spangenberg and Beukes, "Padda en akkedis—oor twee gedigte van Richard Wilbur en Ernst van Heerden," p. 31.

23. Jarrell, *Poetry and the Age*, p. 228.

24. Quoted in Hill, *Richard Wilbur*, p. 80.

25. Marvell, *Poems*, p. 12.

26. Quoted in Hohl, *Alberto Giacometti*, p. 138.

27. The carved cliffs could refer to Thorvaldsen's "Lion of Lucerne"; Honour, *Romanticism*, p. 133. It is possible that the poet also has Borglum's Mount Rushmore in mind.

3. *THINGS OF THIS WORLD* (1956)

1. Browne, *Religio Medici*, pp. 9-10.

2. Herbert, *The Works of George Herbert*, p. 160.

3. Littler, "Wilbur's LOVE CALLS US TO THE THINGS OF THIS WORLD," p. 55.

4. Fraser, "Some Younger American Poets: Art and Reality," p. 475.

5. *Virgil with an English Translation*, p. 264; hereafter cited parenthetically in the text as *Virgil*.

6. Dickens, *Bleak House*, p. 82.

7. Donne, *Paradoxes and Problems*, p. xxiv.

8. White, *The Vivisector*, p. 420.

9. Wordsworth, *The Prelude, Selected Poems and Sonnets*, p. 111.

10. Tennyson, *The Poems of Tennyson*, p. 1600.

11. Farrell, "The Beautiful Changes in Richard Wilbur's Poetry," p. 192.

12. Nemerov, "From 'What Was Modern Poetry?,'" pp. 238-39.

13. *Iambi et Elegi Graeci*, 1:16.

14. Gregory, "The Poetry of Suburbia," p. 548.

15. *Quintus Curtius*, 1:386. The relevant passage reads "*adeo ut rex in misericordiam versa ne ipse quidem, quamquam cupiebat, temperare oculis potuerit.*"

16. Ovid, *Metamorphoses*, p. 31.

17. Aristotle, *Poetics*, p. 68.

18. In *The Norton Anthology of Poetry*, p. 1137.

19. Williams, "Wilbur's BEASTS," p. 27.
20. Webster, *The Duchess of Malfi*, pp. 295–96.
21. Quoted in Hill, *Richard Wilbur*, p. 99.
22. Chandlery, *Pilgrim-Walks in Rome*, pp. x–xi.

4. *ADVICE TO A PROPHET* (1961)

1. Anderson, *A Critical Introduction to the Old Testament*, p. 182.
2. Scott, *The Journal of Sir Walter Scott*, p. 155.
3. *The Jerusalem Bible*, p. 1517.
4. Holmes, "Wilbur's New Book," p. 74.
5. Chaucer, *The Works of Geoffrey Chaucer*, p. 17.
6. White, *Riders in the Chariot*, pp. 274–75.
7. Bowness, *Modern European Art*, p. 158.
8. Boardman, *Greek Art*, p. 76.
9. Dry, "Wilbur's OCTOBER MAPLES, PORTLAND," pp. 61–62.
10. Hopkins, *The Poems of Gerard Manley Hopkins*, p. 71.
11. Scott, "Typography, Poems and the Poetic Line," p. 156.
12. Browning, *Poetical Works*, p. 673; hereafter cited parenthetically in the text by the title.
13. Ellis Davidson, *Gods and Myths of Northern Europe*, p. 26.
14. Donne, *The Complete English Poems*, p. 60; hereafter cited parenthetically in the text by the title.
15. Quoted in Spence, *Myths and Legends of Babylonia and Assyria*, p. 128.
16. Snodgrass et al., "Writers and Wrongs," p. 125.
17. Thucydides, *The Peloponnesian War*, p. 34.
18. Keats, *Letters*, p. 249.
19. Housman, *Collected Poems*, p. 89.
20. *The Poems of Gray, Collins and Goldsmith*, p. 676; hereafter cited parenthetically in the text by the title.

5. *WALKING TO SLEEP: NEW POEMS AND TRANSLATIONS* (1969)

1. Dickey, *Babel to Byzantium*, p. 171.
2. Michelson, "Richard Wilbur: The Quarrel with Poe," p. 258.
3. Boyers, "On Richard Wilbur," p. 79; hereafter cited parenthetically in the text by the title.
4. Gilbert, *The Savoy Operas*, p. 371.
5. Taylor, "Two Worlds Taken as They Come," p. 104; hereafter cited parenthetically in the text by the title.
6. Quoted in Wind, *Pagan Mysteries in the Renaissance*, p. 50.
7. Shelley, *Selected Poems*, p. 157.
8. Hayes, "Counterpoint in Herbert," passim.
9. Lear, *The Complete Nonsense of Edward Lear*, p. 257.
10. *The Norton Anthology of Poetry*, p. 1215.
11. Bergamini, *The Universe*, p. 120.
12. Heyen, "On Richard Wilbur," p. 624.
13. Homer, *The Odyssey*, p. 184.

14. *The Golden Treasury*, p. 441.
15. Ker, *John Henry Newman: A Biography*, p. 266.

6. THE MIND-READER: NEW POEMS (1976)

1. Kinzie, "The Cheshire Smile: On Richard Wilbur," p. 17.
2. Browning, *Poetical Works 1833–1864*, p. 864.
3. Pallottino, *The Etruscans*, p. 178.
4. Dante, *Inferno*, p. 81.
5. Michelson, "Richard Wilbur's *The Mind-Reader*," p. 136.
6. Lewis, *Christian Reflections*, pp. 191–208.
7. Marsh, *The Gospel of St John*, p. 146.
8. Plato, *The Republic*, p. 397; hereafter cited parenthetically in the text by the title.
9. Cocke, *The Drawings of Raphael*, p. 5.
10. Day, *Brass Rubbings*, p. 11.
11. Pinsky, *Sadness and Happiness*, p. 71.
12. Kesey, *Sometimes a Great Notion*, pp. 105–6; the ellipses at the beginning of each paragraph appear in the original text.
13. Carroll, *Alice in Wonderland and Through the Looking Glass*, p. 186; hereafter cited parenthetically in the text as *Alice in Wonderland*.
14. Forster, *Two Cheers for Democracy*, p. 120.
15. Forster, *Howard's End*, p. 31.
16. de Caussade, *The Sacrament of the Present Moment*, pp. 83–84.
17. Longfellow, *Poetical Works*, p. 266.
18. Tillyard, *The English Epic and Its Background*, p. 10.
19. Shakespeare, *The Winter's Tale*, p. 94.
20. *Encylopedia Americana*, 6:288.
21. Attwater, *The Penguin Dictionary of Saints*, p. 268; hereafter cited parenthetically in the text by the title.
22. Of course, the "pink girl" would have been familiar with the Colman/Carroll version, not the Granger/Kerr.

7. NEW POEMS (1987)

1. Rossetti, *Poems and Translations*, p. 138.
2. Bunyan, *The Pilgrim's Progress*, p. 296.
3. That is the AV translation, of course; modern scholarship has turned the thunder into a mane.
4. Goethe, *Faust*, p. 49.
5. Hecht, "Richard Wilbur: A Poet Called to Praise," p. 70.
6. Campbell, *The Dictionary of Birds in Colour*, p. 263.
7. Cowper, *Poetical Works*, p. 270.
8. At least I *think* it is a nonce term. I have not been able to trace it to any source.
9. Burnet, *Early Greek Philosophy*, pp. 298–99.
10. Plimpton and Stewart, "An Interview with Andrew Wyeth," p. 88.
11. Who T. W. W. might be I cannot tell. I have racked my brains, but my only candidate, Thomas Woodrow Wilson, is a nonstarter.

12. James, *Selected Literary Criticism*, pp. 85-86; hereafter cited parenthetically in the text by the title.

13. Woolf, *The Haunted House and Other Stories*, p. 49.

14. Forster, *Aspects of the Novel*, p. 27.

15. Shakespeare, *King Lear*, p. 202.

16. Herrick, *Poems*, p. 261.

17. Zimmer, *The Art of Indian Asia*, 1:97.

18. Quoted in Myers, "Neo-Classical Criticism and the Ode for Music," p. 400.

19. *Medieval English Lyrics*, p. 99.

20. Leigh Hunt, *Collected Poetical Works*, p. 291.

CONCLUSION

1. Athanasius, *St. Athanasius on the Incarnation*, p. 33.

2. Billiart, *Thoughts of Blessed Julie Billiart*, p. 49.

bibliography

Abbott, Craig S. "Wilbur's PRAISE IN SUMMER," *The Explicator* 39 (1981): 13–14.

Abbruzzese, Margharita. *Goya: The Life and Work of the Artist Illustrated with 80 Colour Plates.* London: Thames and Hudson, 1967.

Altieri, Charles. *Enlarging the Temple: New Directions in American Poetry During the 1960s.* Lewisburg: Bucknell University Press, 1979.

Anderson, George W. *A Critical Introduction to the Old Testament.* London: Duckworth, 1959.

Anon. *Pearl.* Edited by E. V. Gordon. Oxford: Clarendon Press, 1953.

Aristotle. *Poetics.* Translated by S. H. Butcher and introduced by Francis Fergusson. New York: Hill and Wang, 1961.

Athanasius. *St. Athanasius on the Incarnation: The Treatise 'De Incarnatione Verbi Dei.'* Translated and edited by a Religious of C.S.M.V. Introduced by C. S. Lewis. 1944; Reprint. London: A. R. Mowbray, 1953.

Attwater, Donald. *The Penguin Dictionary of Saints.* Harmondsworth: Penguin, 1965.

Aubin, Robert Arnold. *Topographical Poetry in XVIII-Century England.* New York: Modern Language Association of America, 1936.

Auden, W. H. *The Dyer's Hand and Other Essays.* London: Faber, 1962.

Beddoes, Thomas Lovell. *Works.* Edited by H. W. Donner. London: Oxford University Press, 1935.

Benedikt, Michael. "Witty and Eerie." In *Richard Wilbur's Creation,* ed. Wendy Salinger, pp. 101–5. Ann Arbor: University of Michigan Press, 1983.

Bennett, Joseph. "From 'Five Books, Four Poets.' " In *Richard Wilbur's Creation,* ed. Wendy Salinger, pp. 38–41. Ann Arbor: University of Michigan Press, 1983.

Benoit, Raymond. "From 'The New American Poetry.' " In *Richard Wilbur's Creation,* ed. Wendy Salinger, pp. 162–68. Ann Arbor: University of Michigan Press, 1983.

Bergamini, David. *The Universe.* New York: Time-Life Books, 1974.

Billiart, Julie. *Thoughts of Blessed Julie Billiart.* Edited by a Sister of Notre Dame (of Namur). London: Burns Oates and Washbourne, 1934.

Bixler, Frances. "Richard Wilbur: 'Hard as Nails.' " *Publications of the Arkansas Philological Association* 11 (1985): 1–13.

Blake, William. *The Poems of William Blake.* Edited by W. H. Stevenson, text by David V. Erdman. London: Longman, 1971.

Bloom, Harold. *Figures of Capable Imagination.* New York: The Seabury Press, 1976.

Boardman, John. *Greek Art.* London: Thames and Hudson, 1964.

Bogan, Louise. "Verse." In *Richard Wilbur's Creation,* ed. Wendy Salinger, pp. 30–31. Ann Arbor: University of Michigan Press, 1983.

Bowness, Alan. *Modern European Art.* London: Thames and Hudson, 1972.

Boyers, Robert. "On Richard Wilbur." *Salmagundi* 12 (1970): 77–82.

Bradbury, John M. *The Fugitives: A Critical Account.* Chapel Hill: University of North Carolina Press, 1958.

Bridges, Robert. *Poetical Works of Robert Bridges Excluding the Eight Dramas.* London: Oxford University Press, 1913.

Brodsky, Joseph. "On Richard Wilbur." In *Richard Wilbur's Creation,* ed. Wendy Salinger, pp. 203–6. Ann Arbor: University of Michigan Press, 1983.

Browne, Sir Thomas. *Religio Medici, Hydriotaphia and the Garden of Cyrus.* Edited by R. H. A. Robbins. Oxford: Clarendon Press, 1972.

Browning, Robert. *Poetical Works 1833–1864.* Edited by Ian Jack. London: Oxford University Press, 1971.

Bunyan, John. *The Pilgrim's Progress.* Introduced by G. B. Harrison. London: Dent, 1954.

Burnet, John. *Early Greek Philosophy.* London: Adam and Charles Black, 1930.

Butts, William, ed. *Conversations with Richard Wilbur.* Jackson: University Press of Mississippi, 1990.

Campbell, Bruce. *The Dictionary of Birds in Colour.* London: Michael Joseph, 1974.

Cambon, Glauco. *The Inclusive Flame: Studies in Modern American Poetry.* Bloomington: Indiana University Press, 1965.

———. *Recent American Poetry.* Minneapolis: University of Minnesota Press, 1962.

Carroll, Lewis. *Alice in Wonderland and Through the Looking Glass.* Kingsport: Grosset and Dunlap, 1946.

Chandlery, P. J. *Pilgrim-Walks in Rome: A Guide to Its Holy Places.* New York: The Messenger, 1903.

Chapman, Raymond. *Faith and Revolt: Studies in the Literary Influence of the Oxford Movement.* London: Weidenfeld and Nicolson, 1970.

Chaucer, Geoffrey. *The Works of Geoffrey Chaucer.* Edited by F. N. Robinson. London: Oxford University Press, 1966.

Ciardi, John. "Our Most Melodic Poet." In *Richard Wilbur's Creation,* ed. Wendy Salinger, pp. 52–56. Ann Arbor: University of Michigan Press, 1983.

Clark, Kenneth. *Civilisation: A Personal View.* London: British Broadcasting Corporation and John Murray, 1969.

———. *Leonardo da Vinci: An Account of His Development as an Artist.* 1939; Reprint. Harmondsworth: Penguin, 1959.

Cocke, Richard. *The Drawings of Raphael.* London: Paul Hamlyn, 1969.

Cowper, William. *Poetical Works.* Edited by H. S. Milford. 4th ed. with corrections and additions by Norma Russell. London: Oxford University Press, 1967.

Crabbe, George. *The Complete Poetical Works.* Edited by Norma Dalrymple-Champneys and Arthur Pollard. 3 vols. Oxford: Clarendon Press, 1988.

Creely, Robert. *The Collected Poems of Robert Creely: 1945–1970.* Berkeley: University of California Press, 1982.

Cummings, e. e. *Complete Poems.* 2 vols. London: Macgibbon and Kee, 1968.

Dante. *The Comedy of Dante Alighieri the Florentine.* Translated by Dorothy L. Sayers. 3 vols. Harmondsworth: Penguin, 1949.

Day, David. *Brass Rubbings.* Cheadle: Carcanet, 1975.

de Caussade, Jean-Pierre. *The Sacrament of the Present Moment.* Translated by Kitty Muggeridge. London: Collins, 1981.

Deneke, Rolf. *Gestalten deutscher Dichtung: Eine Literaturgeschichte.* Frankfurt: Hischgraben-Verlag, 1967.

Deutsch, Babette. "Scenes Alive with Light." In *Richard Wilbur's Creation,* ed. Wendy Salinger, pp. 36–37. Ann Arbor: University of Michigan Press, 1983.

Dickens, Charles. *Bleak House.* Introduced by Sir Osbert Sitwell. London: Oxford University Press, 1948.

Dickey, James. *Babel to Byzantium: Poets and Poetry Now.* New York: Farrar, Strauss and Giroux, 1968.

Dinesen, Isak. *Out of Africa.* New York: Vintage Books, 1972.

Donne John. *The Complete English Poems.* Edited by A. J. Smith. Harmondsworth: Penguin, 1971.

———. *Paradoxes and Problems.* Edited and introduced by Helen Peters. Oxford: Clarendon Press, 1980.

Donoghue, Denis. *Connoisseurs of Chaos: Ideas of Order in Modern American Poetry.* New York: Macmillan, 1965.

Dry, Helen. "Wilbur's OCTOBER MAPLES, PORTLAND." *The Explicator* 40 (1981): 60–62.

Duffy, Charles F. " 'Intricate Neural Grace': The Esthetic of Richard Wilbur." In *Richard Wilbur's Creation,* ed. Wendy Salinger, pp. 176–86. Ann Arbor: University of Michigan Press, 1983.

Eliot, T. S. *The Complete Poems and Plays of T. S. Eliot.* London: Faber, 1969.

Ellis Davidson, H. R. *Gods and Myths of Northern Europe.* Harmondsworth: Penguin, 1964.

Encyclopedia Americana. 30 vols. Danbury: Americana Corporation, 1979.

Farrell, John P. "The Beautiful Changes in Richard Wilbur's Poetry." In *Richard Wilbur's Creation,* ed. Wendy Salinger, pp. 187–202. Ann Arbor: University of Michigan Press, 1983.

Fermigier, André. *Pierre Bonnard.* London: Thames and Hudson, 1987.

Flavius Vopiscus of Syracuse. *Divus Aurelianus. 3: Scriptores Historiae Augustae With an English Translation by David Magie Ph.D.* 3 vols. London: William Heinemann, 1932.

Forster, E. M. *Aspects of the Novel.* 1927; Reprint. Harmondsworth: Penguin, 1962.

———. *Howard's End.* Edited by Oliver Stallybrass. London: Edward Arnold, 1973.

———. *Two Cheers for Democracy.* Edited by Oliver Stallybrass. London: Edward Arnold, 1972.

Fraser, G. S. "Some Younger American Poets: Art and Reality." *Commentary* 23 (1957): 454–62.

Frost, Robert. *Complete Poems.* London: Jonathan Cape, 1951.

Fussell, Edwin. *Lucifer in Harness: American Meter, Metaphor and Diction.* Princeton: Princeton University Press, 1973.

Gilbert, W. S. *The Savoy Operas: Being the Complete Text of the Gilbert and Sullivan Operas as Originally Produced in the Years 1875–1896.* London: Macmillan, 1962.

Goethe, Johann Wolfgang. *Faust.* Introduced by Max von Boehn. Berlin: Carl Albert Kindle, 1940.

———. *Wilhelm Meister's Apprenticeship and Travels.* Translated by Thomas Carlyle. London: Chapman and Hall, 1890.

The Golden Treasury. Edited by Francis Turner Palgrave. London: Oxford University Press, 1907.

Golffing, F. C. "A Remarkable New Talent." In *Richard Wilbur's Creation*, ed. Wendy Salinger, pp. 32–33. Ann Arbor: University of Michigan Press, 1983.

Graves, Robert. *The Greek Myths*. 2 vols. Harmondsworth: Penguin, 1960.

The Greek Anthology with an English Translation by W. R. Paton. 5 vols. London: William Heinemann, 1917.

Gregory, Horace. "The Poetry of Suburbia." *Partisan Review* 23 (1956): 544–53.

Gunn, Thom. "From 'Imitations and Originals.' " In *Richard Wilbur's Creation*, ed. Wendy Salinger, pp. 70–71. Ann Arbor: University of Michigan Press, 1983.

Hall, Donald. "The Battle of the Bards." *Horizon* 4 (1961): 116–21.

———. "Claims on the Poet." In *Richard Wilbur's Creation*, ed. Wendy Salinger, pp. 57–63. Ann Arbor: University of Michigan Press, 1983.

Hamer, Enid. *The Metres of English Poetry*. 1930; Reprint. London: Methuen, 1969.

Hayes, A. M. "Counterpoint in Herbert." *Studies in Philology* 35 (1938): 43–60.

Hecht, Anthony. "The Motions of the Mind." *Times Literary Supplement* 20 May 1977: 602.

———. "Richard Wilbur: A Poet Called to Praise." *Dialogue* 85 (1989): 64–70.

Herbert, George. *The Works of George Herbert*. Edited by F. E. Hutchinson. Oxford: Clarendon Press, 1941.

Herrick, Robert. *The Poems of Robert Herrick*. Edited by L. C. Martin. London: Oxford University Press, 1965.

Heyen, William. "On Richard Wilbur." *The Southern Review* 9 (1973): 617–34.

Hill, Donald L. *Richard Wilbur*. New York: Twayne Publishers, 1967.

Hohl, Reinhold. *Alberto Giacometti: Sculpture, Painting, Drawing*. London: Thames and Hudson, 1971.

Hölderlin, Friedrich. *Sämtliche Werke*. Leipzig: Im Insel Verlag, n.d.

Holmes, Theodore. "Wilbur's New Book—Two Views: I. A Prophet Without Prophecy." In *Richard Wilbur's Creation*, ed. Wendy Salinger, pp. 72–75. Ann Arbor: University of Michigan Press, 1983.

Homer. *The Odyssey*. Translated by E. V. Rieu. Harmondsworth: Penguin, 1946.

Honour, Hugh. *Romanticism*. 1979; Reprint. Harmondsworth: Penguin, 1981.

Hopkins, Gerard Manley. *Poems of Gerard Manley Hopkins*. Edited and introduced by W. H. Gardner. London: Oxford University Press, 1948.

Horace. *Satires, Epistles and Ars Poetica With an English Translation by H. Rushton Fairclough*. London: Heinemann, 1929.

Housman, A. E. *Collected Poems and Selected Prose*. Edited and introduced by Christopher Ricks. London: Allen Lane, 1988.

Hunt, Henry Leigh. *Collected Poetical Works*. Edited by H. S. Milford. London: Oxford University Press, 1923.

Hymns Ancient and Modern Revised. London: William Clowes, n.d.

Iambi et Elegi Graeci Ante Alexandrum Cantati. Edited by M. L. West. 2 vols. Oxford: Clarendon Press, 1971.

James, Clive. "As a Matter of Tact." In *Richard Wilbur's Creation*, ed. Wendy Salinger, pp. 144–52. Ann Arbor: University of Michigan Press, 1983.

———. "When the Gloves Are Off." In *Richard Wilbur's Creation*, ed. Wendy Salinger, pp. 106–18. Ann Arbor: University of Michigan Press, 1983.

James, Henry. *Selected Literary Criticism*. Edited by Morris Shapira. Introduced by F. R. Leavis. Harmondsworth: Penguin, 1963.

Jarrell, Randall. "From 'Fifty Years of American Poetry.' " In *Richard Wilbur's Crea-*

tion, ed. Wendy Salinger, pp. 85–86. Ann Arbor: University of Michigan Press, 1983.

———. *Poetry and the Age*. 1953; Reprint. New York: Vintage Books, 1955.

Jensen, Ejner J. "Encounters With Experience: The Poems of Richard Wilbur." In *Richard Wilbur's Creation*, ed. Wendy Salinger, pp. 243–64. Ann Arbor: University of Michigan Press, 1983.

The Jerusalem Bible. London: Darton, Longman & Todd, 1966.

Jobes, Gertrude. *Dictionary of Mythology, Folklore and Symbols*. New York: The Scarecrow Press, 1961.

Jonson, Ben. *Poems*. Edited by Ian Donaldson. London: Oxford University Press, 1975.

Karsavina, Tamara. *Theatre Street: The Reminiscences of Tamara Karsavina*. 1930; Reprint. London: Dance Books, 1981.

Keats, John. *Letters of John Keats: A New Selection*. Edited by Robert Gittings. London: Oxford University Press, 1970.

———. *Poetical Works*. Edited by H. W. Garrod. London: Oxford University Press, 1970.

Ker, Ian. *John Henry Newman: A Biography*. Oxford: Oxford University Press, 1990.

Kesey, Ken. *Sometimes a Great Notion*. 1966; Reprint. London: Methuen, 1985.

Kinzie, Mary. "The Cheshire Smile: On Richard Wilbur." *The American Poetry Review* 6 (1977): 17–20.

Lear, Edward. *The Complete Nonsense of Edward Lear*. Edited and introduced by Holbrook Jackson. London: Faber, 1957.

Legouis, Émile, Louis Cazamian, and Raymond Las Vergnas. *A History of English Literature*. Translated by Helen Douglas Irvine. London: Dent, 1967.

Leibowitz, Herbert. "Review of *The Mind-Reader*." In *Richard Wilbur's Creation*, ed. Wendy Salinger, pp. 120–22. Ann Arbor: University of Michigan Press, 1983.

Leithauser, Brad. "Richard Wilbur at Sixty." In *Richard Wilbur's Creation*, ed. Wendy Salinger, pp. 282–91. Ann Arbor: University of Michigan Press, 1983.

Levey, Virginia. "The World of Objects in Richard Wilbur's Poetry." *Publications of the Arkansas Philological Association* 7 (1981): 41–51.

Lewis, C. S. *Christian Reflections*. Edited by Walter Hooper. 1967; Reprint. London: Collins, 1981.

Littler, Frank. "Wilbur's LOVE CALLS US TO THE THINGS OF THIS WORLD." *The Explicator* 40 (1982): 53–55.

Livingston, Myra Cohn. "Review of *Opposites*." In *Richard Wilbur's Creation*, ed. Wendy Salinger, pp. 140–41. Ann Arbor: University of Michigan Press, 1983.

Longfellow, Henry Wadsworth. *Poetical Works*. London: Routledge and Kegan Paul, 1889.

Marsh, John. *The Gospel of St John*. Harmondsworth: Penguin, 1968.

Martz, Louis. *The Poetry of Meditation: A Study in English Religious Literature of the Seventeenth Century*. New Haven: Yale University Press, 1962.

McLuhan, Herbert Marshall. "Edgar Poe's Tradition." *Sewanee Review* 12 (1944): 24–33.

McMullen, Roy. *Degas: His Life, Times and Work*. London: Secker and Warburg, 1985.

Mann, Thomas. *Death in Venice, Tristan, Tonio Kröger*. Translated by H. T. Lowe-Porter. 1928; Reprint. Harmondsworth: Penguin, 1955.

Marvell, Andrew. *The Poems and Letters of Andrew Marvell.* Edited by H. M. Margoliouth. Rev. ed. Pierre Legouis and Elsie Duncan-Jones. 2 vols. Oxford: Clarendon Press, 1971.

Medieval English Lyrics: A Critical Anthology. Edited and introduced by R. T. Davies. London: Faber, 1963.

Meredith, William. "Wilbur's New Book—Two Views: II. A Note on Richard Wilbur." In *Richard Wilbur's Creation,* ed. Wendy Salinger, pp. 76–77. Ann Arbor: University of Michigan Press, 1983.

Michelson, Bruce F. "Richard Wilbur: The Quarrel with Poe." *The Southern Review* 14 (1978): 245–61.

———. "Richard Wilbur's *The Mind-Reader.*" In *Richard Wilbur's Creation,* ed. Wendy Salinger, pp. 132–38. Ann Arbor: University of Michigan Press, 1983.

———. *Wilbur's Poetry: Music in a Scattering Time.* Amherst: University of Massachusetts Press, 1991.

———. "Wilbur's Words." In *Richard Wilbur's Creation,* ed. Wendy Salinger, pp. 265–81. Ann Arbor: University of Michigan Press, 1983.

Mills, Ralph J. "The Lyricism of Richard Wilbur." In *Richard Wilbur's Creation,* ed. Wendy Salinger, pp. 78–84. Ann Arbor: University of Michigan Press, 1983.

Milton, John. *Complete Poems and Major Prose.* Edited by Merrit Y. Hughes. New York: Odyssey Press, 1957.

Myers, Robert. "Neo-Classical Criticism and the Ode for Music." *Publications of the Modern Language Association* 62 (1947): 399–421.

Nemerov, Howard. "From 'What Was Modern Poetry?' " In *Richard Wilbur's Creation,* ed. Wendy Salinger, pp. 232–42. Ann Arbor: University of Michigan Press, 1983.

———. *New and Selected Poems.* Chicago: University of Chicago Press, 1960.

The Norton Anthology of Poetry. Edited by Alexander W. Allison et al. 3d ed. New York: W. W. Norton and Company, 1983.

Oliver, Raymond. "Verse Translation and Richard Wilbur." *The Southern Review* 11 (1975): 318–30.

Ommanney, F. D. *The Fishes.* Time-Life International, 1970.

Ovid. *Ovid With an English Translation: Tristia, Ex Ponto.* Translated by Arthur Leslie Wheeler. London: William Heinemann, 1953.

———. *The Metamorphoses.* Translated and introduced by Mary Innes. Harmondsworth: Penguin, 1955.

Pallottino, M. *The Etruscans.* Translated by J. Cremona. Harmondsworth: Penguin, 1955.

Pater, Walter. *The Renaissance: Studies in Art and Poetry.* London: Macmillan, 1910.

Peters, W. A. M. *Gerard Manley Hopkins: A Critical Essay Towards the Understanding of His Poetry.* London: Oxford University Press, 1948.

Phipson, Emma. *The Animal-Lore of Shakespeare's Time, Including Quadrupeds, Birds, Reptiles, Fish and Insects.* London: Kegan Paul, Trench and Co., 1883.

Pinsky, Robert. *Sadness and Happiness: Poems by Robert Pinsky.* Princeton: Princeton University Press, 1975.

Plato. *The Republic.* Translated by B. Jowett. New York: Random House, n.d.

Plimpton, George, and Donald Stewart. "An Interview with Andrew Wyeth." *Horizon* 4 (1961): 88–101.

bibliography

Plutzik, Hyam. "Recent Poetry." In *Richard Wilbur's Creation*, ed. Wendy Salinger, pp. 66–68. Ann Arbor: University of Michigan Press, 1983.

The Poems of Thomas Gray, William Collins and Oliver Goldsmith. Edited by Roger Lonsdale. London: Longman, 1969.

Pope, Alexander. *The Poems of Alexander Pope: A One-Volume Edition of the Twickenham Text With Selected Annotations.* Edited by John Butt. London: Methuen, 1963.

Prideaux, Tom. *The World of Delacroix: 1798–1863.* New York: Time Inc., 1966.

Pushkin, Alexander. *Eugene Onegin: A Novel in Verse. A New Revised Edition Translated by Babette Deutsch. Edited with an Introduction by Avraham Yarmolinsky.* Harmondsworth: Penguin, 1964.

Quintus Curtius with an English Translation by John C. Rolfe. 2 vols. London: William Heinemann, 1946.

Reibetanz, John. "What Love Sees: Poetry and Vision in Richard Wilbur." *Modern Poetry Studies* 11 (1982): 60–85.

Relph, E. *Place and Placelessness.* London: Pion, 1976.

Rochefoucauld, Duc de la. *Reflections; or Sentences and Moral Maxims.* Translated by J. W. Willis Bund and J. Hain Friswell. London: Samson Low, Son and Marson, 1871.

Rosenthal, M. L. "From 'Speak the Whole Mind.' " In *Richard Wilbur's Creation*, ed. Wendy Salinger, p. 34. Ann Arbor: University of Michigan Press, 1983.

———. "From 'Tradition and Transition.' " In *Richard Wilbur's Creation*, ed. Wendy Salinger, pp. 64–65. Ann Arbor: University of Michigan, 1983.

Rossetti, Dante Gabriel. *Poems and Translations: 1850–1870 Together with the Prose Story 'Hand and Soul'.* London: Oxford University Press, 1913.

Rourke, Constance. *American Humor: A Study of the National Character.* 1931. Reprint. New York: Doubleday Anchor Books, n.d.

Rubin, Louis D., Jr. *The Faraway Country: Writers of the Modern South.* Seattle: University of Washington Press, 1963.

Salinger, Wendy. "Introduction." In *Richard Wilbur's Creation*, ed. Wendy Salinger, pp. 1–23. Ann Arbor: The University of Michigan Press, 1983.

Sayre, Robert F. "A Case for Richard Wilbur as Nature Poet." In *Richard Wilbur's Creation*, ed. Wendy Salinger, pp. 153–61. Ann Arbor: University of Michigan Press, 1983.

Scott, Charles T. "Typography, Poems and the Poetic Line." In *Linguistic and Literary Studies in Honor of Archibald A. Hill IV: Linguistics and Literature/Sociolinguistics and Applied Linguistics,* ed. Mohammad Ali Jazayery, Edgar C. Polomé, and Werner Winter, pp. 153–60. The Hague: Mouton Publishers, 1979.

Scott, Walter. *The Journal of Sir Walter Scott 1825–32 from the Original Manuscript at Abbotsford.* Edinburgh: David Douglas, 1891.

Seneca. *Ad Lucilium Epistulae Morales.* Translated by Richard M. Gummere. 3 vols. London: William Heinemann, 1917–25.

Shakespeare, William. *King Lear.* Edited by Kenneth Muir. London: Methuen, 1972.

———. *The Winter's Tale.* Edited by J. H. P. Pafford. London: Methuen, 1963.

Shelley, Percy Bysshe. *Selected Poems.* Edited and introduced by Timothy Webb. London: J. M. Dent, 1977.

Snodgrass, W. D., Richard Wilbur, and Aidan C. Matthews. "Writers and Wrongs: W. D. Snodgrass, Richard Wilbur and Aidan C. Matthews in Conversation." *Crane Bag* 7 (1983): 122–26.

Sonnino, Lee A. *A Handbook to Sixteenth-Century Rhetoric.* London: Routledge and Kegan Paul, 1969.

Southworth, James G. "The Poetry of Richard Wilbur," *College English* 12 (1960): 24–29.

Spangenberg, D. F. and Frans Beukes. "Padda en akkedis—oor twee gedigte van Richard Wilbur en Ernst van Heerden." *Standpunte* 37 (June 1984): 28–33.

Spence, Lewis. *Myths and Legends of Babylonia and Assyria.* London: George Harrap, 1916.

Spenser, Edmund. *Books I and II of The Faerie Queene, The Mutability Cantos and Selections from the Minor Poetry.* Edited by Robert Kellog and Oliver Steele. New York: Odyssey Press, 1965.

Steiner, George. *Extraterritorial: Papers on Literature and the Language Revolution.* London: Faber, 1972.

Stepanchev, Stephen. *American Poetry Since 1945: A Critical Survey by Stephen Stepanchev.* New York: Harper and Row, 1965.

Stern, Carol Simpson. "Richard Wilbur." In *Contemporary Poets,* ed. James Vinson and D. L. Kirkpatrick, pp. 926–28. London: St. James Press, 1985.

Stevenson, Robert Louis. *A Child's Garden of Verses; Underwoods; Songs of Travel.* London: Thomas Nelson, n.d.

Stitt, Peter. *The World's Hieroglyphic Beauty: Five American Poets.* Athens: Georgia University Press, 1985.

Taylor, Henry. "Two Worlds Taken as They Come: Richard Wilbur's *Walking to Sleep.*" In *Richard Wilbur's Creation,* ed. Wendy Salinger, pp. 88–100. Ann Arbor: University of Michigan Press, 1983.

Tennyson, Alfred Lord. *The Poems of Tennyson.* Edited by Christopher Ricks. London: Longmans, 1969.

Thucydides. *History of the Peloponnesian War.* Translated and introduced by Rex Warner. Harmondsworth: Penguin, 1954.

Tillyard, E. M. W. *The English Epic and Its Background.* London: Chatto and Windus, 1954.

van Heerden, Ernst. *Etikette op My Koffers: Bladsye uit 'n Amerikaanse Reisjoernaal.* Cape Town: Human and Rousseau, 1961.

Viereck, Peter. "From 'Technique and Inspiration—A Year of Poetry.' " In *Richard Wilbur's Creation,* ed. Wendy Salinger, p. 50. Ann Arbor: University of Michigan Press, 1983.

Virgil. *Virgil with an English Translation by H. Rushton Fairclough.* 2 vols. London: William Heinemann, 1957.

Warlow, Francis W. "Richard Wilbur." *Bucknell Review* 7 (1958): 217–33.

Webster, John. *The Duchess of Malfi.* In *Five Stuart Tragedies.* Edited and introduced by A. K. McIlwaith. London: Oxford University Press, 1953.

Wells, Frank W. *The American Way of Poetry.* New York: Columbia University Press, 1943.

White, Patrick. *Riders in the Chariot.* 1961; Reprint. London: Jonathan Cape, 1976.

———. *The Vivisector.* London: Jonathan Cape, 1970.

Whitehead, Alfred North. *Science and the Modern World: Lowell Lectures, 1925.* Cambridge: Cambridge University Press, 1926.

Whitman, Walt. *Leaves of Grass and Selected Prose.* Edited by Sculley Bradley. New York: Holt, Rinehart and Winston, 1949.

Whittemore, Reed. "Verse." In *Richard Wilbur's Creation,* ed. Wendy Salinger, pp. 42–45. Ann Arbor: University of Michigan Press, 1983.

Wilbur, Richard, George Steiner, E. H. Gombrich, Katherine Chorley, John Paul Russo, Elsie Duncan-Jones, and Richmond Lattimore. "Eight Responses and a Poem." *P N Review* 16 (1980): 31–33.

Wilbur, Richard. "The Genie in the Bottle." In *Mid-Century American Poets,* ed. John Ciardi. New York: Twayne, 1950.

———. *The Mind-Reader: New Poems.* London: Faber, 1977.

———. *New and Collected Poems.* San Diego: Harcourt Brace Jovanovich, 1988; London: Faber, 1989.

———. *On My Own Work.* Isle of Skye: Aquila, 1983.

———. "Poe and the Art of Suggestion." *University of Mississippi Studies in English* 3 (1982): 1–13.

———. *The Poems of Richard Wilbur.* New York: Harcourt, Brace and World, 1963.

———. "Poetry and Happiness." *Shenandoah* 35 (1984): 452–71.

———. "The Poetry of Witter Bynner." *The American Poetry Review* 6 (1977): 3–8.

———. *Responses: Prose Pieces 1953–1976.* New York: Harcourt Brace Jovanovich, 1976.

———. "Symposium on Lowell's 'Skunk Hour.' " Edited by Anthony Ostroff. *New World Writing,* 21 (1962): 133–37.

———. "Talking to Joan Hutton." *Transatlantic Review* 29 (1968): 58–67.

———. "Commentary: WALKING TO SLEEP." *Dreamworks* 1 (1980): 106–10.

———. "The Writer's Role: Responses to Hortense Calisher." *The New Criterion* 1 (1983): 31–40.

Wilde, Oscar. *Complete Works of Oscar Wilde.* Introduced by Vyvyan Holland. London: Collins, 1966.

Williams, Ann. "Wilbur's BEASTS," *The Explicator* 37 (1979): 27–28.

Williams, William Carlos. *In the American Grain: Essays.* Introduced by Horace Gregory. 1925; Reprint. Harmondsworth: Penguin, 1971.

———. *Selected Essays.* New York: Random House, 1954.

Wilson, Edmund. *Axel's Castle: A Study in the Imaginative Literature of 1870–1930.* 1931; Reprint. London: Collins, 1961.

Wind, Edgar. *Pagan Mysteries in the Renaissance.* 1958; Reprint. Harmondsworth: Penguin, 1967.

Winters, Yvor. *Collected Poems.* Chicago: Swallow Press, 1960.

Woodard, Charles R. " 'Happiest Intellection': The Mind of Richard Wilbur." In *Richard Wilbur's Creation,* ed. Wendy Salinger, pp. 229–31. Ann Arbor: University of Michigan Press, 1983.

———. "Richard Wilbur's Critical Condition." In *Richard Wilbur's Creation,* ed. Wendy Salinger, pp. 221–28. Ann Arbor: University of Michigan Press, 1983.

Woolf, Virginia. *The Haunted House and Other Stories.* 1944; Reprint. Harmondsworth: Penguin, 1973.

Wordsworth, William. *The Prelude, Selected Poems and Sonnets.* Edited by Carlos Baker. New York: Holt, Rinehart and Winston, 1954.

———. *The Prose Works of William Wordsworth.* Edited by W. J. B. Owen and Jane Worthington Smyser. 3 vols. Oxford: Clarendon, 1974.

Yeats, William Butler. *The Collected Poems of W. B. Yeats.* London: Macmillan, 1950.

Zimmer, Heinrich. *The Art of Indian Asia.* Completed and edited by Joseph Campbell. 2 vols. Princeton: Princeton University Press, 1960.

index

about the author

Rodney Stenning Edgecombe is Associate Professor of English at the University of Cape Town. He received his honor's and master's degrees from Rhodes University, Grahamstown, where he was awarded the Royal Society of St. George Prize for English (1972). He took his doctorate at Trinity College, Cambridge, winning the 1978/79 Members' English Prize. His other books include *Leigh Hunt and the Poetry of Fancy* (1994), *Wonted Fires: A Reading of Thomas Gray* (1992), *Identity and Vocation in the Fiction of Muriel Spark* (1990), *Vision and Style in Patrick White: A Study of Five Novels* (1989), *Theme Embodiment and Structure in the Poetry of George Crabbe* (1983), and *"Sweetnesse Readie Penn'd": Imagery, Syntax and Metrics in the Poetry of George Herbert* (1980). A book on the poetry of Keble and Newman is forthcoming.

Date Due

'97		